Linda McCartney

Linda McCartney

DANNY FIELDS

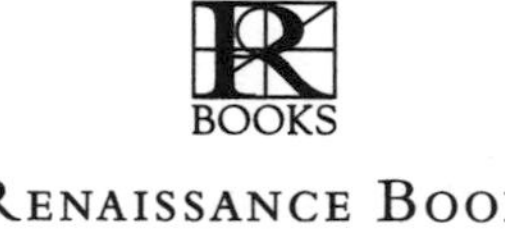

RENAISSANCE BOOKS
Los Angeles

ISBN: 1-58063-104-5

10 9 8 7 6 5 4 3 2 1

Published by Renaissance Books
Distributed by St. Martin's Press
Manufactured in the United States of America
First Edition

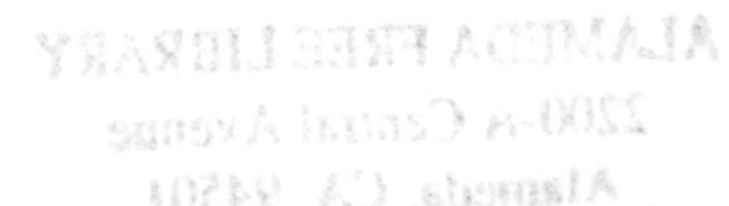

Contents

Acknowledgments

Thank you to . . .

Everyone whose name is in this book, my very greatest thanks, of course; it would be redundant to name you all.

To Mara Hennessey, my partner in this project, without whose work it could never have been done. I will not name all her contributions, in all the realms of the printed and spoken word, because you'll wonder where the author has been all this time, as well you might have done already.

To these wonderful people who were so smart and helpful: Brian Belovitch, Christine Berardo, Bonnie Bordins, Susan Lee Cohen, Wallace Collins, Esq., Gail Colson, Raul Correa, Mark Dillon, Mark Duran, Josh Feigenbaum, Holly George-Warren, Eric Greenberg, Laura Gross, Bill Hennessey, Matt Hurwitz, Sydney Kaufman, Fran Lebowitz, Virginia Lohle, Donald Lyons, Liz McKenna, Dennis McNally, Joe McNeely, Legs McNeil, Belinda Marcell, Maria from *Melody Maker*, Kevin Mazur, Caroline North, Steve Paul, Diana Rico, Jerry Rothberg, Alan Samson, Philip Shelly, Sarah Spurgin-Witte, Ames Sweet, Mim Udovitch, Liz Van Lear, Karla Waples, Judy Weil, Deane Zimmerman, Howard Zimmerman.

To Paul McCartney, without whose "green light" no one would have touched this thing. And I do hope Linda is smiling, with what ironic sense one will never know. To Heather, Mary and James, and to the people at MPL and Eastman & Eastman. Just for being there all these years.

Preface

I wish I didn't have to write this book. I wish Linda was still here, working on her myriad projects, inspiring people and making them feel so much better for her presence, saving the lives of animals, being the wonderful friend that she was, and—this most of all, because it mattered most to her—being the great wife and best friend of one of the most talented men of our century, and mother to their four children.

The public went through a series of mood swings with Linda—she was hated and loved, admired and reviled, able to get her messages across and wildly misunderstood. If you knew her, you adored her; of that there was no question (well, there were some battle royals with a few old friends when she appeared to have abandoned them on the occasion of her marriage to Beatle Paul McCartney in 1969; we'll go into that later). But it is safe to say that when she died in the spring of 1998, there was not a negative opinion to be heard. She had managed to turn it all around and, unless you were a meat-packer or a furrier, she wasn't even vaguely controversial at the time of her passing. In fact, she was beloved. Her friends always thought she deserved to be beloved, and finally the rest of the world agreed. Was it too late, or is it never too late? I think it never is, and convincing you of that is my task here.

In the time allotted, I could not produce an ultimate "biography," down to the last detail and event of her life, plus long exegeses on her work. There is still room for that to be done. Nor did I want to come up with a hagiography—I happen to think she *was* kind of a modern saint, but that's a conclusion one must be left to draw after all the information is presented, and all the information might not lead everyone to the same judgment. Be that as it may.

Linda McCartney, when she was Linda Eastman, came of age in the 1960s, as did most of us who were young enough to change and old enough to understand that it was still possible to do so. Those were very different times, with different values. Lots of them, of course, were fuelled by rock and roll, especially by the Beatles, the Stones and Dylan. We really thought we were radical when it came to politics, art, sex, and mind-altering chemicals. Today, if I were the guardian of someone who is now the age I was then, I would be extremely concerned if he or she went so close to the edge in some of those areas as we did, as I did, as Linda did. "Experiment" was not just a noun or verb back then, it was a command. We were pretty wild, we were different people; "That wasn't me." Yes, it was, but hey, it was a phase, albeit the most spectacular one in our lifetimes; those who didn't rein it in when all the signs pointed to the end of this wonderfully extended adolescence and the return of reality did not present a pretty picture—if they survived at all. I rather thought Linda's picture, in particular, grew more beautiful as the years went by. Some people merely moved beyond the delirium; she triumphed—in a partnership that amazed the world by its intensity and duration, and on her own as well. I think it is a story worth telling.

Chapter 1

"I once went out on a date, to some kind of pub, and I remember thinking, 'This is so boring,' and just sort of walking out and going home."

Linda McCartney

On the first Friday of summer in 1966, the *SS Sea Panther* set sail from a marina on New York's Hudson River shore. On board was a little gathering that would change some people's lives, and a good deal more, for the rest of the century. Linda McCartney (then Linda Eastman) had her mid-twenties epiphany that day. And because it's the day I met her (though I was stranded on the riverbank), I think of myself as having had a whopper of a time as well. So I feel conscience-free, perhaps entitled to use the first person in the telling of this story.

The event itself was "ultra" by definition—a press meet-and-greet with the Rolling Stones, aboard a yacht that went up and down the harbor for about two hours. Among the people invited were those of us who thought ourselves (here was the proof!) clearly A-list in the very tiny, alas, bunch that was known as the "rock press." Well, out of fourteen of us, twelve were invited—to make it look exclusive.

The Rolling Stones!

I cannot tell you how important that group was to a lot of us back then. I know there were not many bands to choose from, or many different "formats" either, but the Stones were It. They were fierce, they were glamorous, they confirmed that behind the sublime glow the Beatles had sent us from England, there was a raging fire. Not "behind"—"along with" is better. They were number one in the charts that week with "Paint It Black," an astonishing song for a *Billboard* chart-topper, if you think of it. After a two-week reign, they were chased back to third place (Sinatra's "Strangers in the Night" was number two) by the Beatles' "Paperback Writer," which was written by Paul McCartney about John Lennon.

The press contingent included two women who worked at *Town & Country* magazine, a glossy periodical for the very rich, or for those who wanted to know more about the very rich than they could find out anywhere else. Not merely about the very rich, but the very rich who were also hanging in there as members of America's pathetically frayed WASP class. To the world's shock, the June issue of *Town & Country* showed a David Bailey photograph of the Rolling Stones on the front cover (still quite the absolute opposite of everything the magazine stood for, but such was the coming power of the rock-and-roll juggernaut) with young socialite Alexandra Chase in an evening gown. Brian Jones was smoking a cigarette. It was all quite revolutionary. The staff members of *T&C* on board the *Sea Panther* were Christina Berlin and Linda Eastman.

Linda was not at all a *Town & Country* kind of girl. Born and raised in affluence, the second-born child and oldest daughter of a distinguished upper-middle-class Jewish family, she was a loner and a rebel who cared far more for horses (she was a champion rider) and photography (pictures of horses, for the most part) than about the social hierarchy celebrated in the magazine. Separated after a brief marriage, she was the mother of a three-and-a-half-year-old daughter and, in her blue gaberdine shirt, loafers, T-shirt and no make-up, looked vividly out of place in an office where hair could be weighed by the ton, false eyelashes by the kilo, and face paint by the gallon. She was a natural woman in a workforce where artifice was the style. But she was very bright, well-mannered, had taken a typing course at her father's insistence, and spoke with a nasal, lockjaw monotone that many aspiring débutantes spent years cultivating. She did her simple editorial assistant job well, and was encouraged to go to the Stones boat ride with Christina—actually, they were the only two at the magazine who wanted to go at all.

A whole book could be written about Christina Berlin, Linda's best and only buddy at work. She's the daughter of the late Richard and Honey Berlin, he having been the president of the Hearst Corporation (which published *Town & Country*, making Christina the boss's daughter), and was William "Rosebud" Randolph Hearst's choice, after he had looked exactingly at all his own sons, to take over the company when he was gone. Not actually blue-blood by birth, Richard and Honey learned very fast, lived in the "best" building on Fifth Avenue, and counted among their closest friends the Duke and Duchess of Windsor and J. Edgar Hoover. In other words, the Berlins were hardly lefties, and their three daughters rebelled, if not politically, then in every other way.

The oldest Berlin daughter, Brigid, was Andy Warhol's best friend and confidante for many years, a star of the earth-shaking movie *Chelsea Girls,* and a ferocious and brilliant woman, now doing theater pieces so exclusive that you need a password to get in. Brigid has boasted of spiking her parents' punch with amphetamine, of which she had once been rather fond herself, and watching the Duchess and J. Edgar, once it hit, dancing on her family's dining-room table. She also spiked, literally, the buttocks of anyone within ten feet of her with a magical meth mixture, earning herself the alternative name, Brigid Polk.

Christina, a few years after this narrative begins, engineered the defection of her lover, Mikhail Baryshnikov, the world's greatest male ballet dancer, from the Soviet Union to the West. We're not bringing any boring people into this story.

Christina had been the only genuine teenager in the VIP press area—courtesy of her father—when the Beatles arrived at JFK (then Idlewild) airport for their first visit to America in 1964. To explain her presence, her father's staff said she was a reporter for the *New York Daily Mirror*, a tabloid in the Hearst empire. She rode to the airport with Murray the K, the self-styled "Fifth Beatle," and behaved herself so well ("I didn't faint at the sight of them") that she was in the Hearst entourage when the Stones arrived in New York for the first time—she was introduced to the band as "the president of your first American fan club" and was instantly noted by Mick Jagger as Someone To Remember. And just the right person on the SS *Sea Panther* that June morning to introduce him to the blonde fox with the Pentax.

So, this was the crowd into which Linda Eastman, single mother and reluctant apprentice at a magazine edited for nobody she could ever want to know, was beginning to drift—the Stones and their people, the Berlin girls, the Warhols (however tangentially, and Linda never liked them much anyhow), the avant-garde rock press (well, the legendary reporter Lillian Roxon, who would become Linda's best friend and bitterest enemy, and me). Perhaps "drift" was not quite what Linda was doing; she was paddling away from the life she had been living, with no particular immediate goal, but with explosive enthusiasm once she saw how much fun New York, the whole world, in 1966, could be.

Oh, 1966. I have to recycle those lines of Wordsworth from *The Prelude*: it's useful when talking about the glorious early-late '60s:

Bliss was it in that time to be alive,
But to be young was very Heaven!

That was extravagantly true in the world of rock and roll—the "British Invasion" was still in full force, and getting better all the time, while America was coming up with true gems of its own: the Byrds, Jefferson Airplane, the Velvet Underground, the *Pet Sounds* Beach Boys, the Grateful Dead, *Blonde on Blonde* Dylan, the Mamas and Papas, Buffalo Springfield, the Doors. Every month there was an album that changed your life, that sounded like nothing you'd ever heard before. And those of us who were thrilled with the music soon discovered that happily there was no real "rock-and-roll" scene already in place, that it was waiting to be invented and that you could just put yourself at the center of it and say your name. Whatever other skills you might also have, like knowing which buttons to press on a handsome 35mm camera, counted for even more points. And Linda happened to be poised to introduce herself into this exciting new world at that very moment.

She was very beautiful, with natural strawberry-blonde hair, classic features, perfect skin, and the fullness of figure that men have always become excited about, no matter that the fashion press at the time was pushing the flat-chested, bony, brittle little bodies of Edie Sedgwick and Twiggy. Linda's bearing was classy, her smile atomic, her accent and her taste impeccable. That afternoon, her Pentax loaded, she shot half-a-dozen rolls of the group being honored; her pictures, to this day, are perhaps the best of the Stones ever taken, certainly the best candid shots, and probably the most famous photos of the band at the height of their youthful sexiness.

What's more, while photographing Mick, and unbeknownst to anybody else on board except Christina, who watched the two of them mouth flirty little messages to each other, Linda Eastman accepted Mick Jagger's offer to meet her early the next week at the trendiest party in town, given by photographer Jerry Schatzberg (Stones in drag, "Have You Seen Your Mother," etc.) in honor of Baby Jane Holzer (an ex-Warhol girl of the year and an ex-Mick flame) and the Rolling Stones, at Schatzberg's loft on lower Park Avenue. Mick asked Linda if she were going to be there, and although she was going with a date, David Dalton, her editor at *Hullaballoo* magazine and occasional boyfriend, she didn't tell Mick that, just that she'd see him at the party. As far as she was concerned, she now had a date with Mick Jagger for that party, and David was very nice, a gentleman (and a passionate Stones fan); he'd understand when the time came to tell him.

So Linda got her first fabulous photographs *and* her first fabulous "date" on that one day. It was one of the very few dates of any kind she'd had since leaving her husband and moving back to New York with her baby daughter. "My father would have liked me to have married a commuter, drink martinis in the evening. He always wanted for me what everyone, I suppose, wants for his daughter," Linda told me some years later. "Singles bars were happening, but I never even went to one. I once went out on a date, to some kind of pub, and I remember thinking, 'This is so boring,' and just sort of walking out and going home. My mind, my karma I suppose, was different from what it was supposed to be." Though she was to make motherhood her first priority, always, Linda was able that day to leave a life that was creatively and sexually non-existent, leave it happily behind her. She entered the history books with all flags flying.

But, before we get Linda dressed up for her first date with a true star, please allow me to introduce myself, as a witness to Linda's life, a friend and perhaps a minor player.

I grew up in New York City too, the wrong part as it happens (Queens), but Linda reminded me of the girls I dated when I was a teenager: Manhattan girls from families richer than mine; strong, smart girls who always looked good and knew how to enter and leave restaurants. That sounds superficial, but it stands for a lot. When I met Linda, it was several years after I stopped dating girls at all, but I knew she was going to be a Best Friend. We had the same taste in music, art, and guys. What more is there to bond about?

Her father had graduated from Harvard Law School, from which I had dropped out after one year. I moved back to New York, to Greenwich Village; a series of weird jobs selling books and putting out magazines about liquor stores (no kidding) got me a job at *Datebook*, a "teen" magazine that by 1966 was buying exclusive Beatles stuff from England and seeing its circulation rise dramatically. The publisher needed someone closer to what was happening, and I faked my way into the position of managing editor. I knew nothing about rock music or the bands or anything, but after a few months of hanging out and listening to the latest albums, I was as qualified as anyone who wasn't actually a practicing musician to be in the hot center of the scene. I would slide notes under dressing-room doors and get interviews with bands like the Byrds, the Rascals, the Mamas and Papas, groups with number one records. "Faked," I think, is the operative word. The Beatles and the Stones I'd never met; they were Up There, and I was Not.

Until the invitation came from Betsey Doster, who worked for Allen Klein (ironies will become apparent later in this story), to come aboard the *Sea Panther* to meet the Rolling Stones. I could bring a photographer.

So I hired someone recommended by the publisher, and the jerk got to my office the morning of the boat ride with plenty of cameras but no film. We were late in departing and it's a long ride from Washington Square, where *Datebook*'s little office was, to the Seventy-Ninth Street Boat Basin, from which the Stones' boat would be leaving. "No matter," he said. "We'll stop in Herald Square and get some film." This guy was clearly a foreigner. You don't "stop" in Herald Square and jump out to buy film; it's traffic hell—you circle the block at one mile an hour. Anyhow, we got to the dock just as the boat was pulling away. I fired the goddamn photographer on the spot and decided, if I wanted to keep my brand-new job in rock-and-roll publishing, that I'd better wait for the *Sea Panther* to come back, attack a disembarking photographer and offer him/her whatever it took to get some pictures of life on the river with the Rolling Stones.

What luck! There was chic and devastatingly clever Christina Berlin, youngest sister of my dear friend Brigid, getting off the boat with a gorgeous, happy girl wearing a Pentax. (And a skirt and matching top, but I only noticed the Pentax.)

"Christina, I *must* meet your friend," I said cheerily. "It looks like she's got some pictures."

"Sure, Danny, this is Linda Eastman. She works with me at *Town & Country* . We both hate it there, I'm sure you'll like each other."

"Nice to meet you, Linda. So listen," I went on, "got any pix to sell?"

Well, *Hullaballoo* had the pick of the pack (*T&C* had already done all the Rolling Stones coverage it was ever about to do; Linda was moonlighting with her first freelance assignment from *Hullaballoo*, a genuine rock magazine), but she promised she'd show me what it didn't want.

Great. I was covered.

By the way, some accounts of this auspicious day say that Linda was the only photographer on the boat. We know this is not true; there were, first of all, "official" photographers hired by the Stones' management office. You don't stage an event this glamorous without some tried and true professional photographers, 1940s movie variety. These pro-bozos barely knew who the Stones were, and you can tell that from their pictures, which were sent out by the Stones organization. They were so dry and formal, almost nobody used them. They make Linda's pictures look all the more wonderful. The Stones, as seen in photographs by efficient older men in brown suits and white shirts, look thoroughly bored, as if they wished they were doing something else; in Linda's pictures, and in *all* Linda's work, the subjects are playing right into her lens, being cute, arrogant, beautiful, sexy, graceful, sensitive, or all the above.

Photo sessions are among the most despised things that musicians are required to do. They are one step less repulsive than meeting the staff of local radio stations. But working with Linda was fun: there was portraitist-subject content, and everyone understood what was going on. "She took my favorite pictures of me" is something said to me often by people who had posed for Linda.

Back at *Datebook*, I was making some mischief that would have national implications, and which resulted in pitting the Beatles against America's ever-vigilant fringe-right religious extremists, including such enchanting fellowships as the Ku Klux Klan.

As managing editor of a magazine for teenagers, I was eager to stand out from the pack. The publisher wanted us to emulate the formula of the incredibly successful *16* magazine, the most widely circulated fan magazine ever, with newsstand sales of a million and a half copies and a readership of close to four million teenage girls. *16*, under the inspired direction of its editor-in-chief and inventor, the great Gloria Stavers, was (even though Gloria was the lover of Lenny Bruce and adored dangerous men) cuddly and innocent. In *16*, no one ever got laid; the readers were pre-sexual (they wouldn't be today at that age) and there was certainly no politics unless smuggled in under the disguise of a poetic obituary for Bobby Kennedy *et al.* Typical *16* cover lines (these from the October '66 issue) were "BEATLES EXPLODE—THOSE NASTY LIES WE HATE! 50 FREAKY NEW PICS;" or, about members of Paul Revere and the Raiders (although never about "Paul" himself): Fang—"COME HOME WITH ME AND MEET MY FOLKS!" or Mark—"THE LONELY YEARS I'LL NEVER FORGET." Despite what my publisher wanted, in my responsible new position, I was not about to follow that mushy line (by sociological, aesthetic, and/or commercial standards, *16* was the most brilliant magazine of its era and for its audience, but what did I know?). Besides, you couldn't just rise up out of nowhere and compete with Gloria on her own turf. She ruled.

For example, Brian Epstein, the manager of the Beatles, introduced his new American group, the Cyrkle, to the American media at a crowded press conference in a mid-town hotel. *Very* crowded—this was the man who controlled the Beatles (one thought) and, if I haven't yet made it clear, although my friends loved the Stones, the Beatles were alone atop the mountain of Fame Heaven on this planet. Being in the same room as Brian Epstein, even for the most cynical reporters, was an enormous thrill and an Important Thing to cover. Anyhow, Brian paraded the Cyrkle in front of the podium and answered a few questions, including, "Mr. Epstein, are you a millionaire?" which came most aggressively from Lillian Roxon. This was my first encounter with Australian journalism (i.e. the form of reportage that now dominates the world) in action. When the audience left, Gloria entered. She and the Cyrkle were ushered into a smaller room for her exclusive pix and "40 THINGS YOU NEVER KNEW." She was getting solo time with Brian and the group; it was inconceivable that any other entertainment magazine editor would merit this acknowledgment of her power.

Another Gloria story, this one tied in to the boat ride that began this chapter. As I watched weeping while the boat I'd missed sailed out into the river, a limousine pulled up and Gloria got out. She didn't say "Hello"—I was too inconsequential for that—only "Shit!" as she realized that the press event had put to sea without her. A man came up to us and offered, for twenty dollars, to ferry us out to the *Sea Panther* in his motorboat. I didn't have this great amount of cash on me, so I turned to Gloria and said (the first words I ever spoke to her; we would eventually become the closest of friends, as would she and Linda), "Hey Gloria! Want to split it ten and ten and catch up to the boat?"

"Fuck 'em," she said, not to me but to the vanishing yacht. "The Stones aren't worth ten dollars." She got into her car, and sped away.

I told this story when I was being interviewed for the 1992 BBC documentary about Linda McCartney, the excellent *Behind the Lens*. The me-and-Gloria moment wasn't really a story about Linda, but it made the final cut and was aired in the U.K. nearly un-bleeped; I knew Paul must have loved Gloria's line about the Stones, and that's why it stayed in the program.

As I was saying, it was time, I thought, to jump past all this teeny-bopper nonsense and put *Datebook* on the map as a magazine that reflected the rebellious wisdom-mongering that characterized our generation. We'd opened our minds with drugs that the older, boring, warring age group could not even comprehend; we were collectively the new improved rhythm section of the universe. Certainly its conscience, as Bob Dylan had demonstrated. Style was being reinvented in swinging London, stoned California, and cool New York—it was up to you to mix the ingredients and give names to the new flavors of life. And we were so gorgeous. Girls were always supposed to be gorgeous, but now so were boys. You had to go to bed with everyone—you didn't really know someone until you'd gotten through the slurping and penetrating part of it, which was not a fate worse than death. What sex you were or what your old tastes and customs had been hardly mattered. We were free to do everything that had ever been forbidden—well, everything that was victimless. And I was free to make some trouble on the cover of a magazine for fourteen-year-old kids. I convinced the owner that it was a good idea, but my time of employment at *Datebook* was so short that I'd been fired long before my contribution to culture hit the newsstands.

You see, *Datebook* had bought the American rights to a series of interviews the Beatles had done in England with Maureen Cleave for the London *Evening Standard*, published in March 1966, in which the boys caused a politely shocked little buzz, though not a lot more, much to the group's satisfaction. They were trying to move away from the "adorable mop-top" phase as fast as their eight legs would carry them. The Beatles were, by this time and particularly in the U.K., so exalted that the royal family was running a tired second to the loftiness of the Fab Four. They could do, say, wear, write anything, and command the attention of the nation. So with Ms. Cleave they pulled no punches. At least Paul and John didn't.

They were long interviews, and buried deep within them were such tidbits as Paul saying (about America), "It's a lousy country where anyone who is black is a dirty nigger." And it was of course the same series of interviews in which John opined, "We're more popular than Jesus now; I don't know what will go first—rock and roll or Christianity."

Yummy! Such good quotes deserved better than the tiny typeface they were accorded in London. They ought to be on the front cover of a magazine. Especially the September *Datebook*, with a cover that featured a big, kissy, color photograph of Paul McCartney.

So we came up with the idea of a "shout-out" issue, and I used the most incendiary quotes (i.e. the two in the last paragraph) on the cover (along with Timothy Leary's already tiresome "Turn on, tune in, drop out!") and as the headlines of two separate stories, one about Paul and one about John. Both were essentially Maureen Cleave's interviews. Nothing substantive was changed, either on the cover or inside, nor were the quotes "taken out of context," as it was later claimed, when trouble arose. Not at all. They'd just been pulled from the body of the interview, enlarged and placed elsewhere. They're called "pull-quotes" in magazine-land, and of course they're commonly used. To say something was used "out of context" implies that the meaning was changed by lifting the quotes from what came before and after. But the meaning had not been changed—John did say, "We're more popular than Jesus now," and he meant it, and it was true.

There follows a quote from the very handy reference book, *Rock Movers and Shakers*, where careers are outlined in careful chronological order, from the section devoted to "The Beatles," sub-section "1966," entry for 31 July of that year: "2 days after U.S. *Datebook* magazine publishes Lennon's interview with Maureen Cleave, citizens of Birmingham, AL, publicly burn Beatles' records and memorabilia, amidst general anger in the Southern states."

The furor spread through America's Bible belt and hopped the Atlantic to South Africa, where the national broadcasting company banned all Beatles' music from that enlightened country's airwaves. In America, though, with the religious right aroused, the controversy had far more profound consequences for the group, then on the eve of their fourth American tour.

In Memphis, outside the Mid-South Coliseum, where the Beatles were to perform on August 19, a spokesperson for the Ku Klux Klan, in full hooded drag, told a television reporter that "the Beatles had made a statement in all the newspapers that they're getting more better than

Jesus." He boasted, "We're gonna try and stop it [the concert] any terror way we can, but it's gonna stop." They didn't stop it, but they assembled 8,000 pro-Jesus supporters for an extremely ugly rally outside the venue. The Beatles were seriously rattled.

A month earlier, they had barely got out of Manila alive, after First Lady Imelda Marcos announced that the Beatles had insulted her, and hence all Filipinos, by not showing up at a garden party she gave in their honor at the presidential palace. But that was a Third World country, and this was America. Wasn't the South, and Memphis in particular, the birthplace of rock and roll? Maybe, but for the Beatles, the South was now a cradle of hatred. Death threats started pouring in, and touring had become not merely no fun, but catastrophically scary. After playing San Francisco on August 29, the Beatles decided they never wanted to perform publicly again, and they never did.

I can't exactly claim that our little attempt to beef up poor *Datebook* magazine led directly to that decision, but it was one of the last nails in the coffin, so to speak. Over thirty years later, in an interview for the *Beatles Anthology* television series, talking about coming off the road once and for all, George Harrison said, "I think the most important thing was the safety aspect . . . It was just becoming too difficult on the nervous system." And the first time I met Paul, after he married my friend Linda, I told him that it was me who had put those quotes on a magazine cover in the summer of '66. "Ah, so *you're* the one," he said.

(Postscript to this frenzied time in America's cultural history: they may or may not have been bigger than Jesus, but Somebody Up There was clearly rooting for the Beatles—the morning after a "Beatles Bonfire" sponsored by radio station KLUE in Longview, Texas, a lightning bolt hit the station's transmitting tower, melting its equipment, knocking out the news director, and leaving Longview KLUE-less until the damage was repaired.)

The Beatles, Jesus, Linda, *Datebook*, Mick, Imelda, Memphis, and the Hudson River on a day in June—what a summer! They don't have summers any more like they did in the still incomprehensible '60s, when it was all about great rock-and-roll groups, nice drugs, people who made and wore silly clothes, believed a new era was at hand, slept with everyone else under thirty, and danced and dreamed to music such as had never been heard, before or since.

Let's get off that cloud and watch Linda create a remarkable new life for herself. "In that short hour and a half on that boat she was happier than I'd ever seen her," Christina Berlin recalls. "Everything started working for her, from that moment. I knew that she could pursue photography, and that she'd be very good. She read people very well, these people related to Linda and that made for great pictures. She had talent, looks and the personality to deal with rock stars. She'd been in the dumps before this, and it certainly wasn't where she wanted to be. Linda was just waiting for something to happen."

Well, it happened that day. A brilliant career as a photographer of rock stars had begun. Her pictures of the Rolling Stones were so good that Linda Eastman was soon one of the most celebrated photographers in the exploding universe of rock and roll. Two of the most exciting and liberating years of her life were now ahead of her; she and her work were recognized, admired, sought after. She produced some of the most memorable images of that era, and she travelled from New York to London to L.A., assembling a portfolio that, in the year 1999, is the core of a show called "Linda McCartney's Sixties: Portrait of an Era," exhibited at dozens of distinguished American museums, attracting big and eager audiences who had either seen Jimi Hendrix or wish they had, but are now getting the chance at least to see—once again—"My favorite pictures of me."

The boredom of life behind a desk at *Town & Country* was at last behind her. Ironically, the relentless pressure from her father to do something worthwhile grew more severe when he learned that her new career centered on the world of rock and roll. "He's always telling me it's going to get me in trouble, it's going to be gone overnight, and I'll be back being an office intern," Linda would complain to me after a bout with Dad. "I was miserable staying where I was, and that state of mind was worse to me than the possibility that this would all be over tomorrow, which of course I never believed. I love what I'm doing, but my family sure isn't making it easy for me to be who I want to be. Too bad." She told another writer, "I said to my father I wanted to quit my job and become a photographer and he shot me a look like, "If you do, you're finished." And I said, "*C'est la vie*."

Linda's family would shift radically from their disapproving mode when her new career brought her, two years later, into a relationship and then marriage with Paul McCartney, no doubt the world's most eligible bachelor. "Linda suddenly became their favorite child," says Nat Weiss, Brian Epstein's American partner and a close friend of Linda's since her first forays as a photographer.

The marriage of Paul and Linda would make history, and lasted until death did them part. But let's stay in 1966 for a while. There's a big party coming up.

Chapter 2

"The problem with shooting groups was the groups. They were obnoxious, excruciatingly self-conscious teenage brats. It was a bloody pain in the neck. But with the Lovely Linda, all this changed . . . Now their eyes were pinned on her."

David Dalton, writer, photographer

Boys, men, dating, heart throbs, conquests, artifice, fashion, flirting—these were really not part of Linda Eastman's life. Horses were more important to her than boys for all her youthful years, then she was married at twenty, separated and a mother at twenty-one. She did not have a lot of girlfriends; girls and Linda had not much to talk about. She loved rock and roll and crawling around damp, dark, little ravines in the country near her house where the lilies of the valley grew.

"I'd lived in Arizona, and I loved Arizona. But I had a husband I was separated from, and a baby to support. So I moved back to New York. I used to think it was scary. I remember the first time I drove into the city, right after I got my license. All that traffic, those buildings. Oh! Scared me to death."

Linda's father, Lee (for Leopold) Eastman, a rich and brilliant lawyer famous for his rich and brilliant clients, would not support her when she came back east in 1964 after her brief, failed marriage (although, no one was going to starve, certainly not an infant granddaughter). Dad, still living in the town where Linda had grown up—Scarsdale, New York—now with his second wife Monique (Linda's mother Louise died in a plane crash in 1962), made patrician paternal noises: "Get a job. Get an apartment. School didn't work for you. Marriage didn't work for you. No time for experimenting now, you have to make it work. Start looking."

Lee Eastman was a universe of a guy. If you didn't know after fifteen seconds that his thoughts at any moment were leaping ahead of yours, your mind was second rate and your physical presence went into a kind of atrophy. He was an A-list guy—not socially, as on dinner-party lists, but with A-list brains, ambition, talent, a 360-degree lens built into his sensory mode. It was a shoulders-back occasion when he asked one to stay around a little longer. But I think he no longer had patience with Linda's lovely shoulders. He strongly suggested that she move thirty miles south, to New York City, and find an apartment and a job.

Luckily, there would be no argument about where this apartment was going to be. It's not as if there's a choice. "Our crowd" (i.e. the Eastmans, younger and older) simply settle in the Upper East Side, where the doorman is the most crucial person in your catalogue of "people who make life a little easier." The stores sell extraordinary quantities of $500 dresses for five-year-old girls who will outgrow them well before the age of six; there are tangelos and *minneolas* (and sandwiches to go) at the two or three fruit stores on a single block. There are hardware stores that specialize in the screws and sprays favored by women who carry $6,000 handbags and have more at home. There are hotels where people live for $40,000 a month, dermatologists who can always find $425 worth of unsavory work to do in half an hour. These are today's prices, but only the figures are different from those of the '60s, not the quality of life. You find the finest dogs, magazines from the fashionable new cities on the Caspian Sea, and restaurants where either you are welcomed, and go a lot, or you are not welcome, and never go back. There are alternative doctors who find and treat parts of your body you never knew existed. Dealers deliver, of course, bearing beautiful inlaid mahogany cases with drugs graded by the color of their vials; they might forgo an instant sale and tell you to wait a few days, if you can, because something is coming that "I know you'll love." There are reading clubs conducted by polymaths who put you through a season with *The Golden Bowl*, a sort of boot camp for stunning matrons of a certain age with pretensions. *Everyone* is smoking . . . cigarettes! One would think this was the vanguard of quitters, but it's really action central for the I-don't-give-a-shitters.

Girls like Linda, with good backgrounds and no money, just assume this is where they're going to live—and, guess what, they somehow find apartments and become the alternative population of the neighborhood. The further east you go, the fewer luxury dermatologists you find (but lots and lots of shrinks), and the streets aren't quite as clean as they were just a few hundred feet closer to Central Park. I wonder why that is. In 1992 Linda recalled:

> I didn't have any money, and I didn't know how you did it, but I knew I was going to find a place for me and Heather on the Upper East Side. Maybe if I'd known the city better when I first started looking, I'd have gone downtown.
>
> I had one hundred eighty bucks to spend on an apartment in the most expensive neighborhood of the most expensive city in the world, but, you know me; I never thought normal.
>
> I had the nerve to start looking in the Sixties—nothing. The Seventies—nothing. My chances were lousy. Then on Eighty-third Street I saw this doorman and asked about the building, and he told me about a woman on the tenth floor who was moving. She was in my situation, a mother and a child. It was an L-shaped room, and she had put in a little thin wall, so it became my tiny, tiny one-bedroom apartment, $180 a month [today an apartment like this would cost at least $2,000 a month]. I was scared, you know, I'd never lived in a city. I got my furniture from the Salvation Army on the West Side. Nice! I was leaving Heather with my stepmother in Scarsdale while I went on this quest . . .
>
> Look, I liked rock and roll in the '50s, and nobody's parents anywhere could deal with that, certainly not my father and

> Monique. We were supposed to do well at school; he graduated from Harvard Law School. I can understand why you may have the same mouth and coloring as your parents, and hopefully the graces and curiosity that make them civilized, if they are, because you're surrounded by that. But I never understood how you were supposed to inherit their professional or religious or sociological preferences. Those are supposed to come from the world you live in, they're not in your genes.
>
> That's the best thing you can do as a parent, and we've tried so hard; nice is best, then happiest, then comes fulfilled and good-looking and talented or even just ordinary, but nice is best, and I believe that may be the one thing, and *should* be the one thing, that you can pass on to your kids. It's certainly the one thing you must be above all. Even if all you can do is stick the both of you in an L-shaped room on East Eighty-third Street, come home exhausted, pay the sitter and be a Mommy until you pass out. But there's no place in that whole situation where "nice" doesn't fit in.

Of course, that's Linda McCartney in 1992 talking about Linda Eastman in 1966. But I believe that her deepest values never changed, and although she was dismayed by her father's disapproval, she was in awe of him—he was her ideal of a "cool" man then and always.

Linda had studied photography at a local arts center in Arizona with a teacher named Hazel Archer, but most of her pictures had been of horses. She became fascinated with the art of taking photographs, and acquired a fine appreciation and knowledge of the work of the American greats, like Dorothea Lange, Ansel Adams, and Walker Evans. Living in New York, she spent lunchtimes at the photography exhibitions in the Museum of Modern Art, and was familiar, not surprisingly, with the European painting galleries at the Metropolitan Museum of Art, just a few blocks from her apartment.

I remember a Sunday in the mid-1980s when she, Paul, and the kids were staying at Stanhope Hotel, near the museum. My room-mate Michael and I had breakfast with them in their suite and then went over to the Met for a VIP visit, an hour before it was opened to the public. I said something about wanting to see my favorite really old masters and Linda gave me precise directions: "Go through there and turn left there . . ." I recognized her familiarity with those galleries and her love of the paintings hanging there—it was that of someone who'd been alone in New York City and knew her way around the town's great treasure troves. She obviously visited the Metropolitan Museum frequently, but that was in the years before I knew her. Because when we were "best friends" we talked about rock and roll, subways, and our other best friends—never about Van Eyck and Co. It occurred to me that she'd probably been glad to say goodbye, for a while, to the fifteenth century when she started her own life as an artist, which she really was, just about from the start.

The day in late 1965 that she met David Dalton in the lobby of the Hearst Building, where they both worked, but at separate magazines, was a crucial one. British, well-born, handsome, and very, very smart, David had a "shit job," like Linda's, at *Harper's Bazaar*, a fashion magazine for women who lived near golf courses in the suburbs of Houston.

"I absolutely hated it, it was horrible, I couldn't get up in the morning," Dalton recalls—which could have been Linda talking, or me, or any of lots of people who didn't know what to make of their lives in the early and mid-'60s.

> What could you do to be part of what was interesting? And make a living at it? Play an instrument, which I couldn't, work in a boutique, which I wouldn't. I hadn't thought of being a photographer, but someone told me to just get a single-lens reflex, learn about f-stops and shutter speeds, focus, and press a button. So I got a Pentax and started photographing groups whenever and wherever I could. Because classic languages, and painting, which I'd studied, went out the window when the English bands started happening. Rock and roll had become the real focus of my life.
>
> So there I was, with my camera, waiting for the elevator to hell, when this beautiful blonde girl, also carrying a Pentax,

> started asking me questions about photography. She wanted to know everything. "If I don't learn to do something well," she said sort of sadly, "then what's to become of me?" She bemoaned the pointlessness of her life, but with tremendous energy. She was Sleeping Beauty . . . just around the corner the blazing path of pop life awaited! I identified with her yearnings, plus I was a boy and she was definitely a girl one noticed.

"Linda was educated, smart, and hungry," David Dalton wrote in *Gadfly* magazine, shortly after her death.

> But she was sleeping a lot, snacking on Ritz crackers and hors d'oeuvres from the deli and was in a fog of low level depression.
>
> I was going that night to Steve Paul's club the Scene, where Atlantic Records was having a party for the Rascals, for "Good Lovin'," which had gone to #1. I'd convinced someone in the Atlantic publicity department to let me shoot the "trade shots," you know, the group and Ahmet Ertegun, the dapper and inscrutable president of the company, all posing for *Billboard*, that kind of stuff. So I asked Linda to come with me, and she was bursting with enthusiasm. A rock-and-roll group, the coolest club in town, *and* I'd be using a strobe light, and thereby unlocking one of the mysteries of the universe, for this incredibly excited, energetic girl, who had never taken pictures with anything but natural light.
>
> She met me at the club in the early evening, record company party time, and that's when it struck me how different she was from the other denizens of that sprawling basement on Forty-sixth Street off Eighth Avenue. She was dressed in a striped long-sleeved T-shirt and an A-line skirt down to the knees. Nighttime fashion in New York's hip boites then was mini-skirts, silver foil sheaths, pop art, net stockings, heels, jewelry, much makeup, and carefully crafted hair.
>
> Linda looked every inch a WASP (even though she wasn't), and she dressed with the studied bad taste that elite WASPS aspire

> to. They had whole stores devoted to this strange phenomenon: Peck & Peck, Best & Co., B. Altman. It was a bizarre cult of exclusive dowdiness. Vassar girls dressed like this, rock-and-roll girls didn't. For a while, she was using the wonderful name of Linda See—it was the name of her ex-husband, an anthropologist in Arizona to whom she'd been briefly married, and from whom she'd been recently divorced. He was the father of Heather, born in 1962.

Linda's divorce from Mel See wasn't finalized until June 1965, exactly three years after they were married, although they had stayed together for only about twelve months.

In the beginning of 1966, Linda stopped using her ex-husband's name and became again Linda Eastman. "I once heard someone make fun of that name [See]—they thought I called myself that because I wanted to be a photographer, like Mr. Dose the druggist and Miss Stitch the seamstress from Happy Families or something. I hated anyone thinking I would be so cute as to do that, so I went back to Eastman. No one had believed that See was a real name anyhow, and it had been mine for such a short time, I thought it was best to ditch it."

Back at the Scene with the Rascals, Linda was almost more excited about the strobe attachment than about being so close to the "big time." By the end of the evening, she had convinced David to let her try it a few times. Once having mastered electronic illumination, she tucked it away and used it very rarely. She liked a soft, natural light, and it became part of her m.o. as a photographer not to set off flashes when capturing a subject. If the focus and composition hadn't been perfect, her portraits might have been a bit flat, but they were the opposite. Shades of gray jumped off the page, colors were either elegantly cool or very intense, but, most of all, people turned themselves beautiful, still, arrogant, innocent, just for her camera.

A few weeks later David Dalton, now having associated himself with the start-up rock magazine *Hullaballoo*, was moving into the music business for real. "My speciality was setting up rock tableaux, with groups like the Shangri-Las, with little stories going on in the frame ('Is she really going out with him?' being whispered by three girls in the background, while Mary Weiss stood in front, as though they were really performing 'Leader of the Pack'). Guy groups were harder to manipulate, and quite a few from England seemed to me to be real working-class wise-asses. Like the Animals, to whose shoot on the Hudson piers I'd invited Linda."

The Rascals had been OK, but they were a mostly Italian-American rock band from New Jersey. The Animals were from Newcastle, not exactly members of the British nobility, and as wise-ass as they came. Their music was gritty and soulful, and Linda was a great fan. We were *all* fans of "We Gotta Get out of This Place," which was a signature song of its time and, what's more, the group had been adopted by a very hip, very decadent New York crowd. There were parties in their honor in penthouses where you wouldn't think they could get past the doorman and in sleazy hotels on West Forty-fifth Street where sailors, prostitutes, and black-sheep offspring of some of America's richest families lived in places like the unbelievable Hotel America, sex, and drug center of the then interesting Times Square area. (Oh, Linda never went near any of that, but she did like to hear about it.)

Dalton continues with the story of him, Linda and the Animals down on the docks.

> I found a very thick length of rope used for tying up ocean liners, and made a knot at one end. I had the Animals straining to burst through the circle of rope. Not a profound metaphor, but graphic.
>
> The image was just OK, but when I looked through the lens, it was fantastic. I mean the way those Zen Cockney masters like David Bailey and Michael Cooper did it. Then I worked it out. It was Linda. She had figuratively magnetized the group and it had done wonders for the composition. Streams of energy poured back and forth between the feral animals and Princess Linda. After I'd shot the picture, Linda asked if she could take some informal pictures of Eric Burdon and the boys. While she was snapping some very tightly framed pictures of Eric, he turned to me and confided a passionate interest in photography. Funny

> that he'd never mentioned it before.
>
> The problem with shooting groups was the groups. They were obnoxious, excruciatingly self-conscious teenage brats. It was a bloody pain in the neck. But with the Lovely Linda, all this changed. Photographing a yobby group like Tommy James and the Shondells was usually full of problems. Now their eyes were pinned on her.

So were Dalton's, by the way, and he and Linda were soon going out together—he was absolutely the first cool man she'd dated since she left her husband. It wasn't love—they were, in many ways, too similar to really excite each other—but why not? It was easier to be a couple in those days than it was not to. "My mother adored Linda," he says, "and of course that was one reason to be suspicious of her as a girlfriend."

For some arcane political reasons, *Hullaballoo* was not invited to the Stones, boat ride, and Dalton needed pictures badly for his magazine. Thank God for Linda. As I've noted, although she was officially carrying a camera as a representative of *Town & Country* , she was actually shooting for *Hullaballoo*, and I was to get the rejects for *Datebook*.

As we know, Linda accepted an invitation to meet Mick Jagger at Jerry Schatzberg's party, although her date for the party was David, fortunately, and always a most courteous and easygoing guy. When Dalton, the day after the boat ride, saw her pictures, he was awed. "It was astounding! They looked like real photographs, whereas mine had always looked like the out-takes. She had a sense of framing the thing. I don't know why this was. I went to art school, I studied all this shit! But she intuitively had it. You have to work in nano-seconds in photography, you can't sort of think about something, because by the time you've thought of it, it's gone. With me, it was always an act of luck or fate, but she had an instinctive sense about it and she loved doing it. She was so good, and the guys totally behaved. Her work was by far better than anything I'd ever done with a camera, even though I was 'teaching' Linda about photography." Dalton immediately gave Linda carte blanche to present herself anywhere as "a photographer from *Hullaballoo* magazine."

Christina Berlin has been around magazines, newspapers, and photographers all her life. "When I saw her pictures of the Stones the next day, they were unbelievable," she says. "They were terrific; they were better than any pictures of the Stones I'd ever seen. I said: "Linda!!!" She was excited too, she was jazzed about it. Because she knew she got them. When we left that boat she knew she had a lot, she knew she had pictures."

The Rolling Stones had not all been jumping for joy at this chance to meet the press and have their pictures taken in such a lovely, nautical setting. Charlie Watts thought this was the silliest thing he'd ever been asked to do, tried to pretend he wasn't even there, and was impossible to communicate with. Bill was, er, pleasant. But it was Brian and Keith with whom the two women hung out, as one would expect. And between Linda and Mick, there was something going on.

All the girls, now women, who hated Linda for marrying Paul McCartney would hate her all the more (if they'd also been fans of Mick Jagger back then—well, there must have been a few of them) if they'd seen the instant fit they made that day. Bear in mind, Mick has seduced hundreds, at least, of girls by now; there's no one he can't have (you can add a lot of boys, gay and straight, to that realm of possibilities). Habitués of New York's hotter nightspots (and no doubt London's and L.A.'s as well) were likely to know quite a few girls who'd had sex with Mick Jagger. The size, shape, feel, taste, and smell of every part of his body, and what he did with those, was practically public knowledge. Brian Jones was in that league as well. In fact, you had to turn over rocks to find people who had *not* had affairs (if something that takes place in a phone booth in under eight minutes can be described as an affair) with Brian Jones.

Linda was so eager to escape from, among other things, the New York courtship rituals and the guys she was "supposed" to be hooking up with. An attractive young woman in the 1960s with the time and energy to look for sex and/or companionship (you didn't even need much time and energy; it was the '60s) could find it/them easily, certainly in the major metropolitan areas. If you didn't mind being asphyxiated by certain colognes (what was it then? Canoe?), waiting until he folded his pants and being a good listener when he started babbling about soybean futures after he came, you were going to get some. But Linda hated that stuff. "Ewww, boys who use Mennen and Old Spice! Why would boys want to smell floral and powdery? That's what I like about San Francisco, I don't think they even sell that stuff out there." She couldn't handle the dating game, she preferred real frogs to the kind that she got fixed up with *and* she was the mother of a girl who was barely three and a half when I met her. Not only do maternal duties take most of your time that's left after work, but somehow men do not whistle at young moms and their drooling darlings. What ordinary bachelor wants to get involved with a family?

Still, I am told women have strange longings within them, that they certainly don't hate *all* men and that they rather like being made love to when the weather outside is frightful. And there are mirrors. Linda knew she was sexy—she just didn't know how to make it work for her. Until along came the boys in the bands.

David Dalton remembers bringing Linda to Schatzberg's party at his studio/residence on Park Avenue South. At one point she came up to him and said, "Mick Jagger wants my phone number. What should I do?"

"I suppose she was pretending, for my benefit, that this was the first time Jagger had come on to her," Dalton says. "I told her, 'Sure.' I was much more impressed than jealous—my respect for the Stones was almost religious. If Mick Jagger had chosen my date from that whole crowd to flirt with, it was like an honor."

"MICK AND ME—PHOTOGRAPHED AND WRITTEN BY LINDA EASTMAN," published in the March 1967 issue of *Hullaballoo*, has to be taken for the quasi-fiction that it is, although it is clearly an important artifact in the history of Linda's life and career, and a milestone in the history of rock-and-roll fan magazines. In the story, Linda runs into a "distracted, uptight" Mick Jagger at the party; he tells her, "I have to get out of here." He then suggests that "we all" go back to the hotel, although we never find out who that "we" included. They talk about music and Mick's life, call a radio station to request something by Otis Redding—which, don't you know, turns out to be "Satisfaction," an "ironical little coincidence." After a while, Mick gets very tired and Linda decides, "I'd better say goodnight and let Mick get his beauty sleep. I thanked him and he promised to look me up the next time he was in New York." Linda leaves the hotel, taking note of the groupies still waiting outside for a glimpse of "the fabulous Rolling Stones." The end.

Linda certainly didn't write it; writing was simply not something that she did, at least back then. But she and a couple of hundred thousand women who were then teenage fans of the Rolling Stones sure do remember "MICK AND ME." It was the ultimate fantasy; by taking his picture you know him well enough to talk to him at a party, well enough to go back to his hotel room with him, where he pours out to you the story of his life. Linda remembered that story too, it kind of haunted her. She remembered it well enough to insist, "I did not write that damn thing!" when I asked her about it many years later. I said "Didn't *you* write it?"

"No." I said.

The first person to know of Mick's interest in Linda was naturally Chrissie Berlin. As soon as they got off the boat, Linda revealed, "I think Mick really likes me. I have a kind of date to meet him at Jerry Schatzberg's party. Can you babysit for Heather?"

Recalls Christina, who is now going to narrate the wonderful and revealing story we might call "Linda Goes to Her First Big-time Rock Party,"

> I was absolutely agog that he found her so attractive. I mean, here I am with three-inch eyelashes, falls [hairpieces], make-up, mini-dress, not the most gorgeous person in the world, but I made an effort—and here's Linda, El Slobbo, and Mick absolutely went bananas over her. You know, she was a very sexual woman, sort of like Simone Signoret or something like that. She didn't give a damn, and after the fling with Mick she developed ways of letting men know that she found *them* attractive. "I think he likes me" was always her way of saying there was a mutual attraction. Anyhow, of course I was glad to babysit. That way I'd get all the dope.
>
> So four days later I went to her apartment, and there was the

ubiquitous chef's salad in the fridge for me—American cheese, iceberg lettuce and packaged ham, along with Heather's bottles.

I made her change clothes. I said, "Linda, look, you natural is one thing, slob is another—you don't have to get up like you're going to the prom but, for God's sake, you've got a date with Mick Jagger." She was in a skirt and a white blouse, no bra, no make-up. I said, "Do you have any make-up? I mean *any* make-up?" She said that she thought she did have a little bit somewhere, and went into this messy bathroom and started rummaging around.

She couldn't find the mascara, and it was such a tiny New York bathroom, with one of those lightbulbs on a clip that you light your basement with clipped on to a towel rack. I had some mascara and blusher, and I told her only the bare rudiments were necessary, just a little something. I made her put on a bra, and we found a decent black dress in her closet, and I made her put some earrings on. She was fighting me all the way, but I kept saying, "Trust me, you'll thank me, if not for yourself then for everyone else at the party. My God, you're still representing *Town & Country*, you know, so please." So she did, and she went out.

She left around eight o'clock. I fed Heather, I watched television, I was determined to stay up until she got home. I was dying to know what had happened. And around five in the morning, a dishevelled Linda walks in, with this little secret smile on her face. She said it had been great, and thanks a lot, and that she was absolutely exhausted. She was pretty cool about it, she wasn't one of those people who'd go into extraordinary descriptions of what it was like. She made it pretty clear that it was private.

I understood Linda. She was totally devoted to her daughter, and at the same time had no sex life at all after her marriage ended. Then she got on this very heady trip. Everything was working for her, the photography, the men, the whole thing. It was ego-building, and that was so much what she needed then, to feel productive and desirable, free to live a whole new kind of life.

We can giggle about earrings and bras, but what was in progress was one of the most remarkable make-overs, professional and personal, of the times—and these were times when make-overs were happening with felicitous frequency (cf the Beatles themselves, Bob Dylan, Janis, all the people who came from nowheres-ville and propelled themselves to the very pinnacle of the culture).

Said Linda about that watershed week: "That is when my life really began—when there was no father or husband watching over me. Photography saved me. It was like, wow, there is life after death. I became, at last, a really free spirit."

Chapter 3

"My father . . . was a very, very bright man . . . [my mother] was attentive and charming—everybody loved her."

Linda McCartney

On March 1, 1962, shortly after ten o'clock in the morning, American Airlines flight number 1, leaving New York International Airport (now JFK) bound for Los Angeles, went into a roll at 1,500 feet and plunged into Jamaica Bay, exploding on contact with the water about fifty feet from the shore. All ninety-five people aboard died in the crash, including Louise Sara Lindner Eastman, fifty years of age, the wife of Lee V. Eastman, a prominent New York entertainment lawyer, and mother of four children, John, Linda, Laura, and Louise Jr. She had been going to visit her son John, a student at Stanford. Mr. and Mrs. Eastman always took separate flights when travelling to the same destination, so that if there were an accident one parent would be spared to look after the children. Which is what happened on that day. Horribly, her husband was waiting at the airport for a later flight when his wife's plane went down.

An investigation determined that the use of an improper tool at the factory caused the wiring in the rudder of the Boeing 707 to short-circuit, sending it into an unwanted full deployment on take-off. The pilot was making a left turn and could not recover control of the craft when it flipped and began to fall nose-down into the bay. No scheduled non-stop flight between New York and L.A., arguably the most important air route in the continental United States (hence flight number 1), had ever crashed before March 1962, nor has any since. At the time, it was the worst single airliner disaster in America's history.

Louise Eastman, born in Cleveland on 9 November 1911, was the only child of Max and Stella Dryfoos Lindner, Linda McCartney's maternal grandparents, who'd been married the year before. Both came from prominent German-Jewish Ohio families who arrived in the Midwest well before the Eastern European Jews began settling there at the end of the nineteenth and beginning of the twentieth centuries. There were 3,500 Jews, the vast majority of them German, in Cleveland in 1880, less than 3 percent of the city's population; by 1920 the Jewish population of Cleveland, then a city of 800,000, was over 75,000. Between the Jews of Middle European and Eastern European ancestry there was almost no social contact, and very little intermarriage.

The older settlers, usually rich manufacturers, had their own clubs and their own houses of worship, the most prominent of which was known simply as "the Temple," where Linda's grandparents were married. "They were a major part of the Cleveland Jewish community," notes Arlene Rich, a Cleveland genealogist. "Linda McCartney's family tree is a Who's Who of Jewish Cleveland."

The Temple's approach to Judaism presents a remarkable parallel with Linda's own attitude towards religion and her ancestry. It is said of the Temple in *The Universal Jewish Encyclopedia* that it is a bastion of "liberal Reform Judaism . . . one of the first to have women on the board of trustees . . . services on Sunday took the place of the traditional Sabbath [i.e. Friday evening–Saturday morning] service . . . more than a place of worship [but] the center of all communal life."

Now, here is the transcript of a conversation I had with Linda in 1992, twenty-six years after we'd met.

D: *Do you feel totally removed from your one-half Jewishness now?*

L: *I'm all Jewish.*

D: *Your mother was Jewish? I thought your mother was a WASP.*

L: *No, my parents were both Jews. I think my mother's people were Alsatian.*

D: *I can't believe that all these years I've been imagining your mother as this horsey, WASPy type.*

L: *She was WASPy, but she was Jewish. You know, Danny, you're much more into all this than I am. I could never get into all that stuff, I'm very not into religion.*

D: *Did your parents observe any Jewish holidays or anything like that?*

L: *I think they tried to have something for Passover once, and we all made fun of it, and we all hated it. I've always hated religion. It's the most guilt-ridden, horrible thing. "My God is better than yours, and I'm going to fight you and kill you because of your religion." I think it's just a sick idea. You know how people are color-blind when it comes to other people—I mean, hopefully they are. Well, I'm religious-blind.*

Linda's mother summered at Bar Harbor, Maine (if one had to pick the sociological polar opposite of the Catskill Mountains, New York's "Jewish Alps," it would be Bar Harbor, Maine), and graduated from Smith College, one of the "Seven Sisters" schools of higher learning for daughters of the American aristocracy, in 1933. She became engaged to "Leopold Vail Epstein, son of Mr. and Mrs. Louis Epstein of New York," according to an announcement on the society page of the *New York Times*: "Cleveland, Dec. 25—Mr. and Mrs. Max J. Lindner of this city have announced the engagement of their daughter, Miss Louise Dryfoos Lindner, to Leopold Vail Epstein, son of Mr. and Mrs. Louis Epstein of New York. Miss Lindner attended the Laurel Country Day School and was graduated in 1933 from Smith College. Mr. Epstein, who is practicing law in New York, studied at Harvard University, and was graduated from law school there in 1933."

Louise and Leopold were married at the bride's home early in 1937. Two and a half years later, when their first child, John, was born, something had changed: "A son was born to Mr. and Mrs. Leopold Vail Eastman of 12 East Eighty-eighth Street on July 10 at Doctors Hospital," it said in the *Times*. Well, if "Eastman" was an Americanization of "Epstein," whence came the story, that persists to this day, that Linda was the heiress to the immense Eastman Kodak film and camera fortune? It happened that rumors linking Linda to the Eastman family of Rochester, New York, just sprang up around her when she began her career as a professional photographer—you know, film, cameras, Kodak film, Kodak photographer, Eastman Kodak, it made a nice kind of sense. "I tried to exploit the rumors to become a photographer," Linda told a British paper after marrying Paul in 1969, when the truth had to come out. "But I'm no relation whatsoever."

"Exploit" is a gentle way of putting it. "She told me her ancestor was George Eastman," recalls Chet Helms, one of the pioneers of the San Francisco mid-'60s rock scene via his Family Dog organization. "It was in 1967, and she was doing the pictures for a book that came to be called *Rock and Other Four Letter Words* that J. Marks was writing." Helms and Linda became close friends and were in touch from time to time over the next three decades; she never said why she had told him she was Rochester Eastman, and he never asked. It had been, they both knew, a fib.

It turned out to be a fib that's been very hard to shake. Informal surveys have convinced me that most people think, to this day, that Linda was an Eastman descendant; it makes a good story, and it's easier to despise the girl who married Paul if she turns out to be a débutante, as well as a bachelor-snatcher.

"Once I went to some club in Hollywood; I remember Alice Cooper was there and Mickey Dolenz," Linda told me on the phone from East Hampton in the early 1990s, "and this guy I'd never met was at the table where we sat, and when we were introduced he said, 'Oh, and are you one of the Kodak Eastmans?' I said, 'Oh the press has said that, and it's not true.' He said, 'I'm so glad you said that, because I *am* a member of that family, and I've hated you for years, thinking you were going around saying that you're one of us.' He was so pleased that I told him I was so sick of that story."

In truth, she had gone around for a few months saying that most casually, although not to anyone in New York, where her real family was known. Anyhow, be wary of trying to exploit rumors; there's a reason they get started in the first place, and if you help them along they will take on an endless life of their own, as Linda learned.

Lee Eastman, né Epstein, came from a very different background from that of Louise Lindner. He was the son of Louis and Stella Epstein (note that Linda's maternal and paternal grandmothers were both named Stella), immigrants from Russia. They met at Ellis Island while being processed for entry into the United States. Leopold Epstein was born in New York City on 10 January 1910 and grew up in the Bronx. Unlike his wife-to-be, he did not have the advantage of private elementary or high schools and spent his undergraduate years at City College, known affectionately as CCNY, where tuition was free, standards were high and most of the students were the bright but penniless children of Eastern European immigrants. Academically, it was, in its heyday in the 1930s, one of the best-rated colleges in America. One had to do very well indeed in high school to be admitted. Today, alas, the school is struggling to recover from a disastrous decline in its reputation as a result of a 1970s decision to admit any graduate of a New York City high school. Unfortunately, many of these graduates were pushed out of their high schools just to make room for younger students and entered CCNY barely literate. An influx of Asians has put some of the sparkle back into the institution, but the cauldron of intellect that CCNY used to be is but a memory, particular to its time and place in New York history. CCNY was not worthy of mention, as we have seen, in the engagement announcement cited above. But from CCNY Leopold Epstein went on to Harvard Law School, where in terms of social and financial standing he was very much an outsider, yet, in terms of intelligence and ambition, probably equal to anyone in his class. And even if they had gone to a free college, it was OK for Harvard Law School boys to date girls from Smith—it was OK for Harvard Law School boys to do just about anything they wanted, and it still is.

"My father married up," Linda told me. "He was a very, very bright man. From a wonderful peasant background and yet so astute, so smart."

Class mobility is not an irrelevant factor in the life of Linda and her family: Paul McCartney's mother, for example, anxious about the perceived gentility of her children, insisted that he and his brother speak English "properly," dropping the heavily accented Scouse dialect of Liverpool, which betrayed at once one's lower-class and Irish-immigrant status. "We were upper-lower class," Paul once told me. Emphasis on the "upper." And Linda's father "married up." So, of course, did Paul, although some of his Liverpool relatives hardly thought that marrying an American Jewish divorcée was a step towards heaven—not that he cared. More about that later.

Distinctions relating to birth are surprisingly powerful among the Jewish élite, like the Lindners of Cleveland, who traditionally married within their crowd. An heiress from a great New York German-Jewish banking family once fell in love with the heir of an immensely rich Russian-Jewish family, whose wealth was not of impeccable origin. (This was many years ago, when the fortunes at stake really were big time.) Her mother objected strongly to the match. "But, Mother," pleaded the heiress, "they're worth a billion dollars, and we only have two hundred million."

"I don't care," retorted Mother. "They're trash. You are expected to do better than that."

The Lindners, on the other hand, were a warm and welcoming family, no doubt eager to bring in some new blood, in the person of brilliant, handsome Leopold Epstein from the Bronx. That borough of first- and second-generation immigrants, however, was not where the newlyweds could be expected to set up housekeeping. So their first home was established on Eighty-eighth Street between Fifth and Madison Avenues, in a handsome red-brick apartment building just a few steps from Central Park, in a neighborhood whose elegance cannot be questioned. But although there is hardly a prettier place to live in Manhattan, Louise was not really a city person, having been raised in the lush and leafy neighborhood of Cleveland Heights (with those summers on the coast of Maine). And there was a young child, and plans for more, so a move to the suburbs was clearly desirable.

Scarsdale, New York, is twenty-eight miles north of the city. It tries hard to be quiet and discreet, with its beautiful, winding, wooded lanes and fine large houses, but it has never succeeded, because it just screams money and always has. It is certainly not garish, nor is it at all the "best" address in the suburban counties surrounding New York City, but for better or worse it is famous for simply being . . . Scarsdale. *The* quintessential wealthy suburb. Like "Beverly Hills," "Scarsdale" needs no explanation—it is very rich, and although it is thought of as a Jewish town, the population is pretty evenly made up of WASPs, Jews, and Catholics. The Eastmans lived in the Murray Hill area of Scarsdale, perhaps the most upscale part of this already upscale town, at 4 Dolma Road, in a sprawling stucco Spanish-style mansion with a tiled roof. It was at this house that the Eastman family was living, when Linda Louise Eastman was born on September 24, 1941.

(There is something a bit peculiar—perhaps it's a Cleveland thing—about the proliferation of the name "Louise" in Linda's family. It was her mother's name, her own middle name and the name of her youngest sister, as in Louise Jr., rare for a female child in any Western culture. Jewish parents generally name their children after a deceased relative, even if it means using only the first initial—Morris might become Marc—and not after a living person, which is considered bad luck. Oddly as well, the two daughters born to Linda after her mother's death are named Mary, after Paul's mother, and Stella, after both of Linda's grandmothers. One would have thought there would be a Louise, or any name with the initial "L.")

Two more sisters, Laura and Louise Jr., were born over the next seven years; the family thrived. Lee Eastman was specializing in show-business law and his clients included the very successful bandleaders Sammy Kaye and Tommy Dorsey, composer Harold Arlen and painters like Willem de Kooning. Music and the visual arts played a large part in the life of Linda's parents. Lee Eastman, not unnaturally, amassed a fine collection from the painters he represented (canvases were a welcome substitute for bills owed), and after his wife's death he endowed the Louise L. Eastman Memorial Lectureship in Art at Smith College. Friends of Louise donated a sculpture by the English artist Henry Moore to the college's Museum of Art. "I was brought up all through my life with art. I was a lover of art," Linda has said.

The Eastmans socialized with their distinguished clients, so Linda grew up surrounded by talented people—and was not unnoticed by them: songwriter Jack Lawrence ("Tenderly," etc.), a client of Linda's father, wrote the song "Linda" for her in 1944, and in 1946, with the great Buddy Clark on vocals, it was a huge hit.

"When Linda was forty-five, I was trying to think what I could get someone who's forty-five years old," Paul remembers. "So I thought, aha! a 45 record. I went into the studio and recorded "Linda," and then "Happy Birthday Linda." I had it pressed, with a label and a sleeve, everything.

"When the original recording became a hit, someone decided to do a television segment of Linda and Jack. This was very early on in the TV era. She was five years old, this showbiz wife of mine. She was at it way before I was. They put her up on a piano while Jack Lawrence sang, and the piano was so hot because of the TV lights, it burned her bum. And she cried. I think she felt guilty about that, and she never cried in front of a camera again."

(Indeed, 1946 was very early in television history; it was virtually the first year that people had TV sets in their homes, and total numbers were minuscule—just one dozen in Washington, DC, for example.)

Paul also bought the publishing rights to the song and had new sheet music printed, showing the grown-up Linda and Linda at seven sitting on a piano holding the original sheet music, with Jack Lawrence at the keyboard. She was not crying, having by then had two years to develop her professionalism.

Linda showed me the newly minted sheet music for the song in 1992, saying: "Look at me then! I didn't realize I was such a cute kid. You never feel that you're wonderful or beautiful when you're young, you know what I mean?"

"God, I loved that song, it was my favorite!" I told Linda at the time, and even sang a few lines: "'When I go to sleep, I never count sheep, I count all the charms about Linda . . .' My grandmother had it on a 78—you know, the records that shattered if you dropped them. I knew all the words, and my cousin and I would do little performances of it when the family was all together . . ."

Linda interrupted me: "Isn't it funny that we should be friends, and that was your favorite song? Danny, can I have a transcript of this tape? Because this moment is a memory." And we sang the rest of the song together. It is a memory indeed.

From her early childhood on, Linda was an outdoors person, who formed a close alliance with her brother John, two years her senior, for the purpose of exploring the woods and streams near their house. Frogs and snakes were the objects of their fascination. John recalled in a eulogy at the New York memorial for his sister, "We got our only spankings for scaring our parents by coming home way too late, each vainly trying to take the blame for the other when there was no blame: neither of us could tell the time."

"Scarsdale was country when I was a kid," Linda told *Fame* magazine. "It was farm country. Everyone thinks I'm this spoiled Westchester girl, but I'm not. I'm a country lover and a nature lover."

Her younger sister Laura, when she was old and sturdy enough, played pony to Linda's commanding rider, as they searched the damper and darker crevasses of the woods for lilies of the valley, Linda's favorite flower for the rest of her life.

Horses became an early passion, and by the time she was a teenager Linda was a champion rider. Her sister Louise, at Linda's memorial in New York in June 1998, spoke about Linda's room at home. "It was painted a beautiful pale blue, with the entire moulding at the ceiling hanging with ribbons won at horse shows. Most of them were blue for first prize, but there were quite a few reds, greens and yellows, but the best were the huge multi-colored ones for the Best of Show. She was very proud of these, and so was I."

On the other hand, there was no boasting of equine achievements outside the family. A friend from high school, looking through the yearbook of Linda's class, 1959, was puzzled by the very few extracurricular activities and club memberships mentioned next to Linda's picture. On being told Linda was probably riding when the other kids were doing things related to the school, her friend was surprised. "She never told anybody about it. I guess she just went and did it, and earned medals as well. It's typical of Linda that she never really sought the approval of her peers—or her teachers. She wasn't a good student, didn't like to read or study. I remember an English teacher who used to pick on her for not keeping up with the classwork. It upset her—and she was rarely upset."

Linda's father assumed that she was at least keeping up with her studies, and was especially pleased that she had asked for and received permission to stay out late two nights a week so that she could go to the local library when it had extended hours. A chance conversation with the librarian ("You must know my daughter Linda very well." Blank stare) put Dad on the pursuit of the truth—instead of the library, Linda was at a hang-out where kids listened to the hot new sounds of the Kingston Trio and the Everly Brothers. Music, not books. Late at night, Linda acted out the old teenage ritual of putting her head under the pillow with a portable radio tuned to the glories of rock and roll.

The teenage Linda Eastman was a natural strawberry-blonde, plump ("chunky," said a high-school classmate), pleasant looking and dressed like every other girl in town. Wealth equalled simplicity: Shetland sweaters, Weejun loafers, plaid kilts with huge safety pins, and button-down Oxford shirts. The Brooks Brothers natural look dominated, whether or not you actually shopped there; the Shetland/plaid/herringbone/button-down style was the standard among upper-middle-class youth (and their parents) in the 1950s. It was called "tweedy." The designer Ralph Lauren became a billionaire in bringing back this look a few years ago—perhaps not incidentally, he and his wife were among Paul and Linda's closest friends in the '80s and '90s.

Hair back then in Scarsdale was simple, clean, brushed back, and worn with a headband. None of the girls wore make-up. The idea, if there was an idea behind it all, was to look as if you went to a British boarding school. Adornment was out—big hair, as on the popular TV show *American Bandstand*—was unimaginable.

Gail Smith, who still lives in Scarsdale, remembers her classmate at Scarsdale High School.

> There was nothing bad and nothing incredible or earth-shaking about her. She loved to sing. I remember our senior breakfast in the school cafeteria—there was a microphone and good piano player, and I recall thinking, "Isn't that something! Linda's gonna get up and sing again." But I can't recall where that "again" comes from—she must have performed at some other event. She wasn't especially good, but she wasn't bad, and she obviously loved singing and had the self-confidence to get up and do it. Kids in those days were very supportive of each other. No one would have been mean or made fun of her for not being an exceptionally good singer. They just thought it was great that she got up and sang at all. She was an easygoing, sweet girl, well-liked, not a belle-of-the-ball type, but nice. She always had a smile on her face.

Gail's husband Joel, who was a year ahead of Linda, remembers offering her rides as she walked to and from school. "She was a very attractive, very nice girl."

The Eastman family spent summers in the 1940s and early '50s in the town of Wellfleet, about twenty miles from the tip of Cape Cod. Itself a Yankee enclave, Wellfleet was just south of the more artistic towns of Truro and Provincetown, where the Eastmans visited such eminent modern artists as Franz Kline.

"We'd pack our station wagon to the limit, with dogs and all our summer belongings hanging out of the car," Louise Jr. recounted at her sister's memorial. "My mother would pack dozens of egg salad sandwiches for the trip.

"Wellfleet was a wonderfully easygoing place. It was a fairly wild landscape, almost primitive. Our house was always full of sand and there were lovely beach parties. It was a completely different life than what we were used to, and I think that its spirit rubbed off on all of us. Linda would make the best spaghetti sauce ever, and blueberry pie, and we would have outrageously noisy games of hearts. My father would promote wild family discussions, and I confess we all became rather loud and opinionated. Somehow these summers prepared the way for a less than conventional life, a quality that Linda never forgot."

The Eastman house was a magnet for Cape Cod's Upper Bohemia, with Louise Sr. the most gracious and elegant of hostesses. "She cared for people," Linda said. "I'm not a people person like she was. She was attentive and charming—everybody loved her. She was vivacious in an understated way, she could scope a roomful of people and know what everybody wanted and needed. I envied that about her, I just never felt comfortable in gatherings. My sister Laura is more like her, I think."

For those who knew Linda later in her life, it is interesting that she felt that way about herself, because she certainly was a "people" person. Perhaps not in the sense of handling crowds in one's living room, or maintaining a salon, but in a one-to-one situation Linda McCartney was unmatchable. "Sit down . . . are you comfortable . . . it is so wonderful to see you . . . would you like anything to eat or drink? . . . oh don't worry about that . . . you look great . . . we've missed you, haven't we, Paul?"

In the mid-50s, the Eastmans forsook Wellfleet for East Hampton. One hundred miles from New York, this beautiful seventeenth-century town near the eastern end of Long Island was being discovered by artists (the great abstract expressionist painter Jackson Pollock worked from his studio there until his death in 1956) and a few savvy New Yorkers. It was indeed a well-kept secret, at first glance an area of potato farms, bays and beaches and, nestled in the dunes, the great estates of ancient blue-blood families who didn't want to be involved in the heady social whirl of Southampton, that famous, exclusive resort to the west.

Of course, East Hampton was a hotbed of quiet anti-Semitism, because, after all, people went there to get away from New York, and getting away from New York meant getting away from the Jews. Still, some very openly Jewish families from Brooklyn and Queens were attracted to East Hampton, with enough of them moving in to build a temple in which to worship. Other Jews who were neither practicing their religion nor very proud of it, such as Lee Eastman, were made uncomfortable by the influx of their more pious brethren, fearing it would stir up the latent anti-Semitism of the area, which it did. East Hampton became two towns; many think it still is. "The Jews go to the restaurants, the gentiles go to the clubs. That's the way it's always been and always will be," says a long-time (Jewish) resident. But it now appears as if there's a third town in there somewhere—Linda's brother John was voted into the hitherto extremely "restricted" Maidstone Club; he is one of a very select number of Jews in the club, but never fear that he and his family don't fit in. His wife Jody is gentile, tall, blonde and elegant; John looks like Robert Redford, incredibly handsome in a way that Jews think only Christians can be; and their children might be any kids at the most exclusive, upper-class schools such as Groton or Foxcroft.

This whole subject, which as you have seen did not interest Linda in the least, has several interesting aspects. Her mother was very active in the Federation of Jewish Philanthropies, and was quite accustomed to being both Jewish and élite her entire life. It was indeed possible to be both, and quite impossible for Louise Sr. to be anything else. And here's an irony: Paul McCartney, upon the birth of his first grandchild, Arthur, in April 1999, a year after Linda died, said to several friends at different times, "He's a very clever little lad. His mother is Jewish and his father is Christian, so he chose to be born between Passover and Easter."

Now, this is astonishing and quite lovely. Mary, Paul, and Linda's daughter and the mother of little Arthur, is of course one-half Jewish. Yet Paul doesn't say "half," he says, "His mother is Jewish." We now have Paul being more upfront about Linda's religion than Linda ever was. No one had ever heard him describe his children as "Jewish" before—Chrissie Hynde thinks that now that Linda is gone, Paul is cherishing everything about her even more than he did during all their years together. Including her religion of birth, which she cared about not at all.

East Hampton is certainly a bit of paradise, and was very important to the senior Eastmans, to John and his family and to Linda and Paul. For many years the McCartneys spent a few weeks there every summer, renting a different house each time but never far from Linda's father and brother, who both had (John still has) sprawling houses on Lily Pond Lane. Bob Dylan once lived on that street, and current residents of the neighborhood include Calvin Klein, Martha Stewart, and Steven Spielberg. On the south side of Lily Pond, which is beachfront, houses sell for $15 million; the Eastmans have always been on the north side of the street, but that is still not exactly a disgrace.

Frequently over the years Linda would say to me, "We're coming to East Hampton for a while, will you be near there?" And I would respond, "Maybe, but are you coming into the city?" and the answer was almost always, "No," as in "What city?" They would come to New York every summer without setting foot in the city itself. From JFK, which is near the western end of Long Island, in the borough of Queens, a car would whisk them eastwards to the Eastmans of East Hampton. When they left, they just did it the other way around, and never ventured into Manhattan unless there was business to be done. In 1989, when the McCartneys rehearsed for their forthcoming tour at Broadway's Lyceum Theater, they would leave the theater every night in a limousine which took them to the heliport on the river; from there a helicopter flew them to tiny East Hampton airport, where a car would be waiting to take them home. In the morning, they'd commute into the city the same way. That was after they finally stopped renting and bought a house in East Hampton, north of the Montauk Highway (equivalent to the wrong side of the tracks, but what did they care?), invisible from the road, on a hill-side above the town.

So, that's East Hampton for now, an important place for Linda for nearly forty-five years.

In 1959, kids of Linda's generation and social class were expected to go to college; in fact it was an obsession to get into a "good" school of higher learning, and Scarsdale High placed its graduates at the country's most prestigious institutions. But for Linda, a future in the halls of academe was very nearly preposterous. She loved horses, nature, art, rock and roll, "bombing around" (driving) her mother's powder-blue Ford convertible with the top down and Alan Freed on the radio, and being alone. At her parents' frequent parties, she preferred to hang out in the kitchen with the hired help; she really didn't have much to talk about with the guests.

But one had to go to college; there was no alternative for a seventeen-year-old girl from a distinguished family. Linda chose the University of Arizona in Tucson; it was fairly easy to get accepted there, considering her quite unremarkable high-school grades, it was far from the pressures of home and, perhaps most important, it was deep in the horse-riding country of the American southwest.

Naturally, the horses in the Tucson area took up more time than her studies, and Linda, without a great deal of reluctance (although her parents were certainly not pleased), dropped out of school well before even choosing a major. Her father refused to support her if she wasn't in school, and Linda faced one of the great crises of her life up to that time. She knew she had to start earning her own way. "All right, I'll be a dental assistant, I said to myself," Linda recalled. "But I went for one interview, and thought, 'Oh my God, no way!'"

She was considering alternative ways of getting by in Arizona, when in March 1962 her mother was killed, and of course she had to return home to Scarsdale.

"I had never really connected with my mother," Linda told Zoe Heller for an article that appeared in *Vanity Fair* in October 1992. "But for my father, it was a disaster. My parents had been very much in love. When de Kooning wrote to my father after the death, he described the relationship as a twenty-five-year love affair."

The family was shattered, and friends were called in to help with Linda's younger sisters, Louise, then twelve, and Laura, fifteen. Of course Linda should have stayed to mend the wreckage of what had been an ideal family. Instead, she returned to Arizona.

"It was a kind of escapism," she said to Heller. "I was very immature. I just escaped." Linda went back to Arizona and her boyfriend, a geology student named Mel See. She became pregnant within weeks of her return and married Mel on 18 June 1962. Their daughter, Heather, was born on 31 December, but by the end of 1964, when her husband suggested that the family go to Africa, Linda told him to go alone and the couple separated. In 1963, Lee Eastman had been remarried, to

Monique Schless Sprayregen, a wealthy New York widow and the mother of three sons, and in 1965 Linda and her baby moved back to the home of her father and his new family.

Chapter 4

"The 1960s were the age of erotic labor . . . It was a time when your erotic energies would be central to your work; wherever your erotic instincts led you, that's where you would try to put your work."

Richard Goldstein

It was the best of times, it was the best of times.

It was some West Coast musician—several take credit for the thought, although it is probably attributable to Jack Cassady of Jefferson Airplane—who said that if you can remember the 1960s, then you weren't there. That is, we were so high all the time that there's a blackout riding on the back of that decade in our minds. Add to that possibility the reality that those of us who were young thirty-five years ago are now beginning to experience certain annoying lapses of memory, whether or not drugs were a part of our lives back then.

Or, the memories are there, but they don't quite agree with others' memories of the same events—this is the Rashomon phenomenon: there is no history, there is no memory, there is no truth. One can certainly begin to feel that way after soliciting recollections of the places and the times from perfectly intelligent, rational witnesses, who may have done a few drugs now and then but are sure of what they know; or from perfectly intelligent, rational witnesses who confess to getting things mixed up occasionally.

"Who was there? I think *you* were there. You weren't? You couldn't possibly have been in New York in June 1968? I could swear you were there. I remember you standing by the window of our hotel room, I remember it perfectly, I remember what you were wearing and who you were talking to. No? Well, maybe you weren't there, but I remember who else was there . . ."

Still, I trust the people I talked to for this book. They were smart then, and if they're still around, they're even smarter. They may have problems with some recollections, but the picture is there, others can fill in some of the missing pieces, and the difference between two accounts of the same event is usually just one of emphasis and perception. One remembers what makes one feel good and what makes one look good, it is to be hoped, for the opposite can be very painful.

There are some things we'll never know—the witnesses are gone, and many things were never that important anyhow. But if we don't remember exactly what we were doing all the time, we remember who we were, who our friends were, and why they were our friends. Besides, we taped each other's phone calls all the time, it was the thing to do, so the past is not lost, just elusive.

What is most pertinent to this story, when it comes to the telling of the past, is that Linda was a most extraordinary person, all her early life indeed, but especially after she burst into the world of international rock-and-roll celebrity in 1966. People usually remember Linda well, their encounters with her, their perception of her in the many roles she played, their one-to-one relationships with her (if they had any), and they also usually remember liking her and what she did and said and who she was.

Because she was fairly famous very quickly, and enormously famous within a few years and for the rest of her life. People retain memories of their moments with very famous people; it's one of the last things you ever forget. And when the person is gone, and there will be no more new memories, the old ones are dusted off, packaged well, and stored away. The unfortunate and embarrassing opposite is when someone famous whom you once knew no longer remembers you—though you will never forget them, and never stop boasting of your acquaintance with celebrities. That's a fact of the pecking order of fame; you can't let it get you down.

I worked for Cream when they first came to perform in America in early 1967; Brian Epstein was a friend of mine and, in partnership with Robert Stigwood, he managed them, so they hired me as their press agent for their three weeks in New York. I couldn't get them any press, I couldn't get them arrested. Eric Clapton may have been God in London, but he was no divinity here, except to one beautiful slim blonde whose name I forget. After Brian introduced the group at a (breakfast) press conference for the band at Max's Kansas City restaurant, guaranteeing a full house of journalists, there was nothing more to be done, no further interest. So Ginger Baker and I sort of bonded, as unlikely a pair of buddies as there ever has been, but we seemed so odd to each other—and I was after all being paid to keep an eye on the band—that we were soon comfortable just hanging out, watching television, having dinner together at Max's and late-night drinks at the bar of his hotel. Ginger Baker and I were Really Friends; as weird as it sounds, we were. Plus I was with the whole group at the theater where they were performing, always in their dressing room, and at their recording sessions with Felix Pappalardi at the Atlantic studios on West Sixtieth Street, from which came "Strange Brew," originally titled "Brain Soup." And I never forgot what it was like hanging out with Ginger, who could?

Well, twenty years later he was back in town, some party at the Hard Rock in his honor, and I really looked forward to a hug and a giggle and remembering those nights when I showed him around New York, where he'd never been before, when Eric and Jack had gone off somewhere and it was just me and Ginger. And guess what, he didn't remember me at all. I wasn't really surprised. Hey, what a life he's had, the people he's met along the way, the travelling he's done. I'm sure there was a "me" in every city Cream went to, and they were a supergroup and I was me; why should he remember? If I were to forget him, I'd have handed in my credentials as a "witness to history" a long time ago. There are people who remember me whom I don't remember: "You heard our band in

Boston and you wrote us a nice letter with good advice, and you said you really liked our music . . ." and I have no idea who this person is, and I say, "Oh yeah, well, it's good to see you again." Ginger Baker was past pretending such things. (I told this anecdote to Paul, who of course knew the awkward phenomenon perhaps as well as anyone on the planet: "Oh, they come over and say, 'I tuned your bass in France,'" he said. "'Don't you remember? We were real mates, we used to sit around, you told me about your mother and father . . .'")

As I said, it's the Fame Pecking Order. So Linda Eastman McCartney is well remembered by anyone whose life she touched. And the '60s are well remembered too, albeit through a purple haze.

From mid-1966 until late 1968, when she moved in with Paul for good, Linda was getting around. I once read an interview with Goldie Hawn, who is of course one half of a great showbusiness couple, where she said, "Before I settled down with Kurt, I was doing some canoodling around. Why not? But then we settled down."

Canoodling, I like that word. It means, to me, checking things out, experimenting with relationships, seeing where they lead. And I think when you're canoodling, it's a big part of your life and a lot of energy goes into it, because after all, in modern terms among modern people, it is the search for a mate. How great when the search ends well—it must mean that the searching was conducted well, because no great romance is ever luck.

"The 1960s," says Richard Goldstein, executive editor of the *Village Voice* and probably the first journalist ever to have a regular column on rock in any publication, "were the age of erotic labor, to use a phrase out of Marcuse. It was a time when your erotic energies would be central to your work; wherever your erotic instincts led you, that's where you would try to put your work. And that's what you would try to do—integrate your sex life with your work, if you could."

Well, if your work was photographing rock stars, if you were a beautiful girl and if you dated some of them from time to time, this Marcusian effort got you labeled a "groupie," and let's face it, Linda got called a groupie and we have to deal with that. What is/was a groupie, and what did it mean to be one?

It is not spilling any beans to record that Linda Eastman was romantically linked with (she preferred to say "dated") some of the most successful, handsome, and talented young men in the world. Whatever you might have heard, there were probably no more than twenty such "linkages" in the two and half years before she settled down into unblemished monogamy with Paul, the number of whose dalliances, by his own admission, is much, much higher.

The Beatles were higher in other ways too, according to photographer Bob Gruen, who became a close friend of John and Yoko Ono Lennon after they moved to New York. (Gruen took the famous picture of John, arms crossed in a New York City T-shirt, with the skyline in the background.) As Gruen recently said,

> The Beatles had them lined up. Twenty-year-olds, thirty-year-olds, sixteen-year-olds, you name it. It was funny learning about it later from John, but the Beatles had access to more women than anybody knew. When their public persona was "I Wanna Hold Your Hand," and they were clean-cut, clean hair, nice guys, they would go out to clubs and people would just put things in their pockets. "Take this joint, take this pill, take this tinfoil"—all kinds of things. The four would go back to the hotel, they had a mortar and pestle, and they'd open up the capsules, put the pills in, open up the tinfoils, pour it in, grind the thing and put a spoonful in their coffee the next morning. And that's how they would go out and be the Beatles for another day. This was a time when everyone was on acid, but this was way beyond that. And the girls everywhere—they were fucking their brains out.

Well, our little behind-the-scenes crowd, the writers, the publicists, the photographers, me, Linda—we were virgins compared to the bands, and the other bands were virgins compared to the Beatles, and none of us were virgins.

I don't think anyone was keeping tabs on Linda, except perhaps the late Lillian Roxon, the great Australian journalist who became her confidante and closest friend. But twenty or so guys is about right, the rest of Linda's friends have figured out. Linda herself sometimes, in moments of exercising her newly found bravado, added people to the list who didn't belong there. The thing is, they weren't just guys, they were stars. There was no one in her life whom anyone we knew would ever have been embarrassed to have been seen with. One can't say that about oneself, and I wonder who can.

She indeed knew what was being said about her far and wide, she always did. Groupie? "I don't care what I'm called, I really don't," she told me. "The way I define the word, I wasn't a groupie. There were girls around who were classic groupies; they were very glamorous and often pretty fabulous, I thought. But I did hang out with groups. If that makes me a groupie, so be it. If people have to pin a single word of description on me, there are certainly others I'd prefer, but still, when you know who you really are, how can you let that get to you?"

She was more succinct with the beautiful model Bebe Buell, a girl who went out with rock stars and was sought after by them. She once said to Linda, "Oh, people are calling me a groupie, and I'm not one of those girls who hangs around hotel hallways and I don't want to be called that."

Linda answered, "They call me that too. I know who I am. I don't give a shit."

Nat Weiss, Brian Epstein's American partner, said of Linda,

> She certainly stood out way above all the other girls who were around the scene. Way above. She was very bright, she was a good mother, I never saw her drunk, I never had any question about the fact that she was a solid person. She had no attitude, she was always very friendly and very intelligent. She was ten cuts above any of the girls who went out with musicians. God knows, I saw thousands of them in that whole scene, and she certainly stood out, she was like no one else. And I have no doubt that from the moment she met Paul, she was in love with him, and compared to any other guy she knew, Paul stood out more and more. She was obsessed with him. And from what he said to me when they first met and became acquainted, he was

convinced—but I don't know if he admitted this to himself right away, he wanted to make sure—that she was the one.

"Everybody got called a groupie," Richard Goldstein remembers.

I guess you were a wife, or an "old lady," or a groupie. Linda was certainly not the kind of person I would see hanging around the Who, for instance; those blank, shrieking girls who offered up lots of decadent sex with musicians, any musicians. They were truly tramps and sluts, or whatever words people use to describe those girls. But there were also very classy groupies, there were some women rock critics who were groupies, and Linda was probably the classiest of all them. And they all got called groupies; what does that mean? Linda's attitude towards men was supportive and sophisticated. She exuded a feeling of wealth and status and sophistication. Also, she had this aura of intense empathy . . . intense empathy. I still remember that quality about her.

There's a word in science fiction that people use today called "Empath." I would say that describes her pretty well. These are people who connect with other people in an intense way, an unusual way, and therefore are very compelling. It's a charisma; you make the other person feel that somebody with a lot of magnetism and strength is interested in you. And for rock stars, that was very unusual and something they yearned for, because it's a very nomadic life, one of tremendous tension and dislocation and craziness.

So somebody like Linda had the quality of appearing like an anchor in many ways, yet worldly, and not aggressive or brassy. She was very warm, she didn't have that kind of brittle quality that a lot of people on the scene had in those days. It was a time of intense brittleness. If you think of the Warhol crowd, you can get a sense of how brittle people aspired to be in those days, and she was not like that at all, not at all. Extremely receptive, very friendly. She worked with me a lot when I went to do interviews, and she really didn't have any reason to do that, because she was already more well known than I was. It was part of her niceness.

From my interview with Linda and Paul, 1992:

D: *Linda, you never did like the Warhol crowd, did you?*

L: *That was your scene much more than mine. I never hung out with those people at Max's Kansas City. The drugs, the amphetamines made me uncomfortable. Mainly, I had a daughter, I had to be home at night, I had to be careful.*

D: *You were the straightest girl in rock and roll.*

L: *Straight, but funky!*

Straight she may have been, but Linda's confidence in her ability to attract men grew astronomically after just a few months of photographing groups and celebrities; her pictures were attracting the attention of magazine editors all over town.

I once had an assignment to interview Warren Beatty at his hotel suite, and I told Linda to come along and get the shots. As he and I talked, she moved around the room taking pictures of him, noiseless as a panther in the night. After about half an hour, she caught my eye and made a "Cut! Finished!" gesture, drawing her index finger across her throat, very broadcast industry, very cool. I said, "Oh, excuse me Warren, my photographer is done, but I wonder if I can have a few more minutes with you?"

"Oh, sure," he replied. "I'll see her to the door, I'll be right back."

He was right back. "Your photographer is so professional," he gushed. "I hardly knew she was here."

"Yeah, Linda is great," I agreed. "And the pictures will be fabulous."

The next day, I called her to ask how she thought it had gone. "Oh, I've got the contacts back already and I love them," she answered. "And Warren is terrific. We had the greatest dinner, and we talked for hours."

"You what?" I exclaimed, naïvely, since I should have been able to put two and two together, or one and one together as it were, by that time.

"Well, he asked me to dinner when he walked me to the door. He's so nice, don't you think?"

"Very smart, and a perfect gentleman," I told her, "and he liked you too."

"I know," said Linda.

From Linda's *Linda McCartney—Sixties*: "I used to go to a club a lot called Ondine's, which was a very small club on the Upper East Side of New York . . . the Doors [were] there for two weeks, and I had my camera and I started taking the pictures that are in my book of Jim Morrison singing . . . [it] was all just me about a foot away from him, before he had released 'Light My Fire,' and before they were discovered. The Doors, because we were friends, we'd go out to dinner. I'd tell them about a restaurant, or we'd walk around town and my apartment became a bit of a hang-out. It was in a residential area and I'll tell you, my neighbors would look at me like 'What is this?! And she has a daughter and she's walking around with all those long-haired guys, my goodness.'"

The neighbors, I certainly think, had no cause to be concerned about the quality of Linda's mothering. When any of her children were young (say, the years between Heather's birth at the end of 1962 until James was in his mid-teens in the early 1990s), being a mother was her very first priority, as anyone and everyone who knew the family will testify to.

Still, in 1966 Linda did, every once in a while, tend to her own needs, and it is not to be expected that the accounts of these episodes would turn up in a promotion for her book of photographs. For example, Jim Morrison, the object of every girl's desire during the short time he was in the public eye as a great beauty (1966–68) and before he became a pudgy drunk, was a bit more than just a friend.

"She really wanted to meet Jim," recalls Elektra's senior vice-president at the time, Steve Harris, who was very close to the group. "They were playing at Ondine's late in 1966, just before the release of their first album, and he was the hottest thing in town. The girls who 'knew' were dropping dead at his feet."

Linda called Steve and arranged to meet him at the club, a disco on the Upper East Side, before the show. They smoked some hash under the Fifty-ninth Street Bridge, the band played, Linda took her pictures and Steve took Linda into the dressing room to meet the band. "Jim paid her no attention that night," says Harris. "But we went back the next night, and after the show I saw Linda and Jim walking out of the club together. She turned to wave and smile at me, and I said to Jim, "Don't forget there's an interview at the office tomorrow." He grunted an OK, and never turned up for the interview.

"He called me the next afternoon, and all he said was, 'Oh, man . . . ,' which took about half a minute to come out. I lectured him about missing interviews, and he said nothing more. I mean, he'd said nothing to begin with except that 'Oh man.'"

Morrison was more alert that night at Ondine's, and described a scene at Linda's apartment remembered with not a little amusement. There was a woman there who left as soon as Linda got home, obviously a babysitter, and Linda and Jim were getting snuggly on her living room roll-away when the door to the bedroom opened.

"Suddenly there was this little kid standing there," Morrison told Harris. "So the chick [he meant Linda—he was such a gentleman] looks at her and says, 'You OK?' The kid says nothing, just sort of nods her head 'Yeah,' and the chick says, 'Mommy is busy dear, go back to bed, I'll come and see you in a little bit.' I dig that chick. She's smart. She was taking pictures during the show. She says she's a photographer."

I myself went to work for Elektra Records several months later as the director of the newly invented Publicity Department; I was therefore the press agent for the Doors. Morrison and I came to loathe each other intensely over the next few years, which story is well documented elsewhere. But I must say, three of my favorite women, who were also three of the most extraordinary people I've ever known—Linda, Gloria Stavers, and Nico—were all convinced that he was, at the very least, a wonderful guy. Nevertheless, Gloria and Nico had horror stories about him, although Linda never did, probably because he was in and out of her life fairly quickly, fortunately for her.

In all of Linda's photographs of people and/or animals, i.e. sentient beings, there are several things happening that make the images so good. The technical aspects—like lighting and composition—are just there, intuitively conquered from the start. When Linda and I were putting together the book *Linda's Pictures* in the mid-'70s, I'd see, much more often than not, contact sheets without a single picture badly lit or out of focus. They weren't all wonderful, or we'd have had nervous breakdowns choosing between them, but they were all proficient, and there were usually several that were wonderful indeed. In work that comes out of a studio, it is not exceptional to see every shot well done, technically at least; lighting is controlled, the camera is on a tripod. But Linda worked with a hand-held camera when she did portraits, and with available light. So her achievement on that level was pretty unusual, most impressive.

But there are other things going on in her work that lift it to another level. One is timing—she knew just when to trip the shutter. Another is the affection she obviously felt for her subjects. She was a person full of love; I heard that from nearly everyone I spoke to who had known her (I certainly never heard the opposite, in case you're wondering why I said "nearly:" some people, a few, just never brought it up). You felt it coming from her, it was quite extraordinary. And people returned the compliment to her lens, they wanted to look their best, to show off what they liked about themselves for this person who was taking their picture; it was instinctive on both sides, which is why you see this "personality" (what is the word? "Soul"? No, we stick with "personality," oxymoronic though it may be) in her pictures of animals. They knew what she felt for them, and they somehow knew how to pose for her. Is this silly, sentimental? So be it.

Sam Andrew, guitarist with Big Brother and the Holding Company, Janis Joplin's wonderful band until they were fired by her new big-time manager, Albert Grossman, in 1968 (Sam did join her new group for a while the next year), remembers her as,

> a wonderful person. She did real non-rock-and-roll things, she brought me a heater for my room at the Chelsea Hotel, and no one did things like that. It was really caring, on the creature comfort level. Jewish-mother kind of thing, although I never thought of her being Jewish back then. She was blonde and

> preppy. Anyhow, I didn't know what Jewish was until I read Lenny Bruce, you know, I was West Coast, father in the Air Force.
>
> So we became friends, and everyone thought we were having this thing. There's some book out now by Alice Eccles and she says that Linda and I went off into the night after a concert at the Fillmore East, and the band was supposed to rehearse but I just ran off, boom, missed the rehearsal and left Janis all alone, so she wound up at Ratner's, haranguing the waiters or something. This is not true, and how can you believe someone who thinks that a band is about to rehearse after a concert? No band is gonna do that, that just doesn't happen. And you know Janis was not so left-alone as in the legends. She always had to carry on about something, even if she had wall-to-wall boyfriends, which she very often did.

Asked what he thought of the g-word, Sam replies,

> If anything I was more of a groupie than she was. I would not use that word about Linda. Oh, I'm not gay or anything, as far as I know, but I always put more value on looks. Linda was never trading on people's fame, or leaving the real person out of the equation, which is what real groupies did. But Linda was far away from that.
>
> When I heard she married Paul, I thought, "Wow! He could have any woman in the world," and Linda was like family to me. Linda! And then I was really happy for him and for her. I thought after all that it made perfect sense, that Paul was really level-headed. I'm not surprised they stayed together. She sent me a telegram after they got married. "You better believe it," she said.

Linda's incredible career, within a few months, had brought her close to most of the giants of 1960s rock and roll. She was photographing practically everyone in the pantheon of the new musical culture. And it's not only how well her instincts served her that amazes us when we look at her photographs from that time, but how good, how prescient her musical tastes were. Whether they've made it into the Rock and Roll Hall of Fame, as by far most of her favorites have, or if they're merely ever more interesting as time goes by (like Blue Cheer, Jackson Browne, Tim Buckley), Linda picked the best.

Jimi Hendrix, while we're on the subject, awed Linda. She never needed to be told to listen to what he was doing because it was going to change the way musicians played and audiences listened—she'd tell *you*. It has always been rumored that there was more to their relationship than mutual admiration, and great admiration it was, but that was it. "Jimi's girls" were known to all of New York for their gaudy glamour: Linda Eastman was very much not one of them.

"She was just fascinated with his persona, his drive, his magnetism, his ability to mesmerize crowds; he was a very powerful figure, with a lot of mystery about him," remarks Eddie Kramer, Jimi's record producer and biographer. "She was so different from the girls Jimi was famous for dating. Linda was educated, an intellectual in comparison with the other women he found so fascinating. Completely different, completely different, but he liked Linda for who she was. I don't think he would have had her around for one second had she not been so talented, if her pictures were not that good. Linda, I always thought, was a woman obviously in charge of her own destiny to a large degree, which women in those days were not."

Linda recalled that Hendrix would visit her at home, and together they'd scrutinize and mark up the black-and-white contact sheets of the pictures she took of him. "With the color slides," she said, "we'd sit on the floor and hold them up to the window, because I didn't have a light-board. The ones he liked he'd chuck into his briefcase—he carried a briefcase with him like a businessman. So Jimi had all my great color shots of him in that briefcase, and I don't know what happened to them, because I never saw them again after he died. They must have gone with him, and that was sort of sad for me."

"When you think of the historical perspective," adds Kramer, "it's interesting, isn't it, that it was Paul McCartney who got Jimi on the bill at the Monterey Pop Festival?" (Although Hendrix had performed in America, especially in clubs in New York, as Jimmy James and the Blue Flames, it was in England, with the Jimi Hendrix Experience, that he first astonished crowds and fellow musicians; the Experience made its American début at the historic Monterey Festival in northern California, in June 1967.) Kramer notes, "That was a very important deal. Paul called the promoters and said, 'You have to put this guy in the show.' Paul was a huge Hendrix fan. I have no way of knowing if Linda was directly talking to Paul about Jimi at that time, but it's a fascinating connection."

Each of these relationships—friendship, fling, or not-quite-definable—retained its own resonance with Linda, I think, for the rest of her life. Not so much as men-I-have-been-with, but much more as a sentimental evocation of a few years that she had loved, cherished the memory of, and abandoned with a fond farewell when the time came. It wasn't required, for Linda to romanticize the memories of these guys, that they had actually "dated"—it would have been enough to have been a friend, to have loved someone's music, to have been at a fantastic concert or recording session, or to have captured the beauty of these people with her camera.

Tim Buckley, the brilliant singer/songwriter who died of a heroin overdose at the age of twenty-eight in 1975, was a boy with whom she had a very brief fling, but whose memory she cherished, almost inordinately, long after the short time they spent together in 1967. I was his publicist at Elektra Records, a close friend and a great fan, and I set up a Central Park photo shoot with Linda and Timmy. Linda loved to work in Central Park, and took many of her best pictures in New York's huge, famous mid-town oasis. The subject(s) could be isolated from the noise and action of the city, obviously, and the backgrounds were beautiful and almost infinite in number. This shoot resulted in dozens of exquisite, fantastically composed photographs, with Timmy looking his most fragile and angelic (he was, at the same time, a tough little devil), and the afternoon ended with Timmy and Linda going back to her apartment for ham sandwiches and an iceberg lettuce salad. Whatever. They were together only a very few more times; his budding drug habit scared Linda, and she preferred to remember the innocent Timmy rather than the one who was getting himself into a lot of trouble.

After he died, she often brought up his name when the two of us talked about the people we had known together, frequently when Paul was there, rather enjoying our reminiscences. "Oh, Tim Buckley! He was wonderful! It's so terrible what happened to him. He was so sweet. What a beautiful voice. Paul, you always liked his music. I wish I could find his records."

Me: "But Linda, I sent you the CD re-releases a couple of months ago, I sent them to your office in London."

"Oh dear, well, I must have them somewhere then. But you could send them again, and make sure you write that they're to be sent right to me."

Me: "I did, darling, but I'll do it again."

"He was very special, wasn't he?"

"Yes, Linda, he was."

On a Saturday afternoon in 1978, Paul and Linda McCartney walked into a cheesy (so to speak) pizzeria on Christopher Street around the corner from my apartment, where Paul handed a dollar bill to the boy behind the counter and asked him for change for the telephone. "I suppose you want to call Danny Fields," said the pizza boy to the superstar.

"How the hell did you know that?" a clearly taken aback Paul asked.

"Oh, I live with him," answered the handsome strapping youth, the late Vance Buck (to whom Elton John's 1992 album *The One* was dedicated). "Come on, he's not home, but I'll take you up to the apartment and you can wait for him."

I got back only after they'd left, to find a note from them: "Your friend let us in, we waited, we'll talk to you later," and propped up next to the stereo turntable were Tim Buckley's first and second albums. That's what they listened to while they waited. Myself, I can never find what I'm looking for among my vinyl or CD albums—there are thousands of them, they're not in any order and I don't particularly care. How they (no doubt Linda, not they) located those two records, I will never be able to figure out.

One night in the spring of 1991, record producer Hal Lindner was putting together a (long overdue) tribute to Tim Buckley at a church in Brooklyn Heights renowned for its rather avant-garde events.

Scheduled to appear in New York for the first time, singing two of his father's songs, was Jeff Scott Buckley, Tim's son. Tim had bolted from Los Angeles to New York while his wife was pregnant with Jeff; father and son had been together only twice in Jeff's lifetime, and only once when Jeff was old enough to know that this was indeed his father. I had never met Jeff, nor to my knowledge had anyone who had hung out with Tim Buckley in his New York days. Linda and Paul were in town, and I asked her if she wanted to come to this tribute to her beloved Tim and meet his son.

"I can't make it," she replied, "but I'd love to send him a note. I don't know if he knows Tim and I were friends, but I'd just like to tell him how great I thought his father was." A few hours later a messenger delivered an envelope to me; in it was a note from Linda to Jeff. I dashed backstage after the show (if indeed it's called "backstage" at a church; I never know) and introduced myself to young Jeff—an astonishingly beautiful and talented replica of his late father, by the way.

"Linda McCartney asked me to give you this note. She was a friend of your father's, and has always been a huge fan of his music."

"I know that they knew each other, I know it very well," he said. "My favorite picture of my father is one that she took, and I keep it with me all the time. It's the one where he's sitting on a step with his feet like this, all pigeon-toed. Please tell her that I can't ever thank her enough for that picture."

Jeff's own career started to take off soon after that. Linda followed it closely in the press, and would ask me about him whenever we spoke. Then she called to say that she and Paul would be in New York to do *Saturday Night Live*, and could I bring Jeff up to their dressing room, as they were both so eager to meet him?

I relayed this summons to him (it was always more in the nature of a summons than an invitation when one was invited into the actual Presence), and he was terrified. "What will I talk about? I'm just not ready to meet them, I don't know if I'll ever be ready, what should I wear?" etc.

Jeff and I were whisked into the McCartney dressing room at 30 Rockefeller Plaza; they both stood up to meet him—Paul greeted Jeff with the famous charm that outshines anyone else's that I have ever known, and Linda hugged him. "We're so happy that you're doing so well," she began, and they continued to make such a loving fuss over him that I soon began to feel *de trop*. One is not supposed to leave until one is signalled to do so (which indeed I have been, from time to time), but I never thought of myself as one of those ones, so I said, "Well, Jeff, I'm going to be off, I'm sure you'll be OK."

He looked at me as if he weren't so sure at all, but Linda saw that and intervened. "Of course he will. You take care of yourself." Bye guys!

Months later, it was reliably reported to me that Paul and one of his children (probably Stella, but I won't put my arm in the fire on that) actually went to the Roseland Ballroom to see Jeff Buckley perform. Paul almost never goes to concerts, it's like the President taking a scheduled airlines flight. And to see Linda's friend's son? Even though he was one of the shining talents of the 1990s—this still blows my mind. Only a '60s cliché will do.

Alone at the house I take on Fire Island each spring and summer, fifty miles and a world away from New York City, puttering in my garden on a dreary Friday afternoon, I had a call from Linda, who was home in England. As always, she didn't bother saying "Hello" or identifying herself, she just started talking.

"I heard that Jeff Buckley drowned in the Mississippi River," she said at once. "What do you know?"

"Nothing, of course I would have heard something, it's a ridiculous rumor." I was getting upset and angry—I mean, friends have died in weird ways—and I kind of barked at her: "Anyhow, how could you know? You're sitting there on your hilltop in the middle of nowhere, how could you know? I'm sure it's not true."

"Check on it, will you?" Linda insisted. "And get back to me right away."

Of course it was true; it had happened the day before. A slightly inebriated Jeff Buckley, aged thirty-one, went swimming with a friend on a river beach, fully clothed, and a wave took him away. His body was recovered on the Memphis waterfront a few days later. And Linda knew about it before any of Jeff's own friends in New York, where he had lived.

Refusing to believe that Linda was actually psychic, I tried to trace the source of her information. When I asked her how she knew that Jeff had drowned, she said she had heard it from "a friend at MTV in New York." More probing revealed that she had heard the story either from a high-profile record producer, or from his girlfriend, who worked at MTV. The news was so devastating that Linda couldn't quite recall; the "girlfriend at MTV," it turned out, was an old friend of mine, and so I told her I hadn't realized that her guy was close to Linda McCartney, close enough to transmit death rumors to. "He's not," she replied. "But I'll ask him." She called back: "He knows nothing about this, he promises. It must be someone else."

But it wasn't "someone else." Linda had given me the producer's name. Now, she'd be evasive from time to time, but never did she lie. This whole episode remains an unsolved mystery; I'll attribute it to . . . I don't know, the power of love, perhaps instinct. And maybe I was wrong to think that Linda wasn't psychic, however that gift might manifest itself. Those Buckley men were strange angels, father and son, after all.

I think one of the most charming stories about Linda's "gorgeous guys" comes from Bob Weir, in 1968 a drop-dead beauty and lead guitarist of San Francisco's still struggling Grateful Dead. In a recent conversation, he told me,

> First of all, I remember her face. Just her face. I remember her, yes. She pinned me right away, she wouldn't avert her gaze. I was the one who met her at the door at the Ashbury Street house when she came to photograph the band. Our manager had told us that Linda Eastman was coming by, that she was the Eastman Kodak heiress and a big-time photographer, a really good photographer.
>
> The word was that she was so pretty and so rich that someone was going to make a play for her eventually and take the prize. She took a lot of pictures of me that day, and then we were going to come back the next day, because some guys couldn't be there. But that night I was getting all kinds of heat from the band, they

were convinced that she was the Linda Eastman of Eastman Kodak, and that since she took all these pictures of me she must have liked me, so the guys were pressuring me to hook up with her. "Do it for your fellow band members," they were saying. She was rich and we weren't; I suppose they wanted the band to marry into all this money. We were really broke.

Their reasoning was, here was this attractive young single lady and we sort of had the same background, my family was well-to-do, so the guys thought it was a perfect match. They weren't kidding. I'd just left home the year before to go be a starving artist and I was pleased with what was happening, but the other guys had been starving for a little longer and it wasn't so much fun. They were actually trying to force-feed me to her, and it got a little uncomfortable for me and for her, you know how guys can be when they've got this plan. So I just went up into the attic and hid. It was getting a little embarrassing, and I guess she was kind of feeling it too. As if she were going to buy us equipment or something. The guys hammered each other all the time, and it was my turn. We couldn't afford a TV, so if we weren't on each other's cases we had nothing else to do. It was a way to keep ourselves amused.

There was nothing romantic going on between me and Linda that day she was first there. I was nineteen, and maybe there was a little flirtation going on, but that's all. We talked about the quality of light—I'd never had a substantial conversation with a photographer before, and she was obviously way into it. I found it interesting to hear her talk about light and shadows and colors, and then we walked around the Panhandle [of Golden Gate Park] and just looked around. It was a whole new experience for me, to start looking at things through a visually oriented person's eyes.

But there was definitely something that she had about her. She was maybe the only photographer that the guys could ever sit still for, for more than two or three minutes. When she was looking at you, it seemed as if she was staring into the window of

> your soul, she was looking around in there. I'm not sure about the other guys, but I certainly felt it. She was an old friend, even though we'd just met. There's probably less than half a dozen people like that in your whole lifetime. I'm a total believer in reincarnation, and I would be real surprised if Linda and I hadn't put in some time together in the past. There was that little flash of recognition. An old friend that you've just met, you know?

Shortly after the Grateful Dead photo shoot Linda went to London to be with Paul, and when Bob Weir heard the news of their marriage in March 1969 his first reaction was, "Atta girl!"

They never met again.

> I guess that's what Paul was ready for, after six years of candy being thrown at him. Obviously, they had to have had a very strong relationship to weather everything they must have gone through, being so famous, the object of every girl's fantasies, it's gotta put a strain on things. But they did it.
>
> After she died Paul said he loved her completely from the moment they met. And I understood how he could have felt that way. I had the feeling that if she'd been sowing her wild oats, she was done with that by that time she came to San Francisco. I talked about this with Jerry [Garcia], and we had both heard that bomb ticking. She was ready for something real, something big. And it doesn't get bigger than what actually happened after that.

Chapter 5

"In those days you could be on the make, have a wonderful time, and be gentle and peaceful and silly. I was just delighted that we were all being so nice."

Derek Taylor

The courtship of Paul McCartney and Linda Eastman was (almost) as extraordinary as their marriage. It lasted, by one reckoning, almost eighteen months—that's the amount of time between their first meeting and the day Linda moved in with Paul for good; they were married over four months later, which stretches the time to nearly two years between the first "Hello" and the only "I do" that either of them would ever say again.

It was like a Jane Austen novel: hero and heroine, both of them fabulous (the degrees of perfection are varied), meet and are instantly in love, although one or both of them may not know it at the very first. Several hundred pages and many, many complications later, the smoke clears away, they become aware of the obvious it's-always-been-you and get married, with presumably nothing now to keep them from living happily ever after.

Alas for the true story of the courtship, Linda told friends before she even met Paul that she wanted to marry a Beatle, preferably John but he was married (this was no obstacle for Yoko Ono), so then Paul. She did not mean to be taken totally seriously; she left no doubt that it was wishful thinking, although perhaps within the realm of possibility after all. Now, Linda's friends tended to be rather prominent people, usually journalists or rock stars, and the story has since been told around the world in countless different versions that she set her sights on Paul McCartney very early on, pursued (virtually to the point of stalking) him, and got the prize she was after. I've always thought it odd that Paul McCartney, the world's most wanted bachelor in the late 1960s, seems to have had no choice in the matter. Linda, with all her virtues, was not a sorceress; Paul must have wanted her to be his wife, unless you believe that he is/was a guy whose arm is easily twisted, which plainly isn't the case.

Linda's announcement of her plan to marry Beatle Paul was an anecdote repeated at—of all places—her memorial ceremony in London, by—of all people—Pete Townshend. He told me,

> When Paul asked me to speak at the memorial, I told him that I was gonna tell the "I'm gonna marry one of the Beatles" story, because I'm the one she said it to originally, and I'm responsible for starting the whole thing. It became a terrible story, completely distorted, and you see it was just a joke, and I wanted people to get it right.
>
> Paul was very emphatic about this. He said, "Pete, if this is your story then it's wrong."
>
> I said to him, "Well, it's not my story. It's just that we were kidding around, and then she said that, and then you see what happens, that she ended up with you, and it looks like she set out to get you." And he said, "It's the other way around. I pursued her."

Pete's speech at the memorial did, as he predicted it would, make some people uncomfortable. Because even if you insist that something was originally just a joke, if it becomes true it seems in retrospect not to have been a joke after all. I think it's quite simple in reality: they pursued each other, and each was successful.

But first Pete's story. The setting is New York's Navarro Hotel, at the time of the Who's first performances in America in the early spring of 1967, at Murray the K's Easter show at the RKO Fifty-eighth Street Theater. Linda and I had met Pete together several months earlier when he was in New York on business and found himself alone and angry at a grand lunch in honor of Herman's Hermits. (Ironically, the story of how Linda and I met Pete was told in my own speech at Linda's New York memorial.) When the three of us had a backstage reunion, Linda caught the eye of the Who's manager, Chris Stamp, brother of Terence Stamp the actor, and even better looking; Linda and Chris became an item. Fast forward about a week into the "item," and Pete's story begins:

> Linda and Chris came up to my hotel room, with people coming in and out, and Linda and I found ourselves together. I made some comment like, "You're really lucky!" She asked, "Why?" I answered, "Because you've got the best-looking man in London." And she said, "Oh, really?" I think I said something like, "You know, I'd like to shag him myself," because I just adored him, and I was always so proud of being with him, proud of how beautiful he was, and when he was with me he just gave me his undivided attention.
>
> I guess I wanted to say something controversial, and maybe I thought Linda was being a bit blasé about Chris, so I added, "After him, you could have almost anybody in the world." And she said, "Oh well, maybe I'll marry one of the Beatles." I asked, "Which one?" and she answered, "John Lennon?" So I told her, "He's married," and she said, "Paul McCartney?," and that's how it went.

So that's the tale that evolved into the story of Linda the Huntress. No wonder it angers Paul, for many reasons. It's rather disrespectful of her memory to portray her as a woman spending two years in a well-focused campaign to snag the Cute Beatle; it can't do Paul's ego any good to hear that people think of him as a prize snared by a wily American divorcée; and, above all, it's not true. It is true that she said what Pete says she said; she said it as well to her friend Lillian Roxon, again making fun of herself. But it was without doubt a two-way street. Bear in mind, when she first spoke of marrying Paul, she hadn't yet met him. When she did, she fell genuinely in love, and so did he. It just took a while for things to really happen.

As Beatles press officer Derek Taylor said to me in London in 1987 when talking about the twentieth anniversary of *Sgt. Pepper*, "In those days you could be on the make, have a wonderful time, and be gentle and peaceful and silly. I was just delighted that we were all being so nice."

The chronology will show that it was Linda's fantasy that became Linda's real wish; and that it was Linda whom Paul wanted from the start. In fact, the first time he proposed marriage, she turned him down—but we're jumping ahead.

Linda's first trip to London as a professional photographer was in May 1967. Her closest friends at that time, in the higher echelons of British rock and roll, were the Animals, whom she'd photographed, with David Dalton as her mentor, about a year earlier.

She had also met Brian Epstein, the manager of the Beatles and, some say, much more than that. He had been in New York many times in the early part of that year, mostly on Beatles business but also trying to get singer/songwriter Eric Andersen for a management deal. One of the most talented young men around at the time, Eric suffered, as did so many other talented guys, because of the enormous shadow cast by Bob Dylan. Dylan was clearly "in a class by himself." but he was not the only person hanging around MacDougal Street in Greenwich Village with a guitar and a suitcase full of songs. Joni Mitchell was another, along with the late great Phil Ochs, and of course Andersen, who was also the most gorgeous boy in New York, or certainly in the top ten. It was noted in *Harper's* magazine that "At the age of 23, he is one of the mainsprings of the folk world. Tall, thin, with cheekbones like Rudolph Nureyev (the ballet dancer), he is what everyone who is eighteen in the Village wants to look like." Andersen wrote great songs, such as "Thirsty Boots" and "Violets of Dawn." had his first album released on the Vanguard label in 1965, had even made a cameo appearance in an early Andy Warhol movie, and Brian was in love with him.

I have to admit it was me—along with one of New York's towering intellectuals, who shall remain nameless—who chased Eric down Bleecker Street one day and into the Café Figaro and asked the question, to which there was only one answer, "Would you like to be in an Andy Warhol movie?" We brought Eric up to Andy's factory, and he was no less thrilled to be there than Andy was thrilled to have someone in his studio who had actually made a record album. The movie was called *Space*. It was the first film where Andy actually panned the camera, i.e. swivelled it on its tripod, thanks to the advice of Paul Morrissey, then paying his first visit to the factory, where he eventually became the director of some of Warhol's most brilliant movies—and a very good friend of Linda and Paul McCartney. These were very early times.

Epstein, among the most impressive gentlemen I've ever known, knew me because of his friendship with a hunky young hustler named Richard Luger, who was "staying" at my loft with his girlfriend, Patti D'Arbanville, now a successful actress. Richard was a very hot boy and Brian had something of a crush on him—this was in March 1967. Several times, at about three or four in the morning, a limousine would pull up outside my shabby building on West Twentieth Street and it would be Brian, looking for Richard. A few times, when Richard wasn't there, Brian would ask if he might come up and "chat" for a while, which we did, far into the night . . . or until it became clear that Richard wasn't going to be back.

Acting the proper john, Brian took Richard to Acapulco for a week, to stay at a villa he'd rented. When he came to my apartment to pick Richard up and take him to the airport, he told me he'd forgotten to bring any records with him; was there something he could borrow, maybe just one, and then he'd get some more in Mexico? I gave him *The Velvet Underground and Nico*, the "banana" album, which had just been released, and said, "This is the greatest music you will ever hear." (I was a Velvet groupie, truth be known, and have never revised that opinion to this day.) A few days after they returned, I ran into Brian at Max's Kansas City and he said, "Goddamn you," with a most inscrutable smile.

"Why?" I asked.

"That fucking album you gave me—I couldn't get any other records at all down there, so it's the only one we had, and it was on the turntable twenty-four hours a day the whole time we were there. It's made a hole in my brain."

I told him I was glad he'd been exposed to some decent music at last (what a wag I was!), and he responded by saying, "Mmm . . . yes," and would I like a ride up to Ondine's in his car.

Bingo! Lou Reed, chief songwriter of the Velvet Underground himself, was in Max's at the time, so I ran over and told him to drop everything, for I was going to introduce him to Brian Epstein who was "crazy" about the VU's début album and maybe could be their manager. Lou was reluctant, I was insistent. The three of us got into the back of Brian's limo, Brian on the left, me in the middle, Lou on the right. Brian and Lou were looking out of the left and right windows, respectively, and sullenly, while I gushed: "Brian's been listening to your record, Lou! He adores it!"

Lou grunted, "Oh?"

"Brian," I said, "didn't you *love* the Velvet Underground album?"

Brian mumbled, "Most interesting."

There was silence for the rest of the ride uptown, two miles which seemed to last a lifetime. When we got to Ondine's, Lou jumped out and announced he was taking a taxi back to Max's. Matchmaking is my middle name, always has been, always will be.

Much speculation has gone down the pike on the subject of the Beatles' awareness of Brian's gayness. It was not much of a secret in the early days of the band in Liverpool, although the subject in general was but dimly comprehended by that city's very conservative working- and lower-middle-class Irish population, whence the Beatles came. Nor was Brian's religious background comprehended all that well, either. "Rich Jewish Liverpool." is Paul's description of Brian Epstein's ancestry. The gay thing can hardly have mattered much to the Beatles, after all the time they spent in the Reeperbahn area of Hamburg, the gay center of Germany's gay capital. Meanwhile, we must deal with the ongoing speculation about Brian and John Lennon: did they or didn't they? Nat Weiss says, "No, and Brian told me everything."

Paul, on the other hand, does not totally write off the story that Brian and John had a brief weekend-long affair in Barcelona. "We'd always known Brian was gay," Paul told me. "I'd always credited the gay thing as a great entrée. We were very lucky, I think, that Brian had such an entrée in London showbiz, New York showbiz, any showbiz."

A good time here to revisit a conversation I had with Paul and Linda in the yard of their modest hillside home near East Hampton, on Long Island.

Paul and I have been talking about Brian. Linda rejoins us with fresh drinks, starts to turn away.

L: *Oh!*

P: *It's me, I'm your husband, sit down.*

D: *Yeah, sit down, we're talking about the movie* The Hours and Times, *in which the John Lennon and Brian Epstein characters spend a weekend in Spain in 1963. And the premise is that Brian is in love with John and that they have sex. That's implied, it's not on screen or anything.*

P: *Well, I'm sure Brian was in love with John, I'm sure that's absolutely right. I mean, everyone was in love with John; John was lovable, John was a very lovable guy.* [According to Nat Weiss, "There is no question in my mind that the Beatles happened because Brian fell in love with John. I mean, that was a motivating force for the whole thing."]

D: *That's not exactly what this is about.*

P: *(to Linda) Hey, this is supposed to be* your *interview.*

L: *Carry on.*

P: *But this is relevant in a way. OK, Brian was a lovable guy. And John was sort of more, you know, very middle class, and Brian was middle class, and they could relate to each other.*

D: *As opposed to working class—John, I mean?*

P: *Yeah, as opposed to working class. So they would kind of know about this, what's expected of them, a little above people, a little superior. Then Brian invited him to come away to Spain. A couple of the guys whom we knew were sort of gay, with a bit of money, were going to Spain. I think the rest of us were a little peeved not to be invited, because somebody was getting a free holiday here.*

D: *Did you think John was going to have a gay sexual experience, or might have?*

P: *No, no, no, it didn't occur to us. And to this day I don't know. Now the gay bit, you tell me what you've heard, because I don't know anything.*

D: *It doesn't matter what I've heard. I want to know now, if you think it's possible that something happened between John and Brian?*

P: *It's more than possible, it's more than possible, but, as I've said, "Come on, this is the fucking Beatles, everyone wants to imagine everything." I never got any clue of anything but total hetero. If I saw John doing something, it would be ass bobbing up and down, fucking some chick. There were no real clues whatsoever of John's possible gay encounter with Brian. There were other clues, there were what straight people might call sexual deviancies. I wouldn't call them that. I'd call it a bit of a lad on the loose. You've got to remember, we all got out of home, we got out on the loose, we got into the Reeperbahn, we got into London, it was all kind of there, and all possible.*

Why all this Brian Epstein stuff? As Paul said, "This is relevant." Brian died in the August of the year this chapter talks about, 1967. From that point on, it seems as if the Beatles were in freefall towards an inevitable dissolution.

Also, Brian was always more visible in New York than any of the Beatles ever were, if they were at all, except looking down from hotel windows or walking through Central Park with thousands of fans in tow. In a 1998 BBC documentary *The Brian Epstein Story: Tomorrow Never Knows*, Paul was the only surviving Beatle to be interviewed. His take on Brian was upbeat, almost adulatory; Brian's friends have said that no matter what Paul and Brian may have gone through, and there certainly were ups and downs, Paul came through for Brian on this show in a big way. "Without Brian, there would have been no Beatles," he concludes.

Besides, while some claim to *know* what happened in Barcelona, Paul leaves it deliberately ambiguous. It is also interesting to me, on a very personal level, that Linda was about to excuse herself from the conversation Paul and I were having about Brian's sexuality, when Paul told her to "sit down."

So, back to Brian and Eric Andersen, about two months after we left them above. Also enamored of Eric's talent and beauty was a prominent publicist named John Kurland, who had very important clients, was no fool and was locked in a struggle with Brian over Eric's future that was the sensation of New York's gossiping crowd. It was very catty, and great fun to watch these gay Titans battle it out for the artistic and professional control of a boy who could not have been more straight, more sweet, or more baffled by what was going on around him. To have the Beatles' manager wanting to guide your career was overwhelming in 1967, when the group was at the height of their importance, when they were indeed in that overworked "class by themselves" of all the entertainers in the world. To have him *fighting* for you was beyond dreaming about. (From Lillian Roxon's *Rock Encyclopedia*: "Beatle manager Brian Epstein was all set to sign him [Andersen] just before Epstein died in 1967.")

Eric, not unaware that he was the "boy Brian Epstein wanted to manage." dropped in at Steve Paul's Scene from time to time and basked in the attention he didn't quite get in the Village, even though he'd headlined at Town Hall and was, according to *The Encyclopedia of Folk, Country & Western Music*, "one of the foremost candidates for Dylan's folk mantle." It was at the Scene one night that Brian invited a select little crowd, including Eric and me, back to his palatial suite at the Waldorf Towers, got us stoned on the best grass anyone had ever had, and played "A Day in the Life." from the as yet unreleased, most anticipated album in the history of recorded music, *Sgt. Pepper's Lonely Hearts Club Band*. I think none of us had ever felt so "in" as we did at that moment. And it was astonishing to hear that track, calculated as it was to amaze and the most ambitious production in the short history of rock—"ambitious" becomes, perhaps, "pretentious" with the passage of time, but I'm not a music critic, and I promise no more of that.

Brian knew Linda Eastman—I had introduced her to him with glowing reviews, mentioning in particular her photographs of the Rolling Stones. He had seen the famous "crotch shot" of Brian Jones and was delighted to be meeting the photographer. "Oh, I can show you a really good print of that," Linda volunteered, and Brian said he was most eager to see that picture and any others that were "so interesting." Linda was planning a trip to London at the time and Brian told her to get in touch with his personal assistant, Peter Brown, when she was there, to arrange a meeting. She was going to England to take photographs for the forthcoming book *Rock and Other Four Letter Words*, photographs by Linda Eastman, text by J. Marks.

"You got me that job," Linda reminded me in the summer of 1992, remembering Marks as not one of her favorite people. "And I thought I was getting $10,000 for it, which was great, but it turned out that it was only $1,000. Still, I spent it all on travelling. I bought tickets to London and to the West Coast. My father advised me not to do it. I said, "Dad, I've got to do it. Don't tell me not to." I mainly wanted to get pictures of Stevie Winwood, and perhaps even the Beatles. My father said, "Don't go to England!" I said, "I've absolutely got to go," and he was very unhappy about it." Linda was soon off on a journey that was going to have more significance for her than any other in her life.

Paul McCartney, in May 1967, was the most glamorous young man in London, perhaps the world. There are currently 177 books about the Beatles, and twenty-three about Paul alone which provide ample descriptions of his lofty status at the time. Publicly, he was "going steady" with actress Jane Asher, with whose utterly fabulous upper-middle-class London family he'd lived since 1963 and who was now in residence at his town house on Cavendish Avenue, in the St. John's Wood area of London, a prosperous neighborhood but by no means Mayfair or Belgravia. Although Paul and Jane would announce their engagement at Christmas, in May Jane was in a play that was touring America and Paul was on the town. On the night of 15 May, he was at a trendy Soho club called the Bag O' Nails, where his friends Georgie Fame and the Blue Flames were performing.

Linda Eastman was with the Animals in another booth. Paul claims she caught his attention right then and there, and it was her smile that did it. It most definitely wasn't what she was wearing, because whatever that was, it was probably not in fashion; but Linda always looked good, and was *so* unfashionable that she appeared to be making an anti-fashion statement at any given moment. When Linda got up to visit the loo, Paul blocked her way, introduced himself and asked, "And who are you?" He was one month short of his twenty-fifth birthday; she was going to be twenty-six in September. He invited Linda to go with him and his friends to another nearby club, the Speakeasy.

After the Speakeasy, Paul suggested that the little crowd, which included the singer Lulu and an artist friend of Paul's, Dudley Edwards, go back to his home to "see the Magrittes." Linda was enthusiastic. Paul had never met a girl in "the clubs" who had ever heard of Magritte. "They were very interested in each other," Lulu recalls. Linda left Paul's home while the little gathering was still in progress, no doubt a shrewd move.

A few days later, on May 19, there was a press conference at Brian's house in Belgravia to celebrate the release of *Sgt. Pepper*. It was limited to the "A" press list of London, and Linda knew about it and wanted to go. Peter Brown, in *The Love You Make*, co-written with Steven Gaines, claims he'd been deluged for weeks by people wanting to attend. Peter says that, in return for one of Linda's pictures of Brian Jones (very sought after, those pictures were), he invited her to this most recherché event of the season.

Photographs show Linda at the party looking very proper, nicely dressed in a striped jacket and medium-short skirt, wearing false eyelashes. Her friends at home would have fainted at the thought. Linda got her pictures of the Beatles and, what's more, got some quality time with Paul, chatting with him while he sat down to take a break from the madness. They didn't meet again until four days short of a year later.

Flying back to New York the next week, after Linda had spent some time photographing Stevie Winwood and his band, Traffic, she found herself sitting next to Nat Weiss, who knew Linda (and her family). "She told me then that she was in love with Paul," Nat recalls. "She said, 'I've got to meet him again, I want to marry him.' Well, lots of girls wanted to marry Paul; get in line. But I sensed this as a defining moment for her, she was in love, no doubt about it."

Linda called me the day she got off the plane, to tell me essentially what she'd been telling Nat Weiss, over and over he says, on the seven-hour transatlantic flight. "I met the Beatles, and I got great pictures," she began, establishing her professionalism, which was hardly necessary. I knew something else was coming. "Listen," she said, "Paul McCartney is so wonderful, I really am in love with him."

"In love? After how long?" I was skeptical about the depth of this emotion.

"You sound like you don't believe me. I don't know why I'm telling you this if you won't believe me," she complained.

"How much time did you spend with him?"

"Maybe an hour or so altogether. That's between the night we met and the *Sgt. Pepper* press conference at Brian's. And we were never alone. You have to believe me, when did I ever say I was in love?"

She had a point there. She never had said exactly that before. It was always, "He's so cool/sweet/smart/talented/groovy/good-looking [pick one or more]. And I think he really likes me."

That was always the kicker: "I think he really likes me," as if she were still, every time, trying to convince herself that she was a desirable woman. Lillian Roxon used to do a great imitation of Linda saying that, and we'd laugh, but it was kind of sad in a way. Come to think of it, she never had been in love.

"Darling, I believe you. You have said you wanted to marry him *before* this."

That wasn't real, Linda insisted, but now it was real. I asked her what she was going to do about it.

"Well, what can I do? Camp out on his doorstep? I don't have his phone number and I don't even know how he feels. I guess I can't do anything for now."

Wow—no "He really likes me." This time was truly different. So was acknowledging that she was unable to do anything . . . for now. Actually, it took a year before she "did" something; by then she had reason to be encouraged. Between May 1967 and May 1968, Paul McCartney called Linda about four times. He must have really liked her.

And that was despite the announcement of his engagement to Jane Asher at Christmas (rather a big surprise to the London crowd, as the Paul-Jane affair had clearly not been doing so well in the last few months); oddly, although Linda's friends expected her to be crushed by the news, she wasn't. Something was giving her reason to believe that Paul's engagement to his long-time girlfriend was not really something to worry about. What confidence she had.

To repeat, Paul and Linda did not see each other again for a year, nor did she initiate any contacts between them. So much for the theory that she ran him down and eventually trapped her man.

The remainder of 1967 saw Linda working hard at photography and motherhood. Celebrity portraits were her strong point and, as she said, "It paid the rent." New York was where Linda lived, but she was not crazy about the rock stars in residence. "New York had no music scene group-wise," she recalled. "It had the Vagrants, the Blues Project, the Young Rascals. New York was where I did most of my work, so the great thing for me was when the English bands and the California bands came to town. They often didn't know many people in New York City, so it got to be hang-out time while I was getting the pictures. You know, just hanging out, sitting in a hotel room, dropping acid, looking at the television or going out and taking pictures and wandering, whatever one does."

Quite remarkably, Linda did not go to the Monterey Pop Festival that June, certainly a fertile place for meeting old friends (Jimi Hendrix, the Who) and making new ones (Big Brother and the Holding Company with Janis Joplin, etc.). The reason she missed this watershed event in rock history is very simple, according to Linda: "I didn't have the money to go there. If someone had rung me and said, 'We'd like to pay you to go to Monterey,' I would have gone."

More work started coming in from magazines like *Life* and *Mademoiselle* and money ceased to be an overwhelming problem. In 1992, she reflected,

> You know, I was getting to the point where I had to get an agent. Remember, I didn't have an agent, I didn't have an assistant, I didn't have anything. I did it all myself on public transport. I guess that's what I'd still be doing if I hadn't married Paul. Taking pictures, but always on an art level, on a satisfying level. Satisfying to me. I'd always have my own integrity. I wouldn't, I think, have taken any advertising or done stuff I didn't believe in. I'd only take pictures I believed in.
>
> I'd be making a very good living, still having a pretty funky life, hanging out. I would have had my own horse, which is my favorite thing. I never would have lived in the city—but I don't know, I'd have to have lived somewhere I could work. It's hypothetical, isn't it?

Actually, not so hypothetical, except for the part about having to make a living. For Linda got to live her funky life, albeit on a very high plane, she got to take pictures on a most satisfying level and she certainly got her horse(s).

Because the next year, 1968, saw the stalled romance between Paul and Linda pick up momentum and indeed flower into the love of a lifetime for the two of them.

Chapter 6

"When you look back now to the beginnings of it all, Linda was made for Paul."

Nat Weiss, attorney and partner of Brian Epstein

At the start of 1968, Linda Eastman was wondering if she would see Paul McCartney again . . . well, she was trying to figure out *how* she could see Paul again.

Since 1966 Paul had been living with his fiancée, Jane Asher, in his London town house, which was by now a residence that had become precisely what the master of the house seems to have wanted. It is easy to surmise that Jane had some problems, therefore, with messiness, curious guests, and drugs, especially LSD, which can make a houseful of even moderate London lunatics seem more like a goat meadow than a home. But she endured, though she must have felt that when she had said "Yes." it was an unrealistic deal she had entered into. Jane had been in the public eye since 1963, at the age of seventeen, when she was a regular on the television show *Juke Box Jury*. By 1968 she was determined to be a serious actress, had joined a theatrical touring company and was away from London much of the time. Occasionally, Paul would hook into Jane's schedule, as he had done the previous summer, renting half the floor of an elegant San Francisco hotel for the two of them, and then a house in Denver, Colorado. In February 1968, the Beatles went to India to sit at the feet of the Maharishi Mahesh Yogi, a twinkling guru they had discovered the year before, and Paul brought Jane; they fled after five weeks, unimpressed.

Jane really wanted her career, and since her work would keep her on the road for long stretches of time, domesticity could not be her priority. As for Paul, the less cozy with home-cooking his life became, the more he wanted someone to come home to, reliably, all the time. Knowing that, it's hard to find logical thinking behind the Christmas engagement announcement. There had been speculation that Paul suggested marriage to "make an honest woman" of Jane, and when that was no longer required the ties were severed. I've always thought that theory far-fetched. More likely, it was probably easier to arrange a way of remaining together rather than dealing with a split up, which would be big news, generating huge amounts of annoying and unwanted publicity for the two of them. And so they kept the pretense going. That included the pretense of Paul's being faithful to Jane. He could be one half of London's most glamorous couple when the occasion was suitably glamorous, and bedding wenches elsewhere when the urge was upon him—Jane didn't have to know about it. Why give that up to have a pot of stew always on the stove, and besides, who was going to make it?

In New York, Linda's career was on fire. She never entered the Fillmore East except via the stage door. A many-times converted theater "in the Second Avenue." as Henry James put it (please, don't laugh; James had lived in ancient Rye, the nearest town to what would one day be Linda and Paul's vast Sussex farm, and she was proud of living near the Master's old residence, pointing it out to visitors—whether she ever read anything of his is another question), the Fillmore East was New York's palace of rock and roll from 1968 to 1971. It was a golden age of rock history and Bill Graham was booking the acts most creatively, lining up the music as a great DJ would line up his show. Linda had a permanent "all access" pass signed by Mr. Graham, having taken the photographs for the opening night poster; the bill on that auspicious occasion was Big Brother, Tim Buckley, and B.B. King. Linda also enjoyed sitting in the audience like any other rock-and-roll fan. I remember the night we went to see Blue Cheer, whose album was great fun but who were dismissed by the critical establishment as too simplistic, or something like that. Well, they were terrific, and it was like any wonderful discovery: a thrill and a joy. I shouted to Linda (their volume level was famous), "I *love* this band. This is a great band! Everyone's taste sucks but ours."

She responded, "Me too! Me too! I love them, they're great." Linda had impeccable taste, especially when it was the same as mine.

Ah, 1968—measured by body blows, I'd rank it as the most amazing year of the second half of the century just ended. Three fabulous guys got shot, Andy Warhol, Martin Luther King Jr., and Bobby Kennedy (and with that assassination went the future of the American presidency); the cutest students at Harvard, Columbia, and the Sorbonne rioted; the North Vietnamese launched the Tet Offensive; Lyndon Johnson abdicated; Prague had its "Spring;" the Chicago Democratic convention brought joy to the world along with Richard Nixon; the Beatles gave you their White Album; the Rolling Stones had *Beggars Banquet*; Yoko Ono made a comeback—and Linda Eastman and Paul McCartney became *de facto* man and wife, although the legalities would have to wait a few months into the following year.

At the beginning of 1968, Linda was a successful and popular photographer: young, rich, and handsome, with little to vex or distress her—except that she was scorned by her father because of the life she chose to live, had a five-year-old daughter she was raising rather uncertainly by herself, and, in spite of her ability to attract the most impressive young men known to the world, had fallen perhaps hopelessly in love with Beatle Paul. Linda was wistful about her situation, but not one to complain.

Three women knew her best, and were her closest friends and confidantes—Lillian Roxon, Blair Sabol, and Robin Richmond. All were formidable media dominatrixes and easily among what Pete Townshend calls the "thirty or so possible people" in New York at that time. Sabol, volatile and fiery in print, wrote a fashion column for the *Village Voice* in which she took no prisoners—years later she would skewer Linda in an article that rattled the foundations and standards of celebrity journalism.

Volatile and fiery in person, Roxon was the New York correspondent for Australia's most important daily, the *Sydney Morning Herald*, a regular columnist for the *New York Daily News*, the author of the ground-breaking *Rock Encyclopedia*, about ten years older than the rest of us, beloved, hilarious, and occasionally exasperating. She would become, publicly and privately, Linda's most outspoken detractor by the time of her death in 1973. In 1968, Linda and Lillian were so close that people suspected Something; Roxon boasted of her bisexuality and probably had a bit of a crush on Linda, but she was in fact Mother Confessor and there was absolutely nothing physical between the two women. Lillian knew more about Linda's romantic escapades than any other single person, and probably more than all of Linda's friends put together; Linda told her everything, and Lillian repeated some of it, only some, to others in our little crowd when it suited her to do so. Lillian and Linda broke each other's hearts—but we're not yet there.

Robin Richmond was a junior editor at *Life* magazine—cultivated, well-bred, smart, eager, and attractive. A few years younger than Linda, she was the girl friend with whom Linda spent the most time, in those heady days when Linda's career and reputation were booming. At *Life*, Richmond had become the local expert on the exotic new worlds of rock and roll, hippiedom, and other alternative lifestyles—it was a photogenic, revolutionary, exploitable new world and the establishment media couldn't get enough of it. If Robin plugged *Life* magazine into this youthful universe, then it was Linda who was Robin's tour guide.

Linda popped into Robin's office almost every day, and they'd go to lunch, preferably at the Palm Court of the then (pre-Ivana Trump) aristocratic Plaza Hotel. "We had to wear skirts, and for Linda that was a big deal," Richmond, now living in New Mexico, recalls. "The first time we went there, we were turned away, because she was wearing some synthetic V-necks in hot pink or hot lime, and blue jeans, with a Gucci bag full of cameras." Chef's salad (presumably more elaborate than Linda's famous home-made "There's-a-chef's-salad-for-you-in-the-fridge" of iceberg lettuce, diced ham, and American cheese) was the girls' standard lunch, and the talk was about magazines, photographs, records, concerts, and bands.

"We'd go to the Scene after it closed and there were those sixties "jams," usually Jimi Hendrix, Jimmy Page, Mike Bloomfield, or we'd go to the Café Au Go Go after it closed, or to a Country Joe recording session, and Linda knew everybody, she was a VIP in that world." In that world, perhaps, but not in the world of Lee Eastman and his wife, Monique, whose homes on Park Avenue and in East Hampton Linda and Heather, with Robin in tow, would visit often.

"She adored her father so much; she was in awe of his intelligence, his success, his confidence," says Richmond.

> But it was very hard for Linda, because he was cold to her and disapproved of what she was doing, very obviously. He'd make snide remarks, and it was all about innuendo: "What a great job Robin has! *Life* magazine!" If there was an opportunity for him to come in sideways, to make a comment of implied disapproval in front of me, he'd never miss the chance. I don't think Linda spent a lot of time, except in my company, with her father and stepmother. It was very uncomfortable for her. It's ironic, because a large part of Linda's attractiveness was her air of complete independence and confidence. She might have been dying on the inside because of her father's loathing of the way she lived, but she never showed it.
>
> We were really close for only about a year and a half, but it was a wonderful friendship. It was an adventure being with her, she had an uplifting quality. I never saw her slugging around depressed because some guy she'd gone out with was in town and didn't call her. She was never "Poor me!," never. It was always, "Let's take a walk, or let's go to a recording session or whatever," she was just ready to seize the moment. You can see it all in her pictures—that's why all those people have those extra-great smiles on their faces. She had such an incredible, engaging quality about her. For Linda there was no agenda, no artifice, no contrivance, no manipulation, it was just having fun,

> it was a game, it was fun. And all the time she was reinventing herself, from the inside out, to be the person she really was. Without even putting on lipstick, because she didn't need it.

Well, to me she was Miss Rock and Roll, impeccable in everything she did, if you can excuse iceberg lettuce as the vegetable course, always. She was not devastated by Paul's betrothal to Jane, but appeared to be riding it out, as though it were not in any way a major impediment to her hopes and dreams. In fact, she was so unrattled, it was as if she knew something that no one else knew, but of course she didn't. When Lillian Roxon gingerly mentioned the subject, Linda commented that, well, it was something to do with Paul and Jane and was not of much concern to her. "I love him, and I'm pretty sure he's not serious about being engaged. Anyhow, they're not right for each other." Pretty good intuitive analysis of the news coming from London, especially since Linda had never met Jane, and hadn't seen or talked to Paul since the previous May. Lillian worried that Linda might be headed for a fall—on the other hand, she was so impressed with her friend's determination that she told me if she had to bet on the outcome, she'd put her money on Linda's ultimate victory: "I'll even lay odds, darling."

The advent of Paul and John's utopian concept called Apple gave Linda Eastman, in a most roundabout way, the chance she wanted and needed to get Paul's attention, and to present herself—without ever saying just that—as the only suitable answer to his long-range needs.

Paul McCartney and John Lennon were so enthusiastic about Apple, and its potential to advance art, science, music, and retail fashion merchandising, that they planned to announce its inception as guests of Johnny Carson on his indisputably number one late-night talk show. Their appearance was booked for May 15, and they flew to New York on the 12th. They tried to sneak into the United States as quietly as possible, but some DJ got hold of their schedule and there was the usual airport nightmare. No hotel wanted to put up with the security and crowd-control problems that the presence of the two big Beatles would involve, and Paul and John were not wild about the idea of being imprisoned in one. The solution was to stash them away in Nat Weiss's luxurious two-bedroom apartment on East Seventy-third Street and hope that their presence could be kept a secret. Weiss himself arranged to stay at the St. Regis, planning to be at his apartment during the day. Before leaving his home in the hands of the Beatles, Weiss replaced his elderly housekeeper because a) he felt that it would all be too much for her, and b) John Lennon had expressed the wish that whoever was cleaning the place be young and attractive. She was; John was happy, and took her frequently to bed. As it happened, the boys were also tidy. "Lennon really surprised me—he was very neat, he would fold all his towels. I've never forgotten that," Nat told me. "Paul too, but that was sort of thing you would expect from him."

One person who knew the Big Secret of the Beatles' New York hideaway was Nat's friend Linda Eastman. Recalling their flight together from London to New York a year earlier, after Linda had met Paul for the first time and couldn't stop talking about him, Nat told Linda that Paul was coming to town and, lo and behold, was going to stay at his own apartment. Not surprisingly, she begged Nat to be allowed to visit and he ran the request past Paul, who approved. And so, during the week Paul and John were in New York, the only two women ever in Nat's apartment were the saucy maid, and Linda. In fact, no other outsiders were permitted in at all, except veteran journalist Al Aronowitz, whom John was impressed by. The routine was that Linda arrived early in the afternoon and stayed until the evening, chatting away with Paul. When she left to go home and be a good mom, Weiss would take Paul and John out to dinner, or to a club to hear music. It was just the three of them; Linda and Paul did not see each other in the evenings, and they did not make love on Seventy-third Street. In retrospect, that week in 1968 was the defining moment—albeit a week-long moment—of their relationship.

The attempt to keep quiet the fact that the Beatles were in town failed within two days of their ensconcement at Nat's apartment. So many, dedicated and relentless were the fans that the news about the two's whereabouts was soon known; after all, it needed only one spotting of Paul and John to set in motion a tracing routine that led to the high-rise where they were staying on the fifteenth floor. Soon the secrecy aspect of their visit was a joke.

Thousands of screaming and fainting girls lined the area around the building where Weiss lived, creating a major nuisance in what was ordinarily a quiet, expensive residential neighborhood. Famous people lived in the area quite anonymously, but no one was as famous as the Beatles, and their followers were not known for mature, discreet behavior.

"The doormen were getting blow-jobs from teenage girls who wanted to get upstairs," Weiss recalls. "The people in the building across the street were hanging out their windows to see what was happening down there; there were so many people in wheelchairs it looked like the shrine at Lourdes. Of course not all of the kids in wheelchairs needed to be in them, but they hoped the Beatles would take pity on them and invite them up. I didn't think it would escalate to that."

Most unhappy about the hysteria raging all about were the other residents in Nat's building, and the building manager, who wrote him a letter that he has framed and hanging on the wall of his study. It says, "Dear Mr. Weiss, Two clients of yours, the Beatles John Lennon and Paul McCartney, stayed at your apartment. These are not run-of-the-mill guests. Crowds of unruly girls have disrupted life in the neighborhood, and certainly in this building. If any such future visits are contemplated by the Beatles or any other clients of yours, we need to be notified one week in advance so that we can review the situation. Yours truly, etc. etc."

It was deemed wise to let slip Paul and John's departure date so that the fans would know when it was time to go home, but this was a two-edged sword: on the one hand, the crowd was indeed gone by the next day, yet on the other, the day they left the frenzied crowd was the biggest it had been, since this was the last chance to See The Beatles until who knew when. Decoy limousines were hired, and Paul and John managed to get out in time to catch their plane back to London. Riding to the airport with them was only one person who was not a part of their organization, Linda Eastman.

Paul and John had come to New York mainly to tout the advent of Apple on the *Johnny Carson Show*, and although the magnificently witty Derek Taylor, Apple's press officer, had come with them to oversee a bunch of telephone interviews on the subject, the Carson appearance was far and away the most important event on their official agenda. Ironically, the night they were scheduled to appear, the king of late-night, Johnny Carson, was not hosting his own show and the Beatles were doomed to face one of the great mediocrities in the history of broadcasting, someone named Joe Garagiola, remembered by few and missed by fewer. He was once a baseball player, as if that qualified him to sit in for the coolest guy on the air. Paul and John (privately) let it be known that they thought themselves incredibly insulted by Carson's absence, and had to work extra hard at summoning forth their reserves of charm in order to hide their true feelings. Making things even more difficult was the presence of Tallulah Bankhead, the heavy-drinking, flamboyant baritone American actress, who kept telling John and Paul how beautiful they were. It was obvious watching the show that the host had little knowledge of who his British guests were, or what they really did; he behaved as if some neighbor's daughter had fainted upon hearing of the night's line-up and that he would be chatting with people who were Very Big, as Big as anyone he'd ever interviewed. In his clumsy, embarrassing way, Joe was actually rather decent.

Paul and John (who had sent his wife, Cynthia, a telegram from Nat's saying he wanted a divorce; Yoko Ono was looming large in his life at the time) arrived back in London on May 20, and with George and Ringo, who were just back from the Cannes Film Festival, they began work on what was to be the Beatles' White Album. John and Yoko did some recordings of their own as well, which would later be on their *Two Virgins* LP. On the 21st, Paul and Jane lunched with Andy Williams (no kidding) and went to his concert at the Royal Albert Hall—it was the kind of thing they did so well together, and also the kind of thing they would not be doing very much more of as the summer wore on.

The glamorous couple also went up north on June 8, where Paul was the best man at the wedding of his brother Mike McGear, who'd changed his last name earlier in the decade so as not to appear to be riding on his brother's reputation. When I told Linda in 1991 that I'd recently interviewed her brother-in-law, I concluded from her reaction that Paul and Mike had fallen out, and they remain, at the time of writing, estranged.

On the day Paul and John flew out of JFK, Linda rode back from the airport with Nat Weiss, her first time alone with him since they'd flown from London to New York in adjacent seats after the *Sgt. Pepper* press conference at Brian Epstein's almost exactly a year earlier. Once again, and even more so than before, Weiss was impressed with the intensity of Linda's feelings for Paul. "She kept going on about how much she loved him, and wanted to know if Paul had said anything about her. Actually, Paul took me aside at the airport and asked me if Linda really owned a horse in Arizona. I told him I didn't know," says Weiss, who wonders to this day why he wanted to know that, of all things. "So I told her he obviously thought she was good company, or she wouldn't have been in my apartment in the first place, and she seemed sort of satisfied with that but insisted on knowing if there was anything else. There was nothing else, but of course his asking her to accompany him to the airport was very significant, very significant. When you look back now to the beginnings of it all, Linda was made for Paul."

Linda told her friends that she felt "something was happening" between her and Paul, but she didn't know where it would go, could only hope that it went in her direction, and meanwhile would continue being a mother, taking pictures, going to the Fillmore, dealing with the unspoken scorn of her father, and lunching at the Plaza with Robin Richmond. Whatever would happen would happen.

Paul's very public appearances with Jane Asher after he'd returned to London in May had been interpreted by some as a sign that their "engagement" was still in place, but his actions in late June 1968 seem to indicate that he had given up on the affair. On the 20th he flew to Los Angeles, ostensibly to make a presentation of a short film about the Apple project to the Capitol Records' executives gathered there for a mini-convention. Two days into his stay, he phoned Linda in New York and asked her to join him there at the Beverly Hills Hotel.

The Beverly Hills Hotel, built in 1912 and massively done over in the early '90s, is a giant pink lodge sort of a building, just west of Los Angeles proper, tucked into twelve florally abundant acres in what was a desert not so long ago, before they brought the water in. ("The look is 'non-manicured,'" gushes the press packet for the hostelry, "but don't be fooled: It takes as much upkeep as the fabulous faces and buff bodies of the Hotel's famous guests.") It is the "Hotel California." and much more, a perennial player in the entertainment industry and a love-nest in a league of its own. Warren Beatty and Leslie Caron, Jennifer Jones and Norton Simon, the Duke and Duchess of Windsor, and the John Ono Lennons famously diddled here.

Many of the lustier moments, about which so much has been written, took place in one of the bungalows tucked away in an eastern corner of the grounds. They're as close to being "bungalows" as the marble palaces of Newport are "cottages." but allow the very rich their attempts at understatement. About twenty discreet little houses, each with four or five opulent rooms, the bungalows have their own driveway from the street that borders the hotel grounds on the east, a driveway usually lined with the limousines of those with access to a great deal of money to spend on accommodation. Of course your little house has full hotel services—the help comes in through a back door, bringing food and flowers, or whatever else can't be delivered by wire. Celebrities have every reason to adore the bungalows of the Beverly Hills Hotel, because one can reach one's private nest without going through the main lobby; for a Beatle in 1968, this combination of luxury, efficiency, and complete privacy was certainly ideal. Bungalow five, the most legendary of all the cottages (the preferred love-nest of Elizabeth Taylor and Richard Burton, Marilyn Monroe and Yves Montand, etc.), with four bedrooms—these days it is available for $4,000 a night—was Paul McCartney's home-away-from-home that June.

"The only time I ever, ever saw Linda display any anxiety was the night before she left for Los Angeles," Robin Richmond says. "She was remarkably, girlishly, coy, and shy and nervous." Paul had left a message with her answering service (this was before machines; some people use human answering devices to this day, but not many), something like, "Tell Miss Eastman that Paul called and said, 'Why don't you come and join me at the Beverly Hills Hotel for a few days?'" Linda found someone to stay with Heather, bought a ticket and was off to L.A. the morning after she picked up the rather cryptic message. Was she supposed just to go to the hotel? Get a room for herself somewhere? Tell him she was coming? She decided it was best just to go, and appear. The details would fill themselves in.

Linda was headed for some kind of romantic showdown. She'd never been summoned anywhere by a man to join him, except perhaps at a recording studio or hotel in New York, certainly never across the continent: this was not for a photo shoot either, and besides, this time Linda was in love with the man who invited her.

Tony Bramwell, a member of Paul's staff at the time, wrote a story about the Beverly Hills meeting in a story published in the *Daily Mail*, a year after Linda's death. The headline promised a revelation about the "extraordinary moment when rock's greatest love affair really began." I have no argument with either premise—that it "really" began there, and that it was rock's greatest love affair, because it was. Paul and Linda would tell people throughout the years that it first happened there, and if one were ever with them in the vicinity of the great pink palace on Sunset Boulevard, they would point to it and get all giggly and cuddly.

It didn't take long at all for Linda to phone Lillian Roxon when she returned to New York to tell her that she and Paul had entered into (hopefully, she said) a true sexual relationship. Lillian quickly made sure the whole town knew about it as well, but Linda didn't mind. When I called her to say, "I hear you finally scored, congratulations," she replied simply, "I really am in love with him, you know; it's not like anyone else, it's kind of like the first time."

Bramwell tells the story with everything but a thousand stringed instruments rising in the background, and when he says, "I could sense that this [meeting at the BHH] meant far more than Paul's other encounters. They just gazed at each other looking astonished," I could not be happier, because although not an eyewitness to this particular history, I believe it 100 percent.

"What are you going to do now?" I asked Linda when she confirmed Lillian's hot news.

"I suppose it's up to him, isn't it?" she said.

I told her that I thought she was being unusually modest about her own powers, but she was deferential as I'd never heard her before: "I *said* it was up to him. I will not call him . . . but we talked about music a lot. Maybe I'll send him some records, he told me he'd like to hear what I liked. Can you get me some advance pressings?"

"Hey," I said, all eager to please, "can you send him some things that *I* like?"

"Only if I like them too."

"Linda! What's up?" I remember imploring her. This was big, need I say. This was deep-sea fishing, even for Linda Eastman, and I was convinced she was in love, after all the flirtations we'd lived through together. Linda always preferred being the conquered rather than the conqueror, but I'd seen her moving towards a target by any means necessary, when the prize was juicy enough. Not this time. Paul was no passive southern California crypto-epicene songwriter—he was Beatle Paul, a northern Englishman very conscious of who should do what and with whom. Women were by his side at his pleasure—and, perhaps not so incidentally in the light of future events, the women hanging out with him during that trip to California, before Linda arrived, were said by some friends to be rather more trashy than aristocratic. Why begrudge anything to the man who had everything? But as anyone can tell you who's possessed concubines by the thousands, of either sex or both, even that gets boring and leaves you wanting something . . . more.

One month after Paul and Linda parted in Los Angeles after their idyll in Beverly Hills, he on his way to London, she to New York, Jane Asher, on a BBC talk show, announced that her engagement to Paul had ended. "She was just totally devoted to her career, and Paul wanted a proper home life," Nat Weiss relates. "He'd been on top of the world for five years and done enough swinging for a lifetime."

There would be one more live-in girlfriend in Paul's life, the dazzling American Francie Schwartz, who was in residence in Cavendish Avenue (along with John and Yoko) for most of the summer of '68, before Linda took her place at Paul's side once and for all.

Francie, twenty-three at the time and an American would-be screenwriter, was one of many hopeful non-mainstream artists who heard Paul's and John's description of Apple as a refuge for creativity that was not fully appreciated by the general public. As might have been expected—as should have been expected—Apple's London office became a repository of unsolicited and un-listened-to cassettes, which John would shovel into cartons for disposal, and its front doorstep became populated not only by the slightly cuckoo Beatles fans who had always gathered there (the "Apple Scruffs"), but by dozens of people with "projects" they felt only the Beatles would appreciate. It became Derek Taylor's unhappy job to shoo them all away periodically, so that the people who worked there could come and go without having to battle an encampment of weirdos.

But Francie was more savvy. She arrived in London from New York, where she'd been writing advertising copy, in early April. She carried with her a "treatment" for a movie about a street musician she'd met in front of Carnegie Hall who wanted to be a concert violinist, sure that the story would appeal to the Beatles.

She frequented the London rock clubs and managed to make a bunch of new friends, including a receptionist at Apple, who got her through the front door one day early in May. Lo and behold, Paul was in the reception area. Francie gave him her picture and told him she could be reached via a trendy hair salon where another of her new friends was employed. While having her hair done there the next day, a note from Paul arrived with his phone number. Etc. etc.—a month or so of cat and mouse, and Francie found herself a *de facto* resident at Paul's house. Jane's clothes were still there, Francie recalls, but Jane was then on tour with the Old Vic company. John and Yoko were living there as well. Paul does not even mention Francie in his semi-official biography by Barry Miles, and Francie's account of the affair in her own delightful book, *Body Count*, and the conversations I had with her leave some uncertainty as to the exact dates of events concerning the Loves of Paul. What makes sense is that Paul and Jane have effectively called it quits by mid-June; Paul goes to California, where he sends for Linda and they become lovers; Paul returns to his house, which Jane has vacated and where the lovely young couple John and Yoko are living; he is lonely; Francie is attractive and available; she and Paul sleep together a few times; and pretty soon he doesn't seem to object if she sticks around the day after and the day after and so on. Francie is not in a great hurry to leave either, although it is no bed of roses from the point of view of a woman who has been jilted by the man she refers to as the great love of her life. "Oh, he gave me great jobs to do, like cutting the matted fur on the back of Martha, the sheepdog, that had shit balls in it. 'Well, would you take care of Martha please?' He never bothered to send her out to a groomer. When Paul was out, which was often, John and Yoko and I would just sit around and talk and watch TV; one night we made opium cookies which made us sleepy, so we went to bed. You know, this was the extent of the 'heroin-related drug activity' of John Lennon in 1968, no matter what anyone says."

As Francie tells it in *Body Count*, she went to recording sessions (although she did not participate, as did Yoko), worked at Apple part-time, sat in Paul's Aston Martin waiting for Paul to finish his visit with another woman, scored drugs for the household, and prepared her American version of Liverpool junk food, beans on toast.

"More often than not," she writes in her book, "I would just be falling asleep around two in the morning when John and Yoko and Paul would crash in, show films, or play tapes from the session. If he wasn't in a good mood, he'd drink hideous Scotch-Coke combinations, throw food at the dogs and cats, drop his clothes in a path from the door to the bed, and ignore me completely . . . Sometimes we'd go to a club, have a good time, then zip home for the ephemeral thing we substituted for love-making."

This fairy-tale romance lasted until late in August.

> One morning I woke up and everything had changed. I went downstairs, the carpets had just been shampooed and I remember them being damp, very damp. Paul had this horrible look on his face. Totally out of the blue, he asked me when I was leaving. I stuck around for a little bit, and I went into the kitchen in tears and called my mother. He came up behind me and put his arms around me and told me not to cry. And then he said, "I'm going out for a while, make dinner will you."
>
> The next morning, I called the accountant and asked him for just enough money for a coach seat to New York. I packed my

> shit and Paul was pretending to be asleep. He was really awake and he didn't say anything. He just looked at me as if he was embarrassed, and I got the hell out of there.

Francie never saw Paul again. By the time he asked her to leave, he had already called Linda and invited her to come to London.

Chapter 7

"Back then, there were a handful of people who had influence and fun. A handful of people, and the people who shagged them."

Pete Townshend

Before leaving for Los Angeles in August 1968 to work on a major photo shoot for *Mademoiselle* magazine, probably the most lucrative assignment she'd ever had, Linda had a phone call from Paul inviting her to stay with him in London. (The excellent biography of Paul by Barry Miles, *Many Years from Now*, quotes Linda as saying the call came in late September, but it was in August; we know that on September 18 the Beatles were recording "Birthday" for the White Album at Abbey Road, and Linda was there, on back-up vocals.) It was so much what she'd wanted, if indeed it signified that he wanted something serious, that she couldn't quite believe that he wasn't perhaps toying with her. So she checked it out with her close friends, who sensed that she was going through some kind of anguish—a condition she'd not been known to suffer from ever before.

Linda and I had dinner at a nice, long-since-gone restaurant on Sunset Boulevard one night, after she'd spent a memorable afternoon photographing Aretha Franklin in a little park in Beverly Hills. She spoke of that experience in a videotaped promotion for her landmark book of photographs, *Linda McCartney—Sixties*:

> Aretha was in tears [when Linda arrived at her hotel room]. Her husband, who was her manager, really "done her wrong," and he'd left. She had all the band and everybody on her back for money, and she was sort of sipping vodka the whole afternoon, she was so upset. I got a few black and white shots of her while we talked. Such a nice person. I guess because there was no one else there, she was talking to me and Andrea, the *Mademoiselle* editor, just talking heart-to-heart. Then she got past that, and got rid of the busy-stuff she had to do, and they put a wig on her and makeup and this white satin dress, and we went outside and you can see the contrast in my book. Aretha for *Mademoiselle* and Aretha just, really, for me. I thought she was such a great person, it was an emotional thing for me.

After recounting the Aretha session while we dawdled over drinks, Linda became silent, nervous, and fidgety. She looked down at the table, and then right into my eyes.

"Paul asked me to come to London," she announced.

I said, "Great!"

"But do you think he says that to lots of girls so that he's never without one? He didn't say anything specific, just to come over and call him when I get there. What if he wasn't serious?"

"How can you take a chance that he's not serious? You love him. What can you lose? At the worst, you'll find out you're one of many—which I don't think, because no one is that callous—it'll cost you a plane ticket, and you'll get enough pictures while you're there to pay for the trip. On the other hand, if he's serious, Linda . . . well, if he's serious you'd better find out. Just go." It was one of my finer lectures.

"Hmm . . ." she replied. "Maybe I should go." As if she really needed convincing.

The next day Linda and I drove out to Malibu, where she was shooting Judy Collins on the beach. I worked for Judy's record company,

Elektra, and she was a good friend as well. Linda and she were particularly close because after they'd met for a shoot I'd set up over a year earlier, they'd bonded, as single, working mothers in the music business and as artists. When I spoke to Judy for this book, I recalled that August when Linda had told me of Paul's invitation.

"She told me about it too," Judy said. "And she was nervous about it, because 'he's always got all these groupies around him.' Well, I told her that was to be expected, but I knew she could deal with it. She could deal with just about anything."

Of course, in the light of subsequent events, I was always amused to recall Linda's need of reassurance at that very critical moment in her life. I don't think she would have been talked out of it, anyhow, nor do I think anyone tried. If she had *not* gone . . . But there was no "if" about it then, and I'm sure Paul would have continued to court her; given his insistence on having the world know that he, Paul, pursued her, Linda, and not the other way around, they were going to come together no matter what.

I don't recall how that day ended. Linda and I went back to New York separately, and after she spent a few weeks in New York getting Heather started at her first school and making all necessary arrangements for her, Linda flew to London in mid-September. I didn't see her again for over a year, until she called me one night in early 1970 to tell me that she and her husband were in town and wanted to drop over. It was as if we'd had dinner two nights ago. One got used to that over the years.

Little did Linda know, as she packed her bags at the end of the summer of 1968 for what was going to be an extremely auspicious journey, that in Cavendish Avenue in London Paul McCartney was trying to figure out how to evict yet another international player before his true love arrived. Happily for all involved, this was in no way a romantic or even sexual companion living under his roof, but none other than Nico, the decadent, beautiful, and tragic chanteuse.

Born in Germany before the start of the Second World War, Nico had been a model, a minor movie star (as in Fellini's *La Dolce Vita*, 1959), the lover of Lou Reed, Jim Morrison, Jackson Browne, Brian Jones and Iggy Pop, and an Andy Warhol "superstar." Worshipfully nicknamed "the Moon Goddess." she was a singer and songwriter of an importance that remains mysterious and unfathomed to this day, and a terrifying seductress of men. Her friends knew her as one of the sweetest people around, while all the cute and talented boys who fell in love with her were scared, very scared. She was divine, a major pain in the ass, and very collectable. Paul certainly knew that, via his flirtation with the avant-garde of the mid-'60s, his excellent taste, and perhaps through Brian Epstein, who, if you recall, had taken to Acapulco early in the year he died one hustler and one album—*The Velvet Underground and Nico*, the "banana" album that's on every music buff's Top Ten Of All Time list. Nico had lived in London, and naturally travelled in the most élite circles. Linda knew her as well—they had many friends in common, among them Paul Morrissey, the brilliant director of many of Warhol's early movies such as *Trash* and *Heat*, and a classy indie filmmaker to this day.

Paul Morrissey and Paul McCartney had known each other since 1967, when the Warhol crowd passed through London after the Cannes Film Festival and gathered at the apartment of the late Robert Fraser, a great art dealer who was very close to Paul McCartney and had invited him over to meet the famous New York artist. Paul brought with him the advance layouts of the *Sgt. Pepper* album cover, about which Andy could only say—to Fraser after Paul had left—that he didn't see his own picture on it, and that was his opinion of it, period.

Morrissey was, to his infinite credit, Nico's main protector (actually her manager, but that's too impersonal a definition of their relationship) when it came to dealing with the real world. In September 1968, he had just arrived in London with Warhol when Paul McCartney called him at his hotel and said, to Morrissey's astonishment, "Hello, it's Paul. Listen, I have a favor to ask of you. Could you come over to my house?"

"I didn't know what he wanted, until he said it was about Nico. I knew she was in London, but not until that moment did I have any idea that she was staying at Paul McCartney's house," Morrissey remembers. "So I went over there, and he showed me the house, and then he said, 'You know I have Nico here, I invited her to stay here about two weeks ago; she had no money and I just thought it was for a few days, and she had nowhere else to go. I like her and she's very nice, but I have to ask her to leave and I don't know how to do this, and I thought since you're here, and you're her manager, maybe you could do that.'"

Although not in love with her, Paul seems to have been slightly scared of Nico, like all the other young men in her life. Let's say "shy with," rather than "scared of." Linda and Paul and I were once looking at her photograph of Nico and me (my favorite photograph of me, by the way, taken in London in the early 1970s), and Paul commented, "It's just beautiful, it nails you there at the period."

"That's the magic of photography," I said. "Guys were so afraid of Nico, you know."

Replied Paul, "I wasn't afraid of her at all."

Morrissey recalls,

> Paul was very polite, and I said, "Oh yeah, sure," because I knew Nico could be something of a burden, and then he told me that a journalist was coming over from New York to interview him and he didn't have any extra bedrooms. So I asked him who the journalist was, because maybe I knew who it was, and he answered, "Oh, do you know Linda Eastman?" and I said that I knew her very well and, "Yes, she's great." I was supposed to understand that Linda was coming to do some in-depth story and needed to be there for a few days. And it made sense to me that he was giving this girl a place to stay, like he did for Nico, and I just thought it was a nice thing for him to do. I knew that there was nothing romantic between him and Nico, or she would have told me before this, or would have made some reference to it. She would have called me from anywhere in the world if that had been what was happening.
>
> But later, when Linda and Paul got married, I tried to think of that time he mentioned that a "journalist" was coming, and I said to myself, "Oh, he did have this glint in his eye when he told me who it was." Then, I remember very vividly, flying into London from Paris on the day after I had read about their wedding, and I was walking around Bond Street looking at stores

> and art galleries, and I didn't even know where the Apple headquarters was, but I was on that street and they came right out of the Apple building, and they walked over to me and called, "Oh, hello, hi, how are you?" I said, "Congratulations!" and I thought, "Isn't this funny, they got married yesterday but they're not on a honeymoon, they're at the office?"

Morrissey had known Linda since the Rolling Stones boat ride. "Andy [Warhol] was really envious of the Rolling Stones because they were on the cover of *Town & Country*, and Brigid's and Christina's father was the president of the company, and he'd always want to know why he wasn't in *Town & Country* if the Rolling Stones were. We'd met Linda at the magazine office once, and on the boat Andy said to her, 'Ooh, I didn't know you were a photographer,' and she said, 'I think I am, now, but don't tell anyone that I'm really not.'"

New York was a much smaller town in the mid-'60s—everybody knew everybody else, more or less, and there were very few places on the circuit of social and artistic acceptability: the Scene, Ondine's, a few other discos and restaurants and, most of all, Max's Kansas City.

"Linda's story is almost like a George Eliot novel, all about circles of people in one village," Pete Townshend said to me.

> I know somebody reading your book will have difficulty with this unless they can put themselves in their own village. There are the principal characters, and they're around from the beginning until the end. When I first got to New York, I thought, "Oh, there are so many people!" But really, back then, there were a handful of people who had influence and fun. A handful of people, and the people who shagged them.
>
> When you guys adopted me in 1967, I felt like I'd been slipped from one place to another. From the London village to the New York village. And one of a handful of people again, with Linda very much one of them. She was sure of who she was, and she knew which village she came from, and it was not the village of the general populace. I don't mean to say that she was any kind

> of snob or anything like that, but I knew that about myself too. And so who could Linda marry? Someone in her own village, metaphorically. Or in the equivalent of her own village in a different country. Paul. It just seems OK. She had to end up with Paul by the end of the novel.

Linda moved into Paul's house, but not into the spare bedroom, and the honeymoon really began there and then, in the final days of the summer of 1968.

The Beatles were having severe problems then, with Yoko Ono apparently having driven a wedge between Paul McCartney and the most important person in his life, John Lennon. And between John and the other Beatles as well.

"She was in the studio with them all the time, I mean *in* the recording studio, not in the control room, with the Beatles, the *Beatles*!" says Nat Weiss, remembering the year the group was headed in the direction of full disintegration. "George ended up yelling at her, "Why don't you get the fuck off my amps?" Something like that. I went to the taping session of "Hey Jude" for the David Frost show [4 September 1968], and she was ordering people around right and left. She felt her own power right there and then."

Francie Schwartz has memories of Yoko that are kinder than most other people's. But her account of the Big Rupture between Paul and John is probably quite accurate. The same story was told many times by John himself. Francie wrote a version of it in *Body Count*, and she told it to me.

> It was in August, and I was living with Paul on Cavendish Avenue. John and Yoko were staying there too, in the living room. Paul never opened his fan mail, I opened the fan mail for him, but he didn't give a shit about the mail. John and Yoko definitely gave a shit about their mail, and everything addressed to John and/or Yoko came to the house.
>
> Paul was upstairs, and there was a note on the mantle, addressed to John and Yoko, typewritten. It was not postmarked so it was suspicious immediately. The two of them opened it up

> and showed it to me. It said, "You and your Jap tart think you're hot shit."
>
> We were appalled, I mean, what can you say? It was unsigned, just the one sentence, typed. Then Paul bopped into the living room. He was wearing suit trousers and suspenders, barefoot with no shirt, his hands in his pockets. "Oh, I just did that for a lark," he said. As far as I'm concerned, that was the moment when John looked at Paul as if to say, "Do I know you?" It was over, it was completely and totally over at that moment. They may have been able to work together, but it was never the same.

It's convenient to say the "end" of the Beatles was a certainty when in April 1970 Paul McCartney announced publicly, in a press kit included in his first solo album, *McCartney*, that he was no longer working with the group but would be a solo artist from then on. (This is discussed later. However, it wasn't until November that Paul filed a lawsuit against the other Beatles, asking that the band be dissolved; the case was not decided until January 1975 when it was ruled that the Beatles no longer existed.)

However, in January 1970, did John and Yoko jump the gun on Paul when they put out their own press release referring to 1970 as "Year One"? Legally and financially, the Beatles' battles dragged on interminably; they certainly were in full swing many years after John's death in 1980, which itself could be the year the Beatles finally, irrevocably, were finished. Yet even without John, or with John making a posthumous contribution, there have been and continue to be "Beatles" projects. For some fans, it was over when the Beatles played their last concert in August 1966; for others, any attempt to say the Beatles could *ever* be over is a sort of sacrilege. It would be like, er, claiming that Jesus was over when he was nailed to the cross. Some would agree, some would not; some things just don't seem to be conclusively ended no matter what happens in the physical universe—the end of which would not necessarily mean the end of Jesus *or* the Beatles. Just ask a fan of either. It's easier to count the angels dancing on the head of a pin.

But Linda and Yoko will forever be known as "the women who broke up the Beatles." As if there were a need to blame something that might never have happened, had already happened, or would have happened anyhow on two women who did nothing worse than love their men, each in her own fashion. It's interesting that no man was ever held responsible for this ephemeral event. Actually, I'd say the responsibility lay with that judge, whatever his name is, who made the dissolution of the Beatles a legal reality in 1975—it makes as much sense as any other theory.

Still, the two halves of one of the century's great songwriting teams, and the engineers who drove the flashiest and most gorgeous locomotive of modern culture, were an unstable entity perhaps from the start—not the start of the Beatles, but of their success, which is and has been beyond the reach of any phenomenon that's come since. Oh, maybe I take that back, maybe it's an overstatement. One supposes the movies of Steven Spielberg have made more money; Bob Dylan has most powerfully rattled the rafters of lyric-writing; Barbra Streisand has elevated the standards of diva-dom; Andy Warhol and Jasper Johns created the first paintings of the twenty-first century; Mrs. Thatcher changed the sexual possibilities of political dominance for all time; the Kennedys invented political glamour (only to see it evaporate); Diana showed us that fairy tales can come true; Jerry Seinfeld single-handedly forever lowered the standard of comedy established by Lenny Bruce, Jack Benny, Lucille Ball *et al.* and was the biggest phenomenon in television history; Bill Gates became the richest man who ever lived; and Oprah Winfrey is now the first black woman billionairess—wow! What competition—but have the Beatles really any competition? This writer (a Stones guy) thinks not, and so the Destroyers of the Wondergroup deserve very close and special attention, as long as there are those (and there always will be) who believe that Linda and Yoko were indeed just that.

Because Yoko Ono was, from the moment of her irruption into the "art world," an amazing, perplexing, deep, powerful, and mysterious presence, much print and analysis have been devoted to her, and she deserves every inch of column space she's received. She demanded and commanded the spotlight at every moment that was opportune, and was forever hard at work to make those moments plentiful. Before, during, and after the times that John Lennon was by her side.

"John was a bully. John was a complete bully," says Nat Weiss. "If he could intimidate you, he would just do it for the purpose of intimidating you. But his weakness was that he liked to be dominated. And that was the basis of his relationship with Yoko."

Whatever one might say about Paul McCartney, even knowing the Beatles as well as Weiss did, it would not be that Paul liked (or likes) to be dominated. The idea is mind-boggling. If Yoko was a dominating person, and the shoe does seem to fit, then she was quite the opposite of Linda, who shrank from the glare of tungsten and carbide, yet was no less a force in possessing and exhibiting a supreme intensity that in many ways reinformed the meanings of love, caring, parenting, partnership, activism and personal artistic potential and realization. For her, humans were judged on merit alone, not because of the attributes with which they'd been born—she was truly the most color-blind and class-blind person I've ever known—and animals were not judged ever, at all.

From Chrissie Hynde's rhyming eulogy, at Linda McCartney's New York memorial, 21 June 1998:

> *Linda McCartney was a pal and an ally*
> *She wasn't an avant-garde intellectual bully*
> *And she sure wasn't here for the fame or the money.*
> *She didn't cry "Peace!" in a room full of furs*
> *She thought animals' skins were theirs, and not hers.*

There is no intention here of doing a Yoko *vs.* Linda, which would be dumb and sexist, for starters. In fact, I'm going to try to bring Yoko into this story only insofar as her and Linda's paths cross, and I am aware of the naïveté of that intention. I don't know Yoko, nor do I really know much about her. Some people for whom I have enormous respect think she is wonderfully delightful, charitable, and admirable; from a distance, that has not been my own impression, but I bow to those who are in a better position to have a well-informed opinion. It's clear to anyone, however, that she relishes attention, much as Linda, certainly until the last fifteen years of her life, shied away from it. I've watched Linda and

Paul being "attacked" by photographers during many of the times I've been with them, and their way of dealing with the flashing strobes was always so very different—he moving into and towards the light, she backing away from it, ever so subtly, but enough to give the impression that she was a cold person and he was a warm one. Warm is an act for Paul, for which I give him a lifetime Academy Award—he is a master, he wrote the book. Really, Linda was much warmer than Paul, if you knew her. He was publicly as charming a person ever to wear the mantle of talent and fame, and Linda was contrastingly shy, a quality mistaken for aloofness and arrogance.

But in 1968 Linda Eastman and Yoko Ono, later portrayed in the media as a reincarnation of St. Francis on the one hand, and a retro-incarnation of the Evil Queen of Outer Space on the other, were indistinguishable, simply the Vile Villainesses "who broke up the Beatles."

"THE TWO WOMEN WHO BROKE UP THE BEATLES," by Julie Goldman, was the headline of a story (well, it's been in some form or another the headline of many stories, but that's the one I'm looking at now) in *McCall's* magazine, July 1971. Egregiously full of errors (Christina Berlin becomes Christina Paolizzi, a naked-nipple-thrusting "socialite" of the '60s, for whom fifteen minutes of fame would have been far too much for her mind to handle) and insensitive locutions like "two American college-girl divorcees, a Jewish princess and a Japanese princess," the story has a telling take on some prevalent sentiments, and sometimes even hits the bull's-eye: "The breakup of the Beatles was very marital, like a divorce . . . The old theme, love versus friendship. As usual, love won. And what could have done this but love?" And who could argue with that?

When Linda died in 1998, it was not at all difficult for people who had known her and Paul to find countless factors in the lives and personalities of both of them that "proved" they were made for each other. They were each other's best friends, they understood each other's needs, their musical tastes were in synch, they were wonderful parents who loved their children more than anything else, they preferred domestic simplicity to glamour, they were monogamous, thrifty, loved animals, nature and horse-riding, etc., etc. And yes, at the end of thirty years they were as one, and it certainly should be hoped that that was the case, or it would not have been the spectacularly successful marriage that it was.

But in 1968 they had not had a life together, shared no parenting responsibilities and actually didn't know each other very well. There was physical attraction, certainly, and sexual compatibility, it would seem, but Linda and Paul both knew that it would be a bad idea to elevate lust, satisfying though it was, to the basis of a long and agreeable relationship, one that would be fulfilling for them and scrutinized very closely by the rest of the world.

It was clear to Paul by this point that Yoko had become by far the most important person in John Lennon's life; even were she to somehow vaporize, John would not come running back to Paul after that unfortunate disappearance. Besides, no simple act of God was a match for her powers, or her hold on John. There were other notable tensions within the Beatles organization, and Paul, as much as he wanted to keep it going, must have realized that the show's run was ending. Most important, John was simply headed in another direction, which was not very Fab Four, to say the least (can anyone picture Paul and Linda posing naked for an album cover as John and Yoko did for *Two Virgins* in November 1968?), and the partnership that had been the creative center of the Beatles was shattered, far beyond the ability of all the king's horses and all the king's men to repair, not to mention beyond Paul's.

And then there was Linda, and everything was right about her. She was beautiful but never gaudy, not spoiled, and not materialistic (i.e. would not squander Paul's money), extremely talented as a photographer and acknowledged as such (very important, this; John had taken up with someone whom he considered, and who certainly considered herself, an "artist" and Paul could do no less). Moving along, Linda came from a very good family well beyond the social class into which Paul was born (ditto Yoko and John again, although the Jane Asher affair had given Paul a heady taste of the delights of being upper-middle, rather than upper-lower, class), and Paul liked the idea that although Linda's mother had been born into wealth, Linda's father—the great authority figure in her life—was a self-made man, just as Paul was, and someone he could deal with as such. Linda had great taste in rock and roll, and an expert's knowledge of the music business. She was born into the world of contemporary art; for someone who had just discovered modern art via Magritte, a surrealist, it must have been very heady indeed for Paul to have a girlfriend who had grown up with the great abstract expressionists of the New York school as members of her extended family. Paul and Linda had both lost their mothers in tragic circumstances, and Linda was a mother herself, impeccably devoted to her young daughter. She was loving, affectionate, warm, patient, and comforting. She could cook, and was never happier than when in the kitchen; the traditional northern Englishman in Paul, always a large part of who he is and how he sees himself, was delighted with that maternal "Eat! Eat!" quality of hers. And he loved her.

Picking up the story, we find Linda moving in with Paul, and the two of them discovering that they did indeed like each other as much as they had hoped they would. After the career-driven Jane Asher and the American Francie Schwartz (and the example of the woman John chose, who, aside from her formidable intelligence, must have represented to Paul a living specimen of everything he did not want in a woman), and after hundreds of one-nighters, Linda just fitted right in. Paul could bring her to the recording studio without upsetting any Apple carts, so to speak, or he could have her reliably waiting for him at home, tending to the pets and the pots (and the pot), a proper and consoling shoulder to cry on after a day at work.

Linda is happy, and of course wanting it to last. There are big troubles ahead, but those waters don't come to a rolling boil until the very end of the year and the beginning of 1969; Linda's biggest problems now are the press, who are beginning to wonder who she is (neither she nor Paul nor Derek Taylor have any intention of dealing with the media until it becomes absolutely unavoidable), the Apple Scruffs (those ultra-fans who camp out on Paul's doorstep and know everything about what's going on inside; they do not like this American divorcée and consider her an interloper, as opposed mainly to Jane, who was a proper English celebrity), and, most urgent of all, her separation from Heather, who has just begun school and is old enough to be very curious about where Mummy is and what she's doing.

Linda calls Heather every night from London when she and Paul are comfy in bed, when it's early evening in New York. Linda explains to Heather that she's far away with someone she likes very much, his name is Paul and he's one of the Beatles (which means nothing to the child), and often hands the phone to Paul and tells him to say hello to her daughter, whom he's never met. From all points of view, this is brilliant; not cunning, but brilliant. Linda is being a good mother (she was always incapable of being anything but that), Heather is learning about the man who is soon going to be a vital part of her own life, Paul is getting to know Heather and at the same time he is seeing Linda in action as a loving mother.

He admitted to Barry Miles that his first conversation with Heather was nervous-making: "I got on the phone thinking, 'Oh my God, if she hates me this could be very difficult' . . . I said, 'Will you marry me?' and she said, 'I can't, you're too old!' and I said, 'Well, maybe I should marry your Mommy, that'd be good.'"

The coziness of it all is a wee bit treacly, to be sure, but it surely must have contrasted splendidly, for Paul, with the daily, mounting tensions in the recording studio; Ringo "quits" the band in a huff (to return in a week, but Ringo was not supposed to have tantrums—that was George's speciality, apparently), and Yoko-John and Paul are not a happy combination. Was Linda cunning? Did she use Heather? Well, of course, and why not? Did Paul know what she was doing? Of course. Was he flattered, amused, comforted and encouraged? Again, of course, and no one could be as comforting and encouraging as Linda. Jane could not have been, for all her intelligence, elegance and class—her career was at the top of her agenda and she has become a great celebrity in Britain, but as Philip Norman observes in the Beatles' biography *Shout*, Jane would not pamper Paul, and Paul liked that stuff. Linda liked doing it.

Someone who knew Linda very well from the late 1980s until her death once said to me, "She must have been brought up with a lot of love, because she was such a loving person. She had to have learned that early in her life." My response: "Wrong!"

I think she was not expressively and warmly loved when she was a child, although I don't doubt that her parents loved all their children very much. Linda was not close to her mother, after all. As we have noted, at family parties, where Mrs. Eastman could work a roomful of brilliant people with incredible ease and aplomb—"the Auntie Mame of Scarsdale" is how a friend of the family described her—Linda would hang out in the kitchen with the hired help. She worshipped her father, but she was afraid of him always, and he was always (until you-know-what happened) a bit dismayed with his restless, independent daughter, her mediocre school grades, and disgraceful career. And that's my theory: Linda was so eager to give what she never got, what she thought every child, family member, friend, and animal deserved: a whole lot of loving. She didn't learn it by watching other people, she learned it by knowing, absolutely and instinctively, what the other person/creature needed most of all at any given time.

When Linda was gone from New York for a few weeks that September, I remember saying to Lillian Roxon, "Wow, don't you think it's odd that we haven't heard from Linda in such a long time?"

"Not at all," Lillian twinkled, in her wise and sly way, "she's going to marry him, you know."

"How can you know that?" I demanded. "You haven't talked to her or heard from her either."

"Mark my words," she said.

Early in October, they went back to New York to fetch Heather and to meet Linda's father, the formidable Lee Eastman, and her brother John. A very bold and significant move, that, on Linda's part, and a juggling act starring the most important people in her life. The risks, the high stakes, are obvious, yet she wasn't worried. She was certain (and Linda's certainty was a force like the wind) that her daughter, father, and brother would be impressed by the boy she was bringing home, the only boy she'd ever brought home—and she knew the boy would be impressed by the blood she came from, and her smart, sad, beautiful child. This was the test of her lifetime, and she aced it. Not to say she wasn't a little nervous, didn't have a bit of stage fright, like Paul says he had when Linda handed him the phone and told him to say hello to

Heather. But she told Paul she hoped he would like her family, and he told her he was sure he would. So was she.

Linda's self-confidence served her well at this critical time. She was the luckiest girl in the world—by the end of the coming winter, she would also be the most hated.

Chapter 8

"Those first few days in Paul's house, I lived in fear of going outside."

Linda McCartney

What Linda and Paul did that October in 1968 is rather amazing.

At Paul's house in London, Linda is in love, but missing and feeling guilty about Heather. Paul does not want to see her torn between himself and her daughter, so he suggests that they go to New York together. He doesn't want it known that he's there.

"It was his idea," Linda told me. "I wasn't totally sure we could carry it off, but he was. He said he wanted to meet Heather, and to know about how I lived and where I lived. My God! He wanted to see New York. He really had never seen New York. He'd been there about six times, but always as a Beatle. Which meant as a prisoner. We figured it could be a disaster if he were recognized, and how could we make sure it would not get uncomfortable, so we did the disguise thing. He loved fooling people into thinking he was not him, that he was an ordinary bloke. Everyone in the world wanted to be him, and he wanted to be ordinary. For a few weeks. I still can't believe the press didn't find out—that's why I didn't call you guys.

"It's not as if I thought I couldn't trust you, but my friends all worked for magazines or newspapers, you know, and Paul just didn't want . . ."

"Oh Linda, I understand, yes sure, we would have betrayed you in a minute! Why should you have trusted us? You did the right thing."

"Well, you know, it was all his idea."

"Mmm . . ."

"How is Lillian?"

"She's not smiling wildly, but she's fine. Will you call her?"

"I don't think so, but send her my love. You'll explain, won't you? This is Paul's idea. I suppose he's right."

That was the essence of the last conversation Linda and I had for well over a year. I called her, she didn't call me. She and Paul had been spotted strolling around New York, and her friends (hence the entire world?) knew they were in town together and that there was a reason she'd clammed up, but I couldn't resist poking around there. I was dying to tell her that Lillian was sure she was going to marry him, and Lillian was always right. I just said that I hoped it would all work out in whatever way she wanted it to, and see ya later.

"It was a dump, she dumped all her friends," Blair Sabol said to me. And she did, and the consequences were very bad.

Linda took Paul hunting for anonymous fashions at the best thrift shops in her neighborhood, and on 125th Street as well, an exotic destination, all things considered. They decided on a frankly hobo-ish old army uniform and a grubby, badly fitting herringbone overcoat. He had a beard, didn't shave and told Miles, ". . . it wasn't a couple of very rich people walking round New York, it was more the kind of people you'd want to avoid . . . we were very free consequently."

Linda said that Paul was recognized a few times, and if people started following them they'd find a handy subway station and escape. But it never became public knowledge, it wasn't in "the columns," or anything that would bring the nuts and the press out in great numbers.

They did the whole "on the town" routine, the Battery and Chinatown and Times Square, movies and neighborhood restaurants, museums, the park, not much that was glaringly upscale (except the Metropolitan Opera, where they walked out on *La Bohème*) or trendy. I've read in accounts put together long after 1968 that they went to Ondine's, which was described as extremely "hip," but it hadn't been a place one went to for quite a while, and one would think they would have avoided any place where they were likely to run into people Linda knew, especially famous ones. Although Paul did phone Bob Dylan (I do hope you're chortling mildly at this concept) and he and Linda took a subway to Greenwich Village, where Dylan owned a big beautiful house on MacDougal Street, and Linda took some pictures of Bob and his wife at the time, Sara, and their baby Jessie.

It was on this carefree trip that Paul impulsively proposed marriage to Linda for the first time, inspired by a storefront Buddhist temple that advertised quickie weddings (it would not have been a legal marriage according to New York State law), and Linda, claiming that her first marriage had given her a negative feeling for the institution of wedlock, refused. Quite obviously, she knew she would be asked again. I rather think it was not the memory of her first marriage, which ended quite amicably, but the impulsiveness of the proposal that elicited Linda's emphatic "no." She wanted it thought out very carefully. This was not to be a relationship jumped into on a giddy walk in Lower Manhattan.

They had dinner at Linda's father's apartment on Park Avenue, which was a cordial event—I don't imagine it was a laugh, but quite cordial. Paul must have been impressed with Lee's and Monique's duplex apartment (she sold it five years after Lee died, for four and a half million dollars), their art collection, and their style. Not to mention Lee's amazing mind and wit. At no time did Lee ask Paul if he was prepared to support his daughter in the style to which she had been accustomed. He did communicate to his daughter that this young man was probably not as bad as the rest of the people in "that world" she belonged to.

Very importantly, Paul was impressed by Lee's knowledge of the music business, and music publishing businesses, especially the legalities involved. Legal issues were coming into Paul's life with some frequency in those days, and he naturally must have anticipated that things might become very complicated back there with the boys in London. Which they certainly did.

Music publishing was extremely intriguing to Paul, because the Lennon-McCartney team had been if not exactly swindled, then soft-talked out of the publishing of all the Beatles songs several years before, and the songwriting partners were never able to totally accept the fact they did not own the copyrights on the songs they had written. Lee had done well with song publishing himself, and in time he would guide Paul's acquisition of an immense catalogue, worth many hundreds of millions of dollars. Meanwhile, he was a good person to know and a prospective father-in-law into the bargain.

The most delicate and central matter to be resolved in the course of these two weeks was how Paul and Heather would get along together. In fact, they became great friends. Linda contrived some professional obligations that would take her away from her tiny apartment on the tenth floor of 140 East Eighty-third Street, leaving Paul and five-year-old Heather alone together. He cooked for her and they played games. He loved her, he loved New York, he loved Linda; on 31 October they all flew back to London, and a new life began for the three of them.

One supposes that there no longer exists any grouping of nutty fans quite like the Apple Scruffs, an amorphous collection of obsessed teenage girls, who inhabited—literally—the pavements around the Beatles' homes and their recording studio in Abbey Road. The composition of the group varied, and its ranks were often swelled by visiting fans and other hangers-on. The Scruffs tagged the name of their number one Beatle on to their own—becoming Peggy Paul or June John, for example—and they stayed at their posts in shifts, in all kinds of weather, waiting for just a glimpse of their particular favorite. A wave and a smile from a Beatle were extra treats; they had a newsletter, knew each other well, exchanged information on comings and goings, and worked in relays so that nobody went in or came out, or took up residence, without the Scruffs knowing all about it. It all seemed quite innocent. The Beatles got to know some of the Scruffs by sight, and there were more of them devoted to Paul—the cutest, the bachelor, and the most accessible since he had a well-known address in London that was not far from the Abbey Road studios—than to all the others put together. Had the put-down "Get a life!" been in usage in the 1960s, it could have been addressed nowhere more appropriately than to this adorable, star-struck little bunch of busybodies.

For anyone to think that all these fanatics would be content just standing there would be to severely underestimate the mentality that drove them. Paul had a part-time housekeeper who was friendly and helpful to Paul's most dedicated followers—certainly she didn't have to sign a legal document that guaranteed she would tell nothing to anybody of what she knew was going on in Paul's life, as all of his employees must do today. There have been countless scenes in British films and television shows in which two "lady's maids," or the equivalent, from different households, find themselves together and reveal all that they know about their mistresses; they serve the dual function of narrators and of characters who move the plot forward by putting information into circulation that their employers might have wanted kept behind closed doors. Paul's housekeeper appears to have been very much in the tradition of those indiscreet servants, enjoying a chat about the goings on of the Master within. Had the Scruffs been satisfied with that, they could have been kept at bay, but not all of them were.

Once Paul began to treat them as little members of his own organization, by letting one of them walk his dog, Martha, for example, there were those who gladly took the inch and started going for the mile. They found a vantage point from behind the house where they could see him sitting on the crapper by standing on an overturned flower pot, told him about it, and even showed him how it was done when he expressed amused disbelief. More disturbingly, they found ways to get past the security system, an electric gate with an intercom, and by late 1968 they were sneaking into Paul's house when no one was home (who would know that better than they?) and taking little souvenirs.

They also gave themselves the privilege of approving or disapproving of Paul's live-in companions; they adored Jane Asher because she was a British celebrity with just the right amount of upper-middle-class hauteur to elicit their respect and deference—and they thought she was "just right" for Paul, as did the London press and almost everyone else who had given up on becoming his wife or long-time companion themselves. They were a bit wary of Francie Schwartz, but not hostile—she was a "wild" but ebullient American with a good sense of humor, and they kind of knew she wouldn't be around for a very long time. But they detested Linda, and terrified her.

They hated the way she dressed—it was as if she just threw something on, anything. Jane was a TV star, always immaculate and gorgeously groomed, as if for an important appearance on daytime television or a glamorous first-night in the West End. Linda was, let's face it, not gorgeously groomed. As she said in her own song, the light came from within, and it certainly was not visible to the Apple Scruffs. Mainly, they hated the fact that Paul appeared to be so happy with her. They wanted him to be happy, but not happy enough to dispense with their adoration. This time, he seemed to need nothing else but that "arrogant American bitch." Linda was not "charming" with strangers, that was just not her. Paul was the charming one when they were together in public, while she always seemed as if she wanted to get away, with him. In any case, the Scruffs decided that they were going to hate her, and they had more than a few resources with which to demonstrate their aversion.

They shouted epithets at her, even when she was with Paul. They booed and hissed. He would say, "Now there, girls, behave properly!" and smile and tell Linda it was nothing to worry about, that it was quite meaningless. But she had just given up her life in America and had moved into a new home in England with her child; this was virtually her first encounter with the natives, and it was very unsettling.

They would swarm around her when she went outside alone, calling her names, telling her to go back to America, trying to trip her so that she'd fall in the street. This is not harmless. Then she wouldn't leave the house on foot any more, so it was arranged that a car would pick her up within the gates, but once it was on the street, assorted Scruffs chased it, surrounded it and pounded on the roof with their fists, screaming words of hatred.

She'd return to the house and find revolting graffiti on the street wall in foot-high letters. When they broke into the house and stole her photographs and negatives, it was too much. What's more, Linda worried about Heather's safety and about the effect on her of this swarm of evil insects, for that is the way she saw them, and certainly she had done nothing to deserve this.

"Those first few days in Paul's house, I lived in fear of going outside," she told me, a good while later. "I thought of Paul telling me how the Beatles used to be prisoners in their hotels when they toured, because there were thousands of people out there who loved them so much that it was dangerous to be among them. Believe me, a dozen people who hate you and wait for you has to be just as bad. I was a prisoner in Paul's house. Heather was five, how could I explain this to her? "Oh, it's OK, they'd hate anyone who lived here with Paul." Please, you can't expect a child to know what that's about. Hate? It's a new life for her, and I have to tell her about hate, about why these people hate Mummy. It was very, very difficult."

On November 5 Paul, Linda and Heather left London for Paul's farm in Scotland. Linda always preferred the country to the city—New Yorker though she was, the city was a place to get away from and the country was home. More than restorative, it was her natural habitat for her whole life.

By the middle of November they were back in London, with Linda feeling better about things. There was that farm up there, you just had to get in a car and you'd be there. I had a picture postcard from her with a two-word message: "Very well." It was one of those postcards they used to give on airplanes to first-class passengers. The "PanAm" (now defunct) logo was stamped on the back, and on the front was a picture of the Taj Mahal, a memorial built by a great ruler for his beloved wife in the seventeenth century. It's funny how things come together, if you wait long enough.

Hunter Davies was the author of the first and only "official" biography of the Beatles, commissioned in early 1968 and published by the end of that year. He was vacationing with his wife, the novelist Margaret Forster, at a rented house on the beach in Portugal when, very late on a night in mid-December, Paul, Linda, and Heather appeared at his front door, "banging and shouting." The trip was a whim and had required the hiring of a private plane; Paul had taken advantage of an open invitation, offered to all of the Beatles via postcards, and unlikely (so the Davies family thought) ever to be accepted.

Davies, who had become friendly with Jane Asher while doing his book, wrote in a 1985 Postscript that appeared in a subsequent edition that it seemed to him and his wife that Linda was "overdoing her adoration for Paul, clinging on to him . . . hanging on his every word. We couldn't see it lasting. We couldn't see what she was giving Paul."

She was giving him what he very much wanted: love and priority.

This was not a woman about to announce to the world that she would rather be known as an actress than as Paul McCartney's girlfriend, as Jane Asher had done. Paul wanted the woman in his life to want, above all, to please him and give him a family. Linda not only came already equipped with a daughter but was one month pregnant that December. Ironically, very close to the day on which Linda became pregnant with the first child conceived by her and Paul, Yoko Ono miscarried the first child conceived by her and John Lennon.

Paul called Linda's father from Portugal, requesting his daughter's hand in marriage, and then he proposed, or, rather, they set a definite date, because since October the couple had been acting as if they planned to be married someday. It was Christmas 1968, one year after he and Jane Asher had become engaged.

"Everything was going well for us, for the three of us, at the beginning," Linda said to me twenty years later,

> Paul and Heather were becoming really close, and that was so important to me. And Paul and I loved each other. He told me he fell in love with me the first time we met, and that was so sweet of him to say, whether or not it was true. What really mattered so much to me was that he always would tell me that he was falling more and more in love with me as time went on. I mean, as the years went on, he would say that.
>
> I was aware that I wasn't liked outside our home. At least the other Beatles had Yoko to compare me to, so I didn't come off all that badly with them. But some of those girls on the sidewalk! They told the housekeeper that I was acting as if I were jealous of them, that I clung to Paul to keep him to myself. I was scared of them. They really wished me harm. Some of them stole whole

carousels of my color slides. Some of them tried to physically hurt me—on the day we were married one girl pushed a flaming newspaper through the front door. Did they want us all to be burned alive? There was nothing I could do about the way they felt, but they made me feel awful, just the idea of them always lurking out there, plotting their next break-in or whatever.

Well, that was for starters. The people at Apple didn't like me because of the way I dressed, because I was American, divorced and—you know, Danny, I was unsure of myself in Paul's London world, and it came off like arrogance.

The papers knew nothing about me except that I was a photographer, divorced, American. They picked up that story about me being the Eastman Kodak heiress; so that's how I got spoiled and snotty, they figured out. It all fitted in for them. Paul was being asked about me all the time, and he said great things about my photographs, that he was with me and that he was very happy about it, but all they wanted to know was if we were getting married, and he kept denying there were any plans for that, or else they really would have come after me.

As far as "hanging on every word"—I did, I still do, I've been doing it for almost twenty-five years. His "every word" happens to be brilliant, because he is. Or, he's telling me something or asking me something—am I supposed to not pay attention? You see, I couldn't do anything right. I wasn't going to change myself; anyhow, I don't know how I could, and I was confident at least that Paul wanted me to be who I was. No beauty make-overs; could you imagine me "mod"? Well, it was rough, but there was always one person in England who was there for me, and it was enough.

A few people in New York received Christmas cards that year, and in January Linda sent me a postcard with a wire-haired terrier on the front and another cryptic message: "Very very very." I guessed I was supposed to fill in something positive, like "much in love," or simply "happy," or maybe not, maybe that was it, just a postcard with no deep meaning connecting two friends across the Atlantic Ocean. She couldn't very well have said "Wish you were here," which could be read as an SOS, and she certainly wouldn't have wanted to imply that anything was less than fine. Linda never complained, she would never lay her own problems on her friends. She thought to do that was unspeakably selfish and, worse, pessimistic. Everything was going to be OK, somehow; or, if it was bad, it could be handled.

Linda's friends in New York were seething. Mainly, Lillian Roxon was seething, and Blair Sabol to a lesser extent, but Lillian was widely loved and never reluctant to express anger or disappointment; when she was hurt—uh oh, watch out. And Linda had really hurt her, especially with one postcard which was probably playful (I must say, Linda did not have a great sense of playfulness) but had the effect of pushing Lillian over the edge. Her anger at Linda for not having called since September (they used to be on the phone at least four or five times a day) turned to fury at this one: "Keep your mouth shut." Just those four words.

"How dare she? What the fuck does she mean? Keep my mouth shut about what? Does she think I'd stoop to her level of behavior? She's run off with the most famous man in the world and now her friends are no longer useful, out with the garbage? She was just waiting to drop us all when something better came along! That little bitch!" Etc., etc.

It was more distressing for Linda's other friends in New York to see Lillian so upset than it was to have been "dropped," if that indeed is what it was, by Linda. Lillian carried this wound, amplified it, went public with her scorn and never relented before her death in 1973.

Linda carried with her, for the rest of her life, profound regret.

> It's the one thing I'm sorriest about in the whole world, that Lillian and I never made up. When I went to England, I was in this whirlwind. And people say that I "cut them off." I can see now how they'd feel that way. But at the time, I had just gone from being this photographer in New York into a whole different world.

> You can't know how hard it was. I was suddenly in the middle of a situation where the Beatles were breaking up, Paul was really upset, there was a whole business and legal thing happening which took everyone's energy and I hated it. I thought it was going to be all peace and love and music, and it was wartime. Plus, everyone hated me, those horrible groupies always in front of the house, calling me names, spitting at me. It was a terrible time; I didn't know what to expect, but not that, not that. Paul was so romantic, and I was wondering what I had to do to make it last, and we were trying so hard to understand each other. This whole thing was going on, it took up my life.
>
> I didn't write, I didn't communicate, I was living what was going on in front of me. I thought about getting in touch . . . isn't it ridiculous that I didn't communicate with you guys? I didn't call you, I didn't speak to you. I'm so sorry about it, about Lillian. I'm so sad. I'm so sad about it, really. God, I loved her, she must have thought I totally un-friended her. I didn't keep our friendship up. It was sad, I tell you. But I didn't know she was going to die! If she hadn't died, I'm sure we would have gotten together again, been friends again.

It was certainly a very sad business; I guess Linda and Lillian have made up by now. But what was it really all about? Why did Linda ignore her best friends back home for over a year? (Especially when she had to know that we were dying to know what was going on. It was kind of embarrassing to be asked, "So, what do you hear from your friend Linda who married Beatle Paul?" and have to answer, "Well, not much.") It was very confusing—the Linda we knew, the Linda we *thought* we knew, would not do that, she would not "drop" us all merely because she'd made the match of the century. When she resurfaced in 1970, it was as if (as has been noted elsewhere) nothing had been wrong, there had been no lapse, we were just picking up where we left off. Has it been a year and a half? My, my, time flies.

Well, it can't always have been terrible. There were certainly blissful interludes. That trip to Portugal doesn't sound like such a nightmare, for example. Except that, with their host and hostess trying to figure out what Paul saw in her, wondering who this new girl was who had taken Jane's place in his life, Linda had to be uncomfortable under their judging scrutiny.

Then again, when it's all wine and roses, what do you do? "Excuse me Paul, I've got to call all my friends and tell them what fun we're having here on the beach." No, that doesn't work. Or, to tell her friends that it wasn't all peachy, that it was very difficult, that it was not at all what they thought, or what she had thought it would be—that would be complaining and, as I have said, Linda didn't complain.

I can only speculate that there was another reason besides the "whirlwind" one: early in 1969, Linda's father and brother were hired by Apple to advise the Beatles on legal matters. As the group split further apart, it was John, George, and Ringo in one camp, Paul and the Eastmans in the other. It is all so very complicated, and thoroughly described in virtually every book about the Beatles. But I strongly suspect that Lee Eastman told Linda not to talk to her friends in New York while all this was going on. We were all in one way or another connected to the media, and Lee might surely have suspected that once we had Linda on the phone, we'd be digging for news. So it was safer just not to speak to anyone outside the family, especially friends who might want to pry. When it was all settled, Linda could pick up where she left off . . . which is what happened. However, this is pure speculation, and no one has ever told me that Linda was so advised. If I were Lee Eastman, though, I would have told Linda not to talk to me, or Lillian, or Blair, or Robin. It was harsh, but it seems all this time later as if it would have been excellent advice.

On March 11 1969, Derek Taylor stopped denying the rumors and wrote a short press release from the Apple offices announcing that Paul McCartney and Linda Eastman would be married the next day, at the Marylebone Registry Office in London. Paul was in the recording studio that day, while Linda was taking care of the paperwork. That night, he managed to find a jeweller who'd just closed his shop, but would open it up so that Paul could buy a wedding ring for £12.

Why such a modest venue? They had wanted a quiet wedding, they said later. Obviously, this event was going to be anything but quiet. On a cold rainy day, with Paul in a gray suit and yellow tie and Linda in a pale yellow coat over a beige dress, the couple (with Heather) entered the registry office through the rear door, went through the necessary ritual, and emerged to find thousands of screaming, chanting, singing, hysterical girls—and, naturally, dozens of representatives from the world's press. The fans were not happy; Heather had to be rescued from the crush by a policeman. Back at Paul's house, where the couple went before going through a ceremony at St. John's Wood church, the crowd had become nasty; kicking, swarming, and actually trying to burn Paul's house down. Police had to come and disperse the angry fans before their little display of jealousy and frustration turned into a riot.

"Just write that the bride wore a big smile," Linda told Ray Connolly of the *Daily Mail* outside the registry office.

The wedding was front-page news all over the world, and the thousands of disappointed fans in London had millions of counterparts elsewhere. Girls wore the black of mourning for weeks afterwards, and, like an answering move in a chess game, John and Yoko were married in Gibraltar eight days later; the adorable mop-top stage of the Beatles existence was no more by the middle of March 1969.

The newlyweds left soon after to visit Paul's father in Liverpool, and from Manchester they flew to New York for three weeks to be with Linda's family and to wrap up the loose odds and ends of her life at her $180-a-month apartment on East Eighty-third Street.

"She married me, and this is something you mustn't do," Paul said, sitting alongside Linda for the filming of the BBC documentary, *Behind the Lens*.

> You're going to have a lot of criticism, whoever you are. People said, "Who does she think she is?" Oh, she thinks she's my wife, that's all. I said that maybe we should go on a talk show and sort of explain who I've married, and show them that you're a nice person, you know, because I think they think you're a pushy American broad . . . In fact, you're the dead opposite of that, so maybe we should have gone on a chat show, but we just thought,

> "No." You know, what can I do? Go on to justify ourselves to the whole bloody world? Sod 'em. We ended up just thinking if they don't find out about us, then they don't find out about us, big deal. We'll know, our kids will know, our friends will know. If our image goes elsewhere, then too bad.

I suppose I can find it within me to forgive Linda for not sitting down and writing me a long and chatty letter. She had just moved from one country to another, was setting up a new family in a new home with a new Daddy for Heather, was now married to the erstwhile catch of the decade, whose child she was carrying, and was instantly notorious, misread and widely loathed, because she ruined a fantasy that had become an obsession with vast numbers of young women. Who did she think she was? And, as she was starting to realize with great dismay, she was right on time to witness her new husband live and suffer through the worst crisis of his adult life, as the Beatles flew apart. It was to be one of the most public and gripping split-ups in the history of showbusiness unpleasantness.

Chapter 9

"I am just an ordinary person and want to live in peace."

Paul McCartney, explaining to a *Life* magazine reporter that he was not dead.

When Linda married Paul, she brought to him not only the prodigious emotional strength that would help pull him through a very hard time, but also her family, corporately known as the law firm of Eastman & Eastman (that is, her father and her brother). As Linda guided her new husband through the devastated landscape of his old career as a member of the Beatles and into a tremendously successful new one as a solo artist, her family took control of his legal and financial position and made him the richest musician in the history of the world. What Paul McCartney would have become without men (and a woman) named Epstein no one can ever know; with his talent and intelligence he was not destined to be a loser. But with the guidance of Brian Epstein, without whom Paul readily acknowledges there would have been no Beatles, he was one half (or one quarter, if you will) of a creative force which no history of the twentieth century can ignore; and in the good care of Lee (né Epstein), John and Linda Eastman, he survived and he thrived once the Beatles were, indeed, history.

She hated "business," she always said, but Linda was plunged into a maelstrom of such activity in 1969 when she married Paul, and it was coming at her from all directions. Not only was her new husband preoccupied on about half-a-dozen separate fronts (management; publishing; Apple; John and Yoko; John, George, and Ringo, etc.) with the excruciating break-up of the Beatles, but now her father and brother had jumped into the fray as well.

It hadn't taken long for Lee Eastman to reverse his position on the subject of his daughter's involvement with the degenerate world of rock and roll when he found himself with a Beatle in the family. Clearly, as a very successful player in the lucrative field of song publishing, Lee could see the possibilities of a connection with this celebrated songwriter—part of a team or not, Paul had written "Yesterday" and "Michelle" by himself, and those two songs alone had earned millions of dollars, although they did not all flow into Paul's pocket by any means. As Lee saw it, they should have done, and he no doubt saw an opportunity to make certain that in the future anything Paul wrote would enrich the ex-Beatle, Lee's daughter, Lee's grandchildren, Lee himself, and his son John. He did indeed accomplish all that.

The concept of music publishing is confusing, and although I wish it could be explained in twenty-five words or less, it can't, so bear with me. Everything will be much simpler if the process is even vaguely understood: the "copyright" (literally, the right to make and sell copies) automatically belongs entirely to the writer, and it exists the moment a song is written or recorded on tape. Simultaneously, the writer owns the related "publishing" rights. Music publishing, as a practical matter, consists of getting exposure for the song (having other people record it, or getting it on a movie soundtrack, etc.) and collection of the money thereby earned; even when the song is played on the radio, on a jukebox or in an elevator, there is money to be collected. When you record your own song, and the recordings are sold, the manufacturer of the record is required by law to pay money to the owner of the copyright. This might be you, the writer, or you might have sold the copyrights and attendant publishing, in which case someone else gets the money.

Although it's only pennies a time, if 100 other people record that song (as with "Yesterday," which has been recorded far more than 100 times) and it's played on the radio millions of times (it's all kept track of), huge amounts of money can be generated.

In 1962, the very young and naïve John Lennon and Paul McCartney agreed to the formation of a company to be called Northern Songs, which would own all the songs they had written and would write until 1973. Northern Songs was to be a division of Dick James's own publishing company. The ownership of Northern Songs was then split. Dick James got half of Northern Songs, John and Paul got 20 percent each, and Brian Epstein 10 percent. Then (at a later date) George and Ringo were given less than 2 percent each out of Paul and John's share. So the great bulk of Beatles' copyrights was not owned by John and Paul, who wrote the songs, and it came to rankle them greatly. John's widow and Paul continue to be rankled to this day.

When Lee Eastman suggested to Paul that his publishing affairs might be handled far more skilfully than they had been, that is, handled by Lee, Paul gladly agreed, appointing Eastman & Eastman (still the name of the company, although Lee died in 1991) to administer all his publishing henceforth. Copyrights (i.e. publishing) have to be "administered," that is, registered, kept track of, accounted for, supervised, money collected from, etc., and whoever administers the publishing gets a standard (and very nice) 10 percent of the income. "I guess Paul figured it's all in the family, Paul trusted his own family, and the company is impeccably reputable by any standards," says Nat Weiss.

With the advice of his father-in-law and brother-in-law, Paul McCartney as we speak is close to being a billionaire (or beyond; does it really matter at this point?) via the publishing he now owns, which includes—besides most of his own solo work—all the songs written by Buddy Holly, Hoagy Carmichael ("Stardust"), the scores of *A Chorus Line*, *Annie*, *Grease,* and on and on. His is the largest independently owned publishing company in existence. The majority share of the Lennon-McCartney catalogue of song copyrights, as a publishing entity known as Northern Songs, slipped through the hands of Paul and of

John's widow when it came on the market in the 1980s, and is now owned by Michael Jackson, the performer, in partnership with Sony.

So, Linda may have hated business ("Give me a lump of bread and a bit of lettuce in the garden, and forget the rest," she told *Playboy* in 1984), but she was the daughter, sister and wife of very shrewd businessmen, and did not object to them becoming immensely rich as a team, although she was not much interested in the details. Linda was not one to forget how disapproving Lee Eastman had been of her for a very long time, but she was quick (always, throughout their life together, with Paul's permission) to forgive. So she was delighted to see her father and Paul bonding, financially, legally and, to some extent, socially. "We're giving my dad a Rolls-Royce for his birthday!" Linda told me one year in the late 1970s, thrilled that everything was continuing to go so swimmingly between her husband and her father.

For the Eastmans had been involved not only with Paul's extensive and complicated publishing enterprises, but with his legal situation vis-à-vis the Beatles as they were falling apart. Lee had moved swiftly in February 1969, convincing Paul to have Eastman & Eastman hired as legal counsel to Apple, the Beatles' own, extremely troubled company. The urgency was because, thanks to Yoko's influence, the Beatles were now involved with an enticingly sharp-talking accountant named Allen Klein as their business manager, and Klein was a player guaranteed to horrify the distinguished Eastman clan. The war between Paul on one side, with Yoko/John and the other Beatles in opposition, escalated explosively with the intervention of two New York parties, each from a very different side of the music business tracks.

Nat Weiss (whose account of anything relating to the Beatles is both penetrating and hilarious) recalls,

> In early '69, Yoko called Allen Klein because Mick Jagger told her that Klein had gotten the Stones a much better recording deal than the Beatles had. Besides affirming what Jagger had told Yoko, Klein also said that he could help her with her movies, and that was the motivating thing—I mean, she wasn't interested in Beatle royalties. She told Lennon about the royalties, and he

called me up about this and said, "Oh, it's going to be a good thing, getting involved with Klein," and this was very difficult for me because Brian [Epstein] had hated Allen Klein. He was an alley cat. But I went to see him since John asked me to.

I went to his office and there he was, eating spaghetti, and he waved a paper and said, "You see!" and he showed me the signatures of three Beatles. I said, "I don't see four." Then he asked me for Brian Epstein's papers. I said, "No. If you want anything, sue me. I'd rather burn them."

I didn't want to get that involved, it was Brian's thing and I could never get any emotional satisfaction out of it. And Neil Aspinall was there, he'd been the Beatles' road manager from the start and he would give his life for any one of those guys. But Allen Klein came in, fired this one, fired that one, tried to fire Neil Aspinall, ripped up Paul's song "The Long and Winding Road," stuck in a female chorus, and then Paul, on the advice of Lee, sued the Beatles.

George came in to see me, and I said, "How can you sign with him?" and George said, "Well, he can do certain things." I said, "Mussolini made the trains run on time but he destroyed a country; this man is no good." It ended up that he ripped off George as well as everyone else, and George had to sue him, and he went to jail for some things he did anyhow.

Paul had been outvoted so that Klein was hired as business manager. Paul had to break up the Beatles at that point, he had to break it up to sue. I never would have imagined it would end that way.

Paul probably wanted to keep the Beatles together, and he couldn't; I think Yoko wanted to separate John from the Beatles, and George didn't know what was happening, and Ringo—as Brian said, "The great thing about Ringo is that he's the least talented, and never uptight about it."

Actually, it was not until late 1970 that Paul filed the lawsuit against the other Beatles; the chaos, dating from the advent of Klein *vs.* the

Eastmans, took nearly two years to reach that point. It was 1970 that was really the awful year, when Linda and Paul exiled themselves to Scotland and Paul nearly went to pieces, but for Linda's presence. The previous year, in comparison, at least the first three quarters of it, was not that bad and saw some remarkably redeeming events, like the making of *Abbey Road*, the Beatles' farewell masterpiece before the split, and the birth of Mary McCartney in August.

Nothing in Linda's life had prepared her for the downside of her relationship with Paul; despised and envied worldwide, Linda now found herself with her Prince Charming losing confidence in himself and sinking into a deep depression. The head-over-heels, somewhat bewildered bride had become the strong one in the relationship. It was a situation she never could have foreseen (unlike Yoko, who started off strong and only got stronger), but then again, she didn't think much about the future until it became the present, and although it was a staggeringly difficult time for her, she was ready to deal with it. There were reserves of determination within her, and a still embryonic ability to inspire others, that no one, least of all Linda herself, ever knew existed until they were needed.

Imagine the irony in this picture. Lovely, talented, buoyant Linda Eastman wins the biggest prize of all, and finds that the fairy tale is not at all rosy. Every woman on earth dreams of how wonderful it must be to be married to Beatle Paul . . . and the reality is that the man, your husband and the father of your kids, is spiralling downwards from within.

"I was very scared," she told me. "I didn't want to give up, but it was a mess, it was unreal, and I had to handle this all by myself. There was no choice. I had to try. We had two children, we'd just been married a year, and my husband didn't want to get out of bed. He was drinking too much. He would tell me he felt useless. I knew he was torturing himself, blaming himself for the break-up, and I was sure that he could get beyond it, but if he didn't believe in himself, what could I do? I could only try, that's all I could do. Let me tell you, my hands were full."

As Paul told Joan Goodman in the *Playboy* interview: "I was impossible, I don't know how anyone could have lived with me. For the first time in my life, I was on the scrap heap, in my own eyes . . . I'd never experienced it before. It was bad on Linda. Let's say I wouldn't have liked to live with me. So I don't know how Linda stuck it out."

It's odd how the external and internal aspects of a life lived in the glare (or perhaps the shadow) of extreme fame come together, align themselves, contradict each other, propel actuality.

In the autumn of 1969, on the one hand, the Beatles as a happy, creative, life-enhancing foursome are dying as a productive unit; on the other, *Abbey Road* is released, an album produced a few months earlier at Paul's insistence that the group members give up their separate pursuits and come together once again to go into the studio with producer George Martin, to do what they always did best, and very likely for the last time. To their fans (and to this day, perhaps), the Beatles never sounded so strong, and therefore the rumors "couldn't be true" that they were in the process of dissolution. Paul, as a singer and songwriter, was as strong and vital as he had ever been on "Carry That Weight" and "You Never Give Me Your Money."

But of course the rumors were true; in September, John told Paul that he was leaving the group, that the "divorce" of the Beatles was at hand. Paul was in a hideous frame of mind, made even worse by an extracted promise not to reveal what was happening to the group because Klein was negotiating a new recording contract for the Beatles; there would be a lot of money upon signing, but there would be no contract at all if the record company knew the truth. With Linda, Heather, and Mary, Paul got the hell out of London and headed for his farm in Scotland, at "the end of nowhere," as Linda would always describe its location, most approvingly.

Helplessly at first, Linda watched her husband virtually dying on the inside, mirroring the death of his band. (Thanks to Linda, in another sense, he had already "died" as a viable bachelor, and she knew very well that millions of girls wished that she was dead, or at least that she'd never been born.) It was very grim.

Exactly what the frightened little family needed at that moment was the news, a front-page story all over the world, that Paul was literally dead. It was a self-perpetuating hoax of a magnitude no one had ever before seen; dozens of "clues" were discovered that "proved" the real Paul McCartney had died in a horrible automobile accident in 1966, and that the person now assuming his identity was an impostor. "IS PAUL DEAD?" seemed to be the most discussed and debated question in the world in the autumn of 1969. Paul's response: "I'm dead, am I? Why does nobody ever tell me anything?" But that wasn't good enough. The story kept gathering momentum as an army of Beatles scholars searched for, and found, evidence of Paul's death in nearly everything the band had done since the fatal crash. (This external ill wind for Paul and Linda, blew some good nevertheless, as the sales of Beatles' recordings spiked worldwide, making the Lads, and all who had a piece of them, a little bit richer yet.)

In their exasperation at the depressing story that wouldn't go away, Paul and Linda agreed to cooperate with a crew from *Life* magazine, which had appeared at the farm no one was supposed to be able to find, and with their two daughters posed for the beautiful cover photograph that appeared on the issue dated November 7. Along with the photographs was an interview, in which Paul, with Linda at his side, revealed that his future was not as a Beatle, but as a husband and father. "I am happy to be with my family, and I will work when I work," he told *Life*'s Dorothy Bacon. "The Beatle thing is over. It has been exploded, partly by what we have done and partly by other people . . . Can you spread it around that I am just an ordinary person and want to live in peace? We have to go now, we have two children at home."

Linda and the children were now the most important people in his life, and that was never to change.

In the pictures, Paul is intense, patriarchal, with his family gathered around him in an empty and hilly windswept landscape. He is anything but playful or moppety. Linda, in a plain dress, unadorned, natural and very beautiful, looks as if she were born in these hills. In spite of the undertones of Marie-Antoinette and her ladies-in-waiting playing at being milkmaids, the overriding impression is one of a pioneer couple with their young daughters, about to farm for sustenance the land they're standing on.

High Park Farm is about fifteen miles from the southern tip of the

Kintyre peninsula, off the western coast of Scotland, a 600-mile drive from London. Getting there by car requires travelling to the north end of Kintyre, where one connects with the only road joining the peninsula to the Scottish mainland, and then south in the direction of Campbeltown, the nearest center of civilization to the McCartney property. The most celebrated previous inhabitants of the area had been Robert Louis Stevenson, the enormously popular author who gave us *Treasure Island* and *Dr. Jekyll and Mr. Hyde*, and Robert the Bruce, who led the Scots to freedom from England in the fourteenth century. There hasn't been much development around Campbeltown since.

Paul had bought the property with its tiny decrepit farmhouse and tiny decrepit outbuildings at the height of Beatlemania, and Linda had loved it since their first trip there in November 1968, mice in the walls and all. She persuaded him to make some improvements, like pouring a cement floor with his very own hands; rustically inclined though she was, Linda preferred something more solid than planks thrown on the dirt under her feet—and the children's—as she cooked and scrubbed.

Drummer Denny Seiwell, who played on the New York sessions for *Ram* (Paul's second solo album), was summoned to the farm in 1971—he knew not why at the time—and remembers clearly what is was like getting there from America.

> You flew to that weird airport in Scotland, and PanAm [after checking out the legitimacy of Seiwell's presence] had us driven down to Campbeltown in a van. It was a five-hour trek, and we were dropped off at a local rent-a-car, checked into a typical little Scottish hotel, and set out to find the farm, which was in the middle of nowhere.
>
> We asked some of the villagers how to get to High Park Farm, and they said things like, "Well, laddie, ye take the wee car . . ." and I'm thinking, "What the hell are they talking about?" We finally found the right road, and they had said that we'd come to a farmhouse, which was on the edge of the McCartney property, but after that there was no real road to their house. Well, the sun was setting in the black hills of Scotland and we beeped the horn

> and this old guy came out, and we said, "How do you find Paul's farm?" and his answer was nearly unintelligible, but he opened this old wooden gate and there were these boulders everywhere. We ruined the car. We ruined about three rental cars; they wouldn't rent us any more cars in this village. Finally we got to the farm. Two bedrooms in the "main house," a kitchen, the kids, the horses, the sheep. Linda cooked up a dinner that was to die for, real simple stuff, and what we [Seiwell and his wife, Monique] saw was nothing but straight, straight love between her and Paul.

"It was the most beautiful land you've ever seen," Linda told Barry Miles. "To me, it was the first feeling I'd ever had of civilization dropped away. I felt like it was in another era . . . so different from all the hotels and limousines and the music business."

This observation of Linda's covers a lot of ground, for as one can tell by not having to read it with much analysis, the *Life* magazine interview shows Paul's attitude towards the Beatles, the press, and his entire career up to that point carrying a surprising amount of, for him, actual belligerence. It is now clear in retrospect that it was the business of music that was bringing him so low—what had once brought him (in spite of a few scary moments, like escaping the thugs of Imelda) joy, success, and accomplishment, with a ride to the moon thrown in as a bonus, was now a source of profound misery.

"Bad things were happening in the business then, in 1969," Linda said to me in that discussion I had with her and Paul in the summer of 1992.

"To whom?" I asked.

"To everybody," she answered. "Everybody. There was a sourness. There were parasites moving in, there was friction. Everybody started getting hugely successful, and with success came craziness, and any beautiful glow attracts a lot of ugly creatures."

"There's only so long a good mood can last," Paul added.

"Oh, there were so many fucked-up things in 1969," I observed. "The Nixon administration came to power."

"And there was repression," said Paul, having distanced himself enough from that time to include, and very astutely, the unattractive political situation facing the "groovy youthquake" of the mid-'60s.

"Kennedy!" exclaimed Linda, who was not what one might define as a scholar of contemporary history.

"No darling," I said. "We're talking about later than that. We're way past Kennedy, we're talking about the Nixon crowd."

"Try and stay with us, Linda," Paul chided her, very lovingly, a bit exasperated, but so affectionate—very Paul and Linda, that, I always thought—like Burns and Allen: "Say "Goodnight, Gracie." If you got in there, it really was a comedy team, as were, say, the Beatles themselves.

We talked that afternoon about the grandiosity of 1968 that had turned to dust in our hands as the decade ended. "I thought I could decide right there that this would turn into that, no doubt about it, and I still don't know how I could have been so sure about anything," I said.

"We [Linda and Paul, presumably] get the same sort of feeling," he replied. "You don't know. We all got liberated at the beginning of it, then we got certain bad habits, drugs and stuff set in, and we couldn't all put it into a nice little system that would take us thirty or forty years into the future. It was just too wild for that, anyone who tried to organize it went out the window, so it just had to run its little thing, its vitality, like a firework. There was kind of a Roman Empire winding up, and then the Beatles broke up, and that kind of gave the signal. Rock and roll lost its vitality . . . for the time being, then it spat back with punk and everything and it was all fine again.

"But we did feel a winding up, didn't we? And I always say, the reason why the '60s keep coming back is that there has been nothing better in the interim."

"Oh, remember flower-power?" Linda put in. "I never went to a love-in, I guess it's too late now . . . Oh! look at that chipmunk, look at that! Over there, that's really life, not *Life* magazine."

If Linda McCartney didn't have a way with words, she had a way with feelings.

"I didn't spend half enough time with Linda as I would have liked to,"

Pete Townshend told me about a year after she'd died.

> I really came to know Paul so much better and to love him and to accept him in a way that I don't think I would have done had he had a more traditional kind of showbiz marriage.
>
> She showed the world a new way of doing it, of doing marriage, like rock and roll showed the world that there was a new kind of music, and it wasn't going to go away. She was there when people had to make decisions about it. Decided that there was something wrong with the world that said it will only last for another couple of years, and then we'll be back to Sarah Vaughan and Frank Sinatra.
>
> But she believed, she knew, that this was not going to go away. This world that we've created is not going to go away, and we can even do it the way they used to. We can be real Americans. We can have a really happy family without going to church on Sundays. We can smoke the occasional joint. We can be good people with good, happy children.
>
> I think that Paul was growing into a feeling of dignity as an artist, as a pop artist, and Linda was essential to it. It was a loss in so many ways when Linda died, but you have to realize it was a loss to pop music too. This is a new business we're in. We're the first people to get old in it.
>
> At her memorial, I said that her presence in Paul's life felt like my property, like their marriage was something that belonged to me. They showed us a way of doing it that was legitimate for us, they created a whole new world around their marriage, the sheer time they were together, and they reinforced all those things I believe in: the Stones, the Beatles, Paul and Linda, they'll all live with me through my lifetime.

An excellent witness to the newlywed Linda and Paul is Ruth McCartney, Paul's stepsister. Paul's father, Jim, who lost Paul's mother in 1956, was remarried in 1964 to Angie Stopworth Williams. Her husband of three years had been killed in a car accident in 1962, leaving her with a two-year-old daughter, Ruth. Such was the frenzy of Beatlemania in '64 that Paul's father and his new bride couldn't get married in Liverpool, but had to take a taxi to a village in northern Wales for the ceremony; on the way, they pressed the taxi driver into service as the best man. Jim and Angie honeymooned the following January in the Bahamas, where the Beatles were making *Help!*, and with Ruth they lived at Rembrandt, the house that Paul had bought for his father.

A few days after Linda and Heather moved into Paul's London house, he took them up to Liverpool to meet the family. "I think they had jetlag, they both kind of seemed like fish out of water," Ruth recalled about her first meeting with Linda and Heather in November 1968. "I was three years older than Heather, and she wasn't allowed to do a bunch of stuff that I could—when you're nine, and someone else is six, you can stay up till seven-thirty, but they've got to be in bed at five, so it's a pain in the ass. I'd spent three years earning all these privileges, and then you've got to back down to pretend to be six, but I'd grin and bear it."

Raised in a traditional, working-class Liverpool Catholic environment, much as Paul was, little Ruth was constantly being astonished at the difference between Linda's and Heather's relationship, and that between herself and her own mother, Angie McCartney.

"We'd had the single mother and daughter thing, but it was totally different," Ruth said.

> I had never been exposed to any Americans before. The whole idea of marrying an American really shocked my Aunt Millie, who said, "You know, she seems like a perfectly nice girl, but she is an American, and on top of that she's Jewish." My Dad would say, "What the hell difference does that make?" and Aunt Millie said, "It's just a culture thing, love. I mean, he might as well have married a black thing." But Aunt Millie had by far the most closed mind in the whole family, I'm happy to say.
>
> Some of the differences in the way Heather and I were being raised surprised me. If Heather didn't finish her supper or was naughty, Linda would say, "Go to your room!" And I was like, "What is that about?" Because in England you were never sent to

> your room. You were made to rake the leaves or wash the car, not just, "Go to your room and sit there." My mother and Paul's father and Paul thought it was very strange. I remember being nine and thinking, "Boy, being sent to my room would be a treat! I've got a nice big bed and teddy bears and books." I just couldn't figure out how that was punishment.
>
> There were all these different little ways, and my Dad would kind of throw Paul a glance, and Paul would give him that look—"Don't ask me! Don't get me involved!" You know, a Linda-is-doing-what-she-needs-to-do kind of look. But everything seemed odd to us about the way they did things—it's just that by the standards of old-fashioned, Liverpool, working-class Irish Catholic families, to be dragging around a kid in a ballet dress and Wellington boots and taking her to a film festival in France was a very strange thing. Also, when my Mum had to discipline me she never did it in front of visitors; she'd call me into the kitchen with some excuse, and then she'd fix me with a look and tell me what I'd done wrong. In English working-class circles, you never castigated a child in front of anybody. But Linda would do it all the time: "Heather, don't be a pain! Go to your room!" We'd think, "Oh poor child, she's being humiliated," but I know that was never Linda's intention. She was a very caring mother, and she and Paul obviously had a very good relationship. She got her head together and did very well in business, so it turned out OK.

Linda encouraged Paul to adopt a let's-hit-the-road, spur-of-the-moment way of living, and Paul was happy to go along with it; it was therapeutic after being a Beatle all those years and good for him to be moving around without schedules, obligations, screaming crowds, and John, George, and Ringo to deal with. Besides, one could easily hire a private plane to take the family to Portugal on a whim, for example—and the freedom to "Just go!" certainly suited Linda's temperament as well. Things would not be quite that simple forever, but in '69 and '70, if an adventure were at hand, they grabbed the moment.

Ruth recalls, "They'd turn up in Liverpool and Heather would be in these muddy boots, and she'd say, "Have you got any shoes?" They'd be mowing the lawn or something in Scotland and the cold, rainy fog would blow in, and they'd say, "Oh, the hell with this! Let's jump in the Rolls-Royce and drive six hours and visit my Dad!" That's the way it went. If they didn't have the time or the inclination to pack, what's the problem? They could just go to Tiffany's or J.C. Penny and get what they needed when they got there."

Alas, the spontaneous jaunts were, in truth, not very joyful, because Paul—as we noted earlier in this chapter—was a mess, and Linda was frightened. She rescued him, and their marriage, not only by being there, but by convincing her husband that he might try making some music: "It's worked for you before, you know," she told him.

Chapter 10

"I've always had the feeling that Paul pushed her into becoming a musician, maybe to bring her closer to him, I don't know."

Leslie Fradkin

Looking back at those long months of depression and creative paralysis, Paul said, "It was Linda who made me realize what a complete fool I was." Between (and during) those awful periods of anxiety about the state of her husband and her household, Linda came up with the most simple and obvious reading of her partner's situation—it was about work. Work for Paul had always involved the Beatles, now there were no Beatles to work with, and hence no work; the consequence was a gaping vacuum at the center of his universe.

It had never been a secret that although Lennon and McCartney were a team, many of the best Beatles songs were the product of one or the other of them. But whichever one of them did not do the major amount of creative work on any given song was always there to criticize, encourage, make suggestions, shut up, sing, or play along with on the recording, split the royalties, no matter—he was *there*. Now for Paul, John was no longer there, and the natural crisis of confidence that one expects to arise from this sundering of so close a partnership had escalated and spilled over into the emotional picture. The cook of the house was now called upon to help rebuild it, and fortunately she found herself up to the task.

Linda had borne the burden of Paul's very wobbly condition all by herself. There were no girlfriends either in England, Scotland or America with whom she could share her problems, and the farm in Scotland and the besieged fortress (the fans were always there, booing and hissing the wife of their idol) in Cavendish Avenue were metaphors for her isolation. Even if she had retained chatty relationships with her friends in New York, it would have been unimaginable for her to get on the phone to the Manhattan yentahood and bitch and moan about her husband's wretchedness. When you're newly married to one of the world's most famous people it would be indiscreet and rather tacky to tell people that he hasn't been out of bed in two days, that happily-ever-after has taken an unexpected downward and very steep turn, and so on. Besides, as I noted earlier, I suspect—*only* suspect—that Linda was advised by her father and brother, as well as by Paul, that it might not be a bad idea if she sort of avoided speaking to her nearest and dearest friends in New York while the legal madness with the Beatles was raging. Nor can I picture her saying, "Gee Dad, Paul is really in a bad way." She had to figure out how to deal with things quite alone.

I asked Linda, once this unhappy era could be looked at as history, what she would have done if she could have foreseen the turmoil that would envelop her household during the first year of her marriage to Paul. "Would I have gone to London? Would I have married him? Is that what you mean? Well, no one looks forward to being confused. Yes, of course I would have married Paul, because it's all turned out to be so fantastic. We survived all that, you know? I can't say I would have handled it differently, except maybe there was a better way to shield Heather from what was going on. But I really wanted her to have a full-time father, and look, she got the best. Still, I might have thought more about how to make it easier for her. My God, if I had trouble dealing with all those changes in my life, think what it was like for her."

Linda's daughter had been taken out of her first school in New York just weeks after enrolling, and was hastily moved to London at the end of October 1968, when she was five years old. She was placed in a new school near Paul's house in London, walking distance if the mob outside wasn't too threatening on any particular day. As Paul told Barry Miles, "She didn't have an easy time because she was American and the kids made fun of her." Heather made few friends at that school, and the farm in Scotland was one of the earth's lonelier places to begin with. Then, in the spring of 1969, Linda and Paul took Heather away from her classes for a trip to the south of France, and that was indeed to be a pattern with the McCartney family for the rest of Linda's life: the family travelled together, wherever and whenever. It was less disruptive for the younger children, because at least they had their older siblings for playmates, but at the beginning it was a very lonely time for little Heather. "She's a very friendly person," said Paul, which was and is true, but it's not much good being friendly when there is no one to be friends with.

Having on her hands a sad little child, a sad big husband, an infant and a world that loathed her, Linda became relentless with Paul, trying to convince him that he was a great songwriter and that he had to do *something* besides making the odd masculine repair to the farm buildings and worrying about the slow death of the Beatles. And so he roused himself from his torpor, renting small studios or working alone at Abbey Road on his first solo album, *McCartney*. The first song he wrote for it was "The Lovely Linda."

When the album came out in the spring of 1970, it included as an insert a "self-interview" by Paul, somewhat circuitous on most points, but most definite when it came to answering the question "Do you foresee a time when Lennon-McCartney become an active songwriting partnership again?": "No." Well, John was supposed to say that first, according to an agreement the partnership had arrived at the previous October, but Paul jumped the gun and John was furious, accusing him of perpetrating a publicity stunt designed to promote the solo album. John told *Rolling Stone* that he, John, had quit the Beatles months ago, but the break-up was supposed to be a secret.

"It's madness when you think of it—who got to tell first," Linda told *Playboy*. In any case, it was Paul's own announcement (as was the *Life* magazine statement the previous autumn, but people wrote that off as being induced by the stress of having to deny that he was "dead"), and now the world knew that the catastrophe of the Beatles break-up was real. Since it was Paul who'd broken the news, Linda now led the cast of "THE WOMEN WHO BROKE UP THE BEATLES," and the scorn heaped upon her by the press and the fans was even worse than it had been at the time of the wedding a year earlier.

It must seem very odd for anyone under forty to read that people could regard the break-up of a rock group as such a significant event, because there is certainly no band today, nor has there been any perhaps since this all happened, capable of making such a gigantic impact simply by affirming that they now no longer exist. It is unlikely that there ever will be such a band again, simply (well, not so simple at all) because music, the music business, audiences and the culture have changed so much in the past thirty years. One potent reminder about the vast popularity of the Beatles is the fact that early in 1964 they held the top five positions on the *Billboard* singles chart. The five biggest records in America, the five with the biggest sales and the most airplay, were by the Beatles. It was unprecedented and almost certainly will never happen again; occasionally, an artist will have two records in the top five, and *that* is a major event in the music industry. All five? Inconceivable now.

Also, there was much going on about "the end of the Sixties," symbolized in the public mind and the media (for lack of something more specific than the general rot that was setting in) by the Altamont festival in northern California—ironically, one of the greatest performances ever by the Rolling Stones, but newsworthy because a deranged homeless person was stabbed to death by a Hell's Angel. Big deal, you may say now, but this was a very serious blow to the "peace and love" generation and its image. Soon, the stars themselves would start dying, but not with the fabulous timing of the unlucky drifter in a bizarre green suit who got himself killed in December 1969. Flower-power was expiring quickly, and although the Beatles, much to their credit, never came near that wretched phrase themselves, they were the ultimate carriers of the Universal Love message—literally, in fact, because in June 1967 they wrote and sang a song that was part of the first live broadcast to be aired around the world thanks to the brand-new satellite technology; it was titled "All You Need Is Love" and it was Great Britain's contribution to a multinational telecast called *Our World*, seen by a record 400 million people.

In these times when nothing nice is Really Big, except things that are horrible, it is poignant to recall an era when there was an attempt to make "nice" dominant. Of course that failed to happen, and the end of the Beatles was the main clue that it never would. And if you were one of the two women blamed for that ending (and, what's more, the nicer, younger, more vulnerable of the two by far), it was a very heavy thing.

Effectively, Paul McCartney's career as a solo musician began in 1970 with the release of *McCartney*, which went to number one in the U.S. album charts and reached number two in the U.K. The acceptance by the public of Paul alone was therapeutic at the very least, and he has never stopped giving Linda the credit for pulling him out of his desolate slump.

Linda McCartney's career as a musician—which was destined to bring down on her even more abuse than had ever before been slung in her direction—began with Paul's next solo effort, *Ram*.

The writing of six of the twelve songs on that album is credited to Paul; the other six are credited to Paul and Linda. Now is the time to recall our little publishing lesson in the previous chapter. The majority shareholder in Northern Songs, which publishes, i.e. owns (a large percentage of) the copyrights of any and all songs written by Paul McCartney (and John Lennon, together or separately) until 1973, is in 1971 a giant conglomerate called ATV. Well, if Paul wrote a song, ATV would collect their percentage of the copyright (publishing) on every record sold; however, if he co-wrote a song with anyone not bound by the Northern Songs contract, as Linda certainly wasn't, then she owned half the copyright and ATV did not get their piece of her piece.

ATV sued Paul for $1 million for trying to put something over on them; their feeling was that Paul could perhaps have co-written a song with David Crosby or Keith Richards, for example, and then things could be politely worked out. But the lawsuit was based on the perceived impossibility of Linda having made any musical contribution to the work of Paul. So, the first cackles of incredulity she had to bear in the long, long process of becoming Paul's musical partner—whether or not that eventually happened is still argued far and wide—came very publicly and loudly, from the company that controlled his own publishing. ATV's lawsuit claimed, in effect, that the songwriter Paul McCartney, of all people, whose copyrights ATV owned a large percentage of, had a) tried to cheat them, and b) insulted their intelligence by asserting that his wife, of all people, could have anything to do with creating music.

Paul defended the songwriting credits by insisting that Linda had indeed collaborated, if only to the point of making suggestions and offering opinions, but the suit was withdrawn when Paul agreed to do a TV special for ATV, which in turn agreed that Linda was entitled to collect whatever money was due to her. With no small amount of irony, Paul noted that the only money coming into their household was from Linda's share of the copyrights on *Ram*, because all his other income was being held up by lawsuits.

Linda's status as a songwriter, the suspicions of ATV notwithstanding, is affirmed by Jimmy Webb in his excellent 1998 book, *Tunesmith—Inside the Art of Songwriting*. Webb, no slouch at generating hits, wrote such remarkable songs as "McArthur Park," "Wichita Lineman," "Up Up and Away," "Galveston," and "By the Time I Get to Phoenix." He ends the book with a dedication: ". . . to the memory of the songwriters who have left us during the writing of this book." There follows a list that includes Sammy Cahn, Cab Calloway, Kurt Cobain, John Denver, Henry Mancini, Laura Nyro, Jule Styne, Jeff Buckley, Irving Caesar, Carl Wilson, Tammy Wynette, Jerry Garcia . . . and Linda McCartney. What a great honor, what vindication, and how much it must please her husband to see that among the posthumous tributes to have come her way.

A much more contributory and active role for Linda in Paul's musical endeavors was being planned by early 1971, when the family was in New York for the recording of *Ram*; she was to start going really and truly professional by singing back-up on other people's albums—no kidding.

Musician Leslie Fradkin was working on his first solo album at the time and enlisted the help of his friend, the much sought-after studio drummer Denny Seiwell, who was then working with Paul, to come over when he had some time and help with overdubs and such. Seiwell walked into Fradkin's studio, and said, "I have a bass player for you."

"You can park your gear over there," Fradkin said to the bassist. "I'll be with you in a minute." Almost thirty years later, Fradkin recalled,

> He didn't look anything like what I remembered, he had aviator glasses on and his hair was slicked back, and then I realized who it was, but I didn't pass out, I was preoccupied with getting my own thing done. So he introduced me to Linda, and said, "Well, she can help out too, she can sing."
>
> My attitude then was, and it's always been, that if he says it's OK, then it's OK. I never felt that she should have nothing to do with his music. I knew that she'd sung on "Another Day" [a true duet featuring Paul and Linda, it went to number one on the British charts], and I knew that she'd done bits and pieces on his first album that they did at home or something.
>
> She had a little trouble with pitch, I vaguely recall. But I thought if she wants to sing, that's fine. The record sounds very good, by the way. Paul seemed anxious about her confidence, and he encouraged her a lot. I've always had the feeling that Paul pushed her into becoming a musician, maybe to bring her closer to him, I don't know, but it was definitely something coming from him, not from her. He was very much the instigator. She was like, "OK, I'll give it a try, but I'm kind of scared, I don't really want to do this."
>
> I think history shows that she grew as a musician and got better and better, and as time went on she actually became, I think, quite good. That thing Howard Stern did I thought was terribly unfair, it was horrible to do that.

"That thing" was a cruel prank played on Linda that, alas, everyone knows about. For years, it was the first thing that came into people's minds when they heard her name.

First you must know that every microphone on a stage goes into a different channel and is mixed at a "soundboard," a huge blinking console that always seems to be set up right in front of your fine orchestra seats. The person operating the device hears everything on stage one microphone at a time, and then mixes the sounds to produce what the audience hears.

During a rehearsal of "Hey Jude" sometime in the mid-1970s, as the band was playing the famous (and endless) "nah nah nah na-na-na nah" coda, the guys at the mixing board, chortling over Linda's contribution, made a tape of it. It was not exactly vocalizing such as Janis Joplin or Aretha might have done, but few singers on earth sound good when their vocals are played back or listened to a cappella. In fact, even the best sound pretty awful, even comical, when you take away all the instrumental backing.

But Linda McCartney was a target waiting to be hit, and here was the ammunition. The tape of her isolated voice circulated around the world, and every raucous, macho, morning jock couldn't wait to play the mortifying morsel. It's still around; as recently as a year before Linda died, it went on to the Internet and got a whole new life.

"I've been in recording studios where everyone was listening to that and laughing their heads off," said Pete Townshend. "I would fucking bang the table and say, 'Just stop! Just stop!'"

"All those things get to you," Linda told *Playboy*'s Joan Goodman, "but I can handle it. I can just wipe it out, I don't dwell on what people say about me. I actually dwell more on what people say about Paul, for some reason. Maybe it's because he can't handle it."

"Of course I've known about that tape," Linda said to me in the late 1980s. "I'm used to people laughing at me. It just rolls off my back now. It didn't always, but now it does."

When she married Paul, all the girls hated Linda. When she participated in her husband's musical work, especially when she appeared with him on stage, all the guys hated her, because this was a Beatle, and how dare she?

In 1971 Paul decided to put together a band with himself and Linda as the core members. He claims he got the name "Wings" when he was praying for Linda in the course of the very difficult birth of their daughter, Stella, in September of that year.

"Paul wanted, I think, to recapture the innocence of when bands just used to get together to bang around in the garage," says Leslie Fradkin. "The public relations mistake he made is that he was already well past the point where the critics would accept that from him, but conceptually he had a wonderful idea."

The untrained singing of Linda and her keyboard playing were no doubt important elements in the "innocence" that Paul was looking for. It was the innocence of beginning. And Linda's voice was, in a sense, a "found object," like the instruments the Beatles would find in the closets and cabinets of the Abbey Road studios, and then use on their recordings.

Pete Townshend had high praise: "I know that there was something about Wings' sound which had a particular kind of quality to it that definitely came from the way that she sang. I've heard people on the inside of Wings boldly state that Paul used to come in and replace all her vocals. And I know that that's bollocks. I know it's bollocks, I know it's nonsense. "'Cause you can hear her. You can hear her voice. You know the human voice is the hardest to imitate. And you know she's in there, she's part of that sound and she's part of the character of it. I think when you're a composer, you work with the elements that are around you that are part of your human palette."

There were eight configurations of Wings between August 1971 and January 1980. Only Linda and Paul McCartney and guitarist Denny Laine were in the group, and on every recording, for the entire time. The group(s) played for millions of people around the world and sold millions of records; if you add up all the people they played for, and all the records they sold, it was more than the Beatles.

The story of Wings is a book in itself; there follows a listing of some critical dates and recordings to which you can refer if necessary—the personnel changes have been omitted. You need only know that the two superb and articulate musicians who contributed to the current book are drummer Denny Seiwell, who played with Paul and Linda during the *Ram* sessions in early 1971, was part of the original Wings line-up and left the group in August 1973; and Laurence Juber, guitarist, a member of Wings from early in 1978 until January 1980, when the group effectively ceased to exist after Paul was arrested for marijuana possession in Japan, spending over a week in jail and ruining a very lucrative and long-awaited series of concert dates. Both Seiwell and Juber are now living in Los Angeles and thriving.

So, in a nutshell (and with great indebtedness to *Rock Movers and Shakers*, by Dafydd Rees and Luke Crampton, Billboard Books, 1991):

- By late 1971 Wings have been formed, after the release of two solo albums, *McCartney* and *Ram*. The group's first album, released in November, is *Wings Wildlife*.
- In early 1972 the band embark on a "minimal" tour of British universities, with two vans, three children, two dogs, and various musicians.
- July 1972 sees the kickoff of a major European tour, in Chateauvillon, France.
- The album *Red Rose Speedway* is released in May 1973 and goes to number one in America and number five in the U.K. Also that month, the TV special *James Paul McCartney* airs on the BBC. In '73, there are three major hit singles: "Hi Hi Hi," "My Love," and "Live and Let Die."
- August '73: Wings record the phenomenally successful LP *Band on the Run* in Lagos, Nigeria.
- In 1974, with *Band* high in the charts around the world, Paul McCartney finally gets a U.S. visa—which has been held up by pot busts in the past few years—and Wings goes to Nashville to record, where Paul also produces Peggy Lee's *Let's Love*.
- *Venus and Mars* in 1975 makes number one in the U.K. and the U.S.; the single "Listen to What the Man Said" is number one in America, number six in the U.K. Wings goes on a thirteen-month tour.

- *Wings at the Speed of Sound* goes to number one in the U.S. and number two in the U.K. in 1976. "Silly Love Songs" tops the U.S. singles charts, reaches number two in the U.K. The "Wings over America" tour begins in May, with Paul making his first appearance in the U.S., in Fort Worth, Texas, since the Beatles' last concert in San Francisco ten years earlier. A UNESCO benefit in Venice to help save the sinking city is such a massive event that the city sinks even further. In December, the world tour ends in London.
- *Wings over America*, the album, makes number one in the U.S. and number eight in the U.K. in 1977. "Maybe I'm Amazed" is in the top ten in the U.S., only number twenty-eight in the U.K.; but "Mull of Kintyre," released in September, becomes the biggest selling British single of all time, yet bombs in America. The album *London Town* is recorded on a fleet of yachts in the Virgin Islands, to be released in 1978.
- Later in 1978, *Wings' Greatest Hits* is number five in America, number twenty-eight in Great Britain. In 1979 Paul's song "Haven't We Met Somewhere Before" is turned down for the movie *Heaven Can Wait*, but makes it into *Rock and Roll High School*, performed by the Ramones, who named themselves after Paul's first stage name (with the Silver Beatles in 1960), Paul Ramon.
- Shortly after getting an award for being the most successful composer in history, having sold 100 million singles and as many albums, Paul is arrested in Tokyo in January 1980 for bringing a bag of marijuana into Japan in his suitcase. His nine days in jail mean the end of the Japanese tour, and Wings falls apart.

The preceding has been disgracefully compressed but it's just there to give a Wings perspective/retrospective, as it were. We are by no means finished with that eventful decade. In fact, let's go back to the pre-Wings years, as *Ram* was being recorded in New York, as recalled

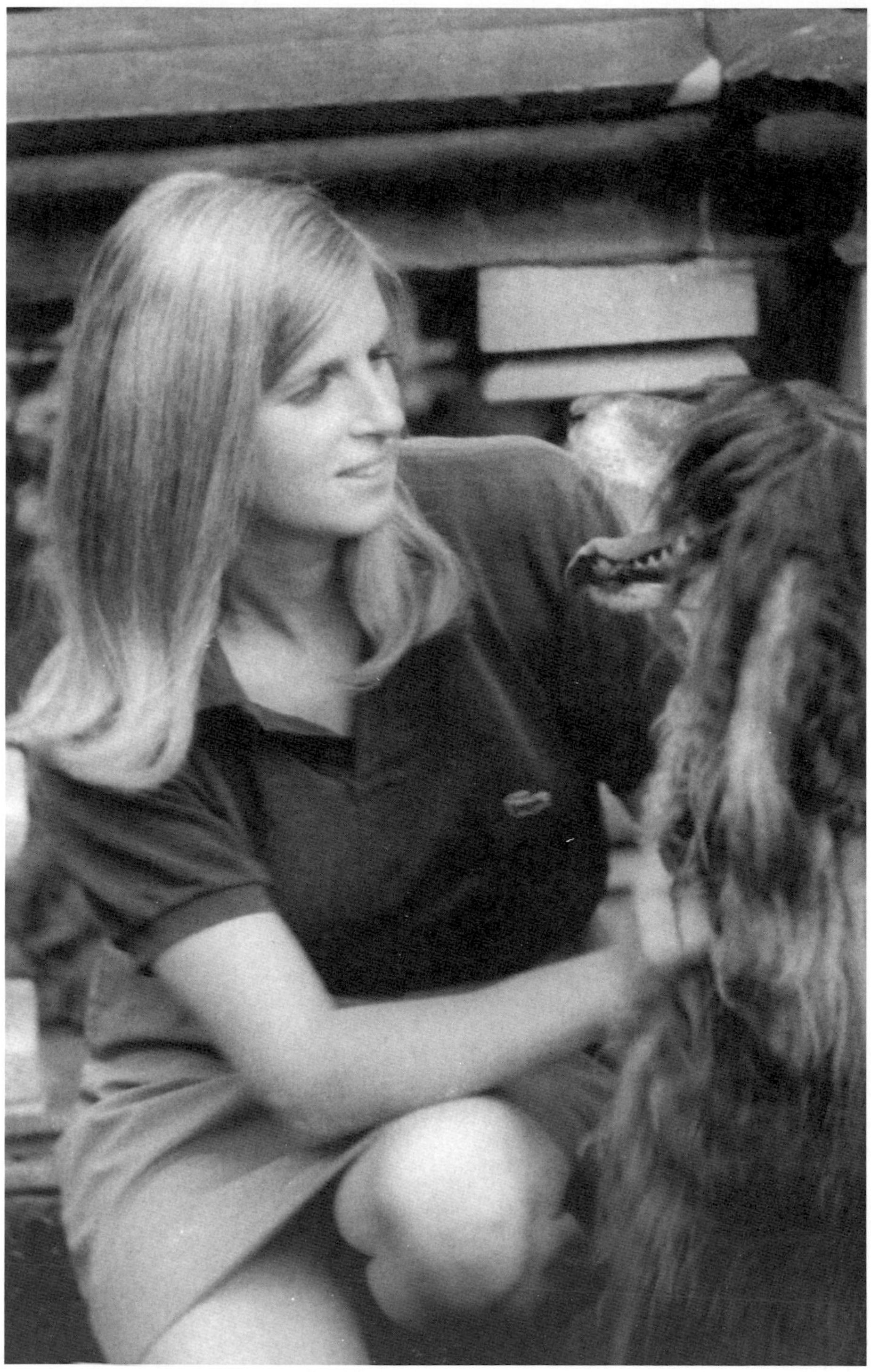

Linda and a new friend, Central Park, New York, 1965.

DAVID DALTON

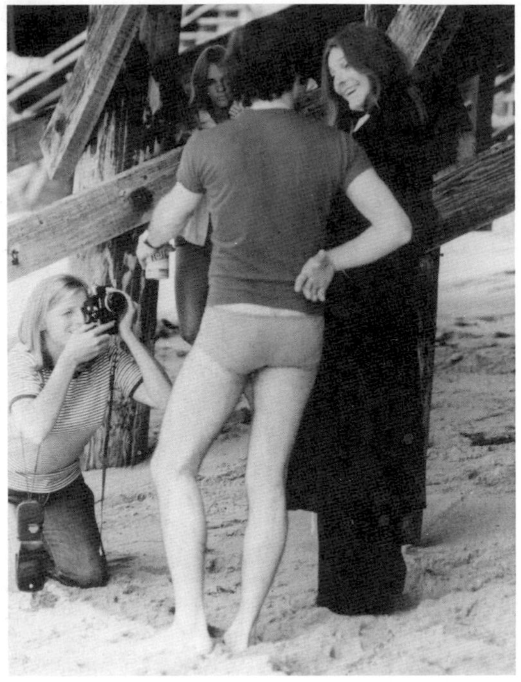

Linda photographing Judy Collins on the beach in Malibu, California, in August 1968. Danny Fields displays his better side.

DANNY FIELDS COLLECTION

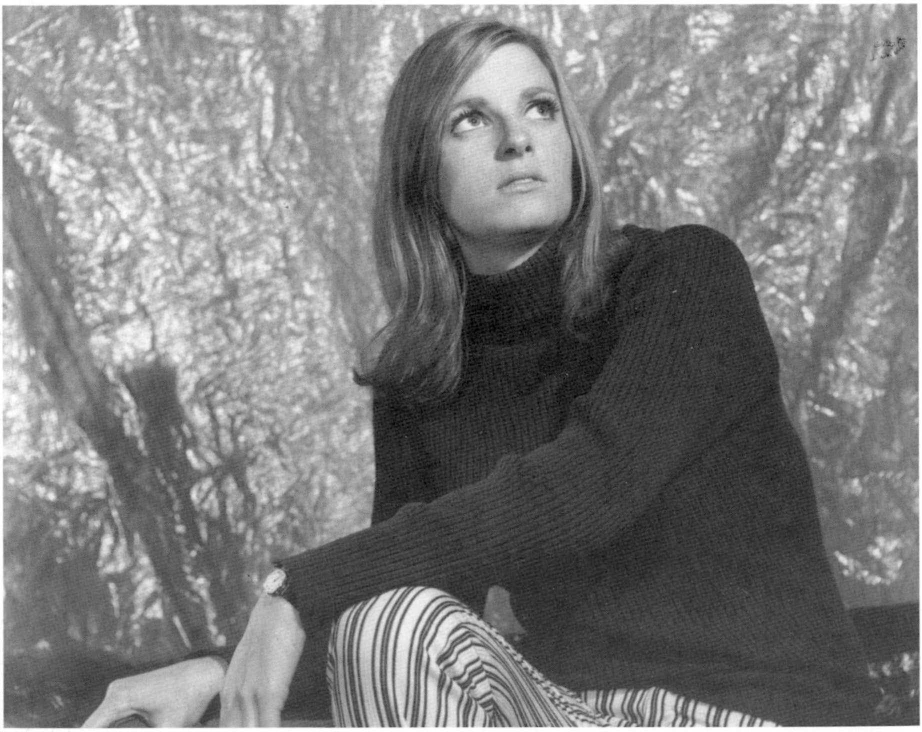

STARFILE AGENCY ARCHIVES

On the other side of the camera, late 1960s.

Danny Fields, Nat Weiss, and artist David Hoff photographed by Linda at the St. Regis Hotel in New York, 1967.

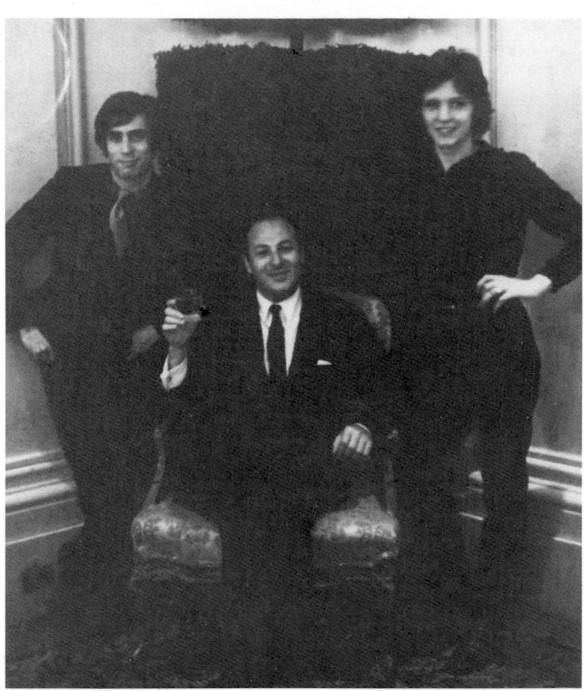

LINDA EASTMAN/DANNY FIELDS COLLECTION

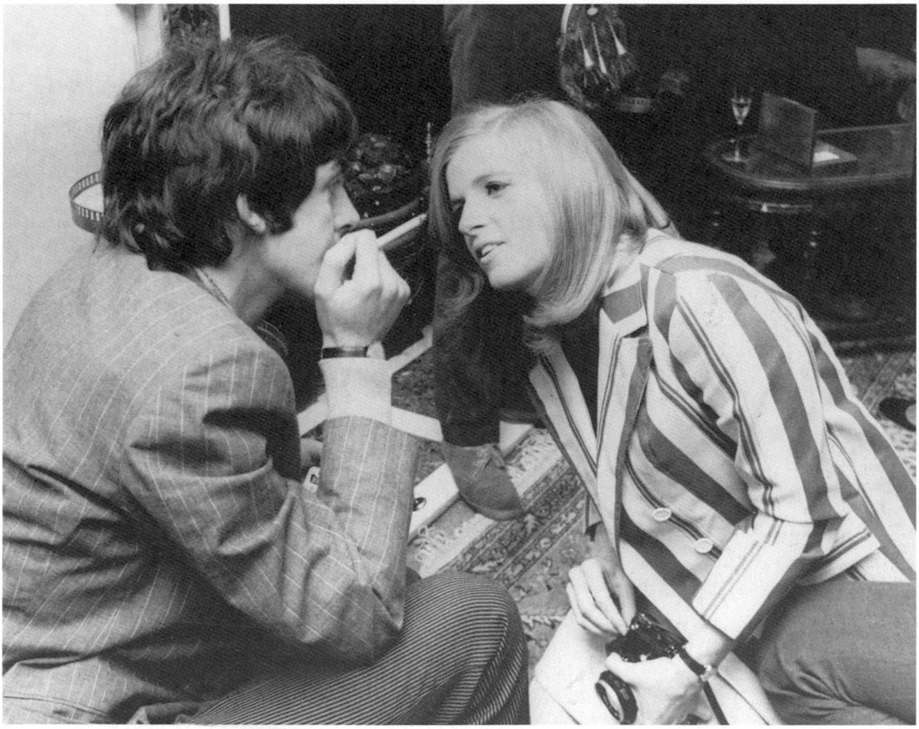

CORBIS/HULTON DEUTSCH COLLECTION

Linda Eastman chats with Paul McCartney at the *Sergeant Pepper* press party at Brian Epstein's London home in May 1967.

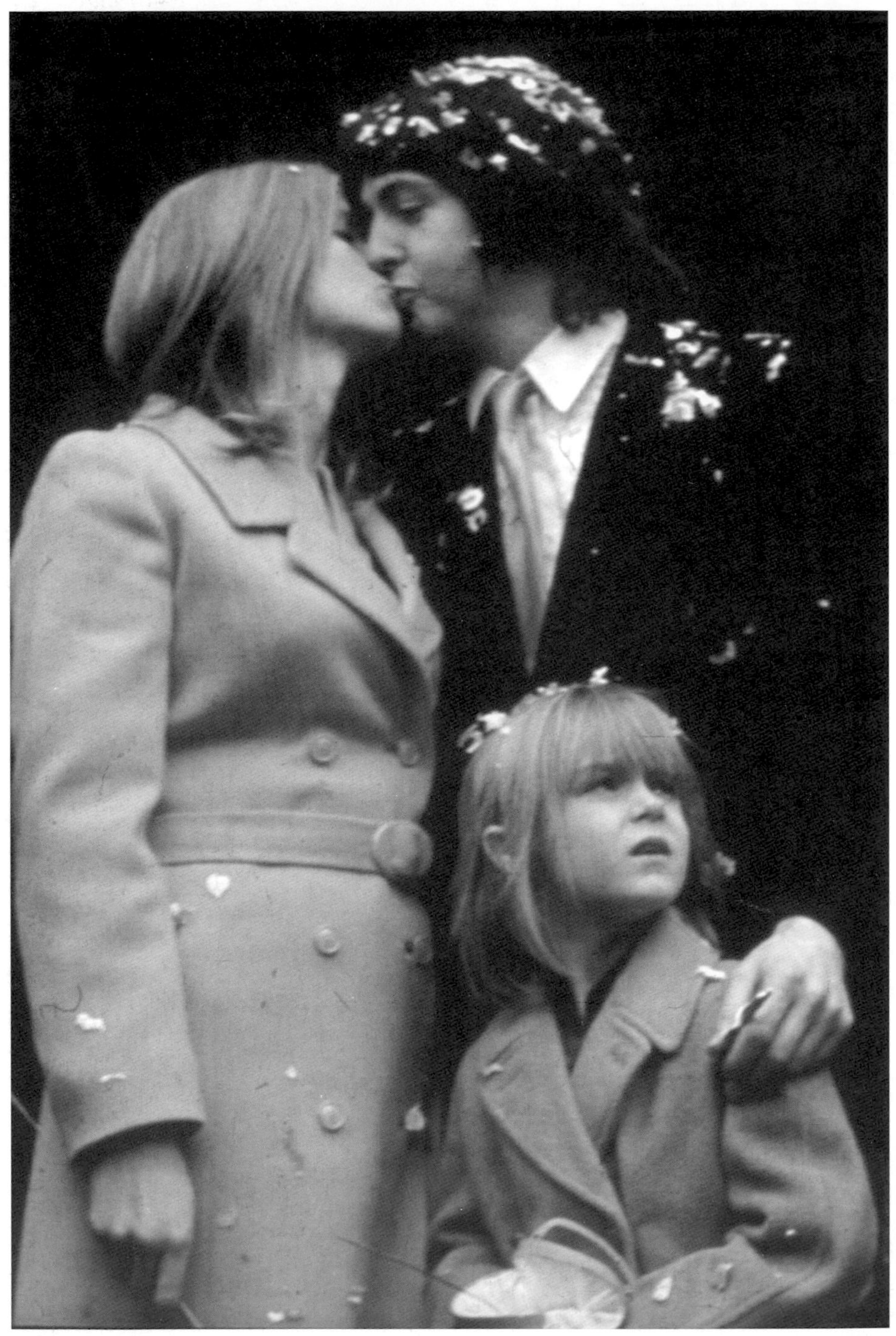

REX FEATURES

Linda and Paul with Heather on their wedding day, March 12, 1969.

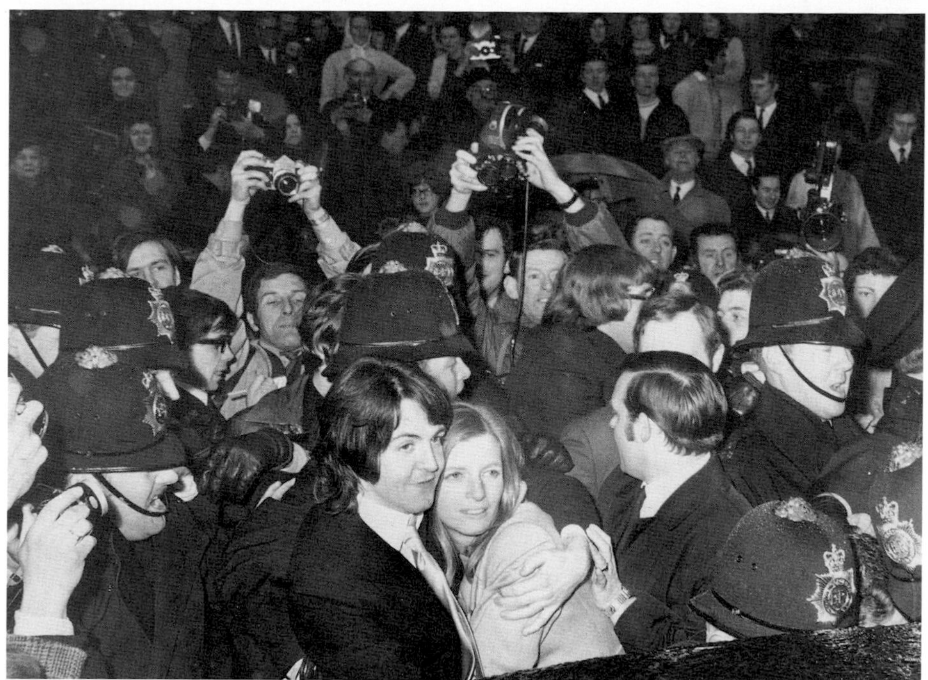

The newlyweds attempt to make a getaway after the marriage ceremony at Marylebone Register Office.

CORBIS/BETTMAN

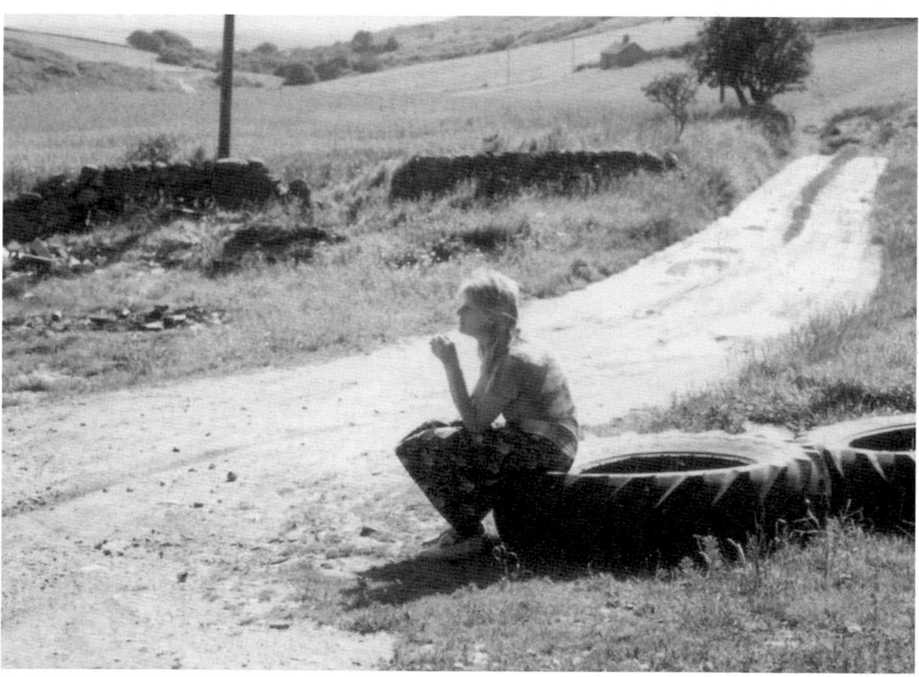

Their farm in Scotland provided sanctuary from the public eye.

LAURENCE JUBER

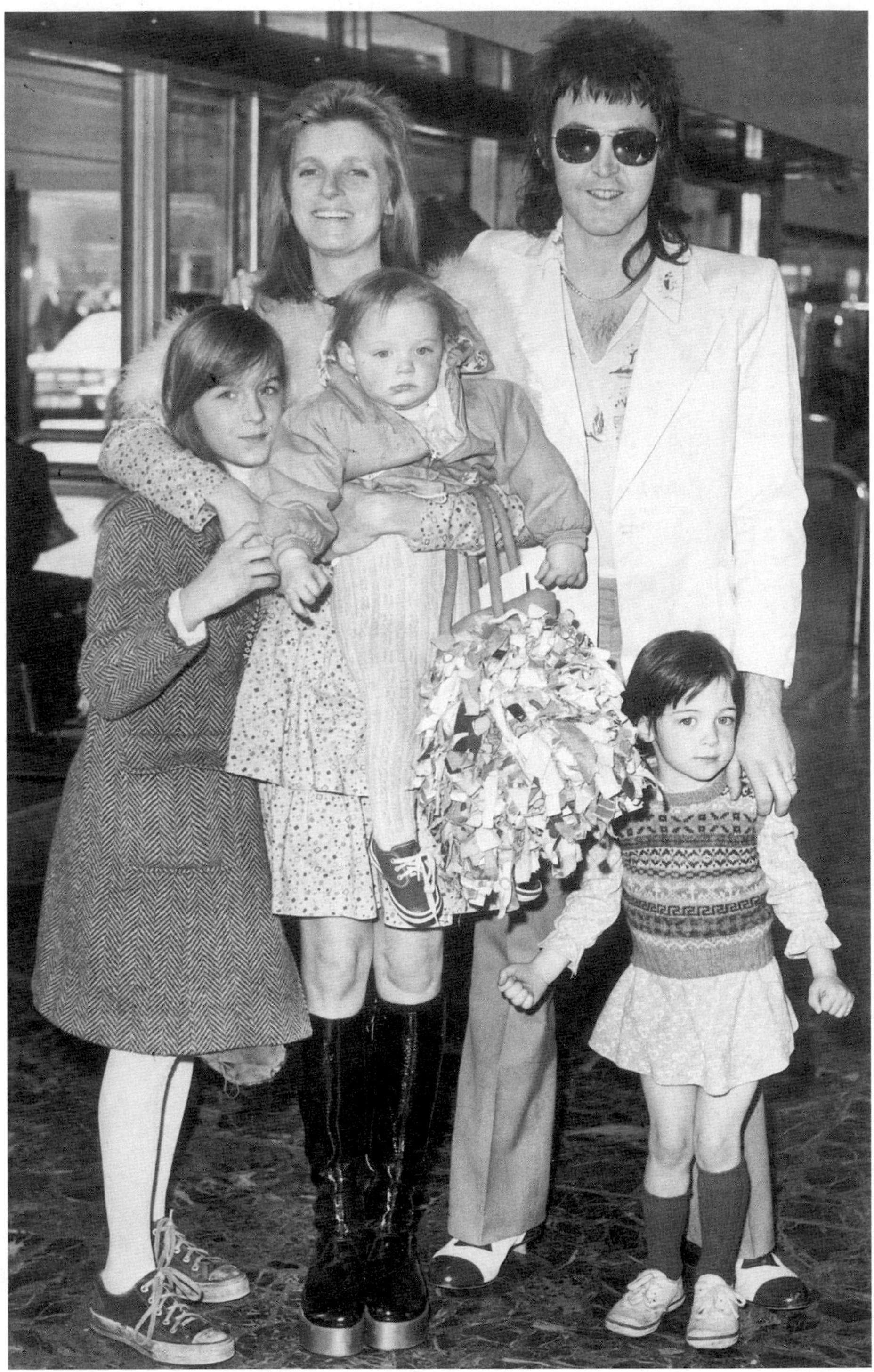

CORBIS/BETTMAN

Traveling with Heather, Mary, and baby Stella.

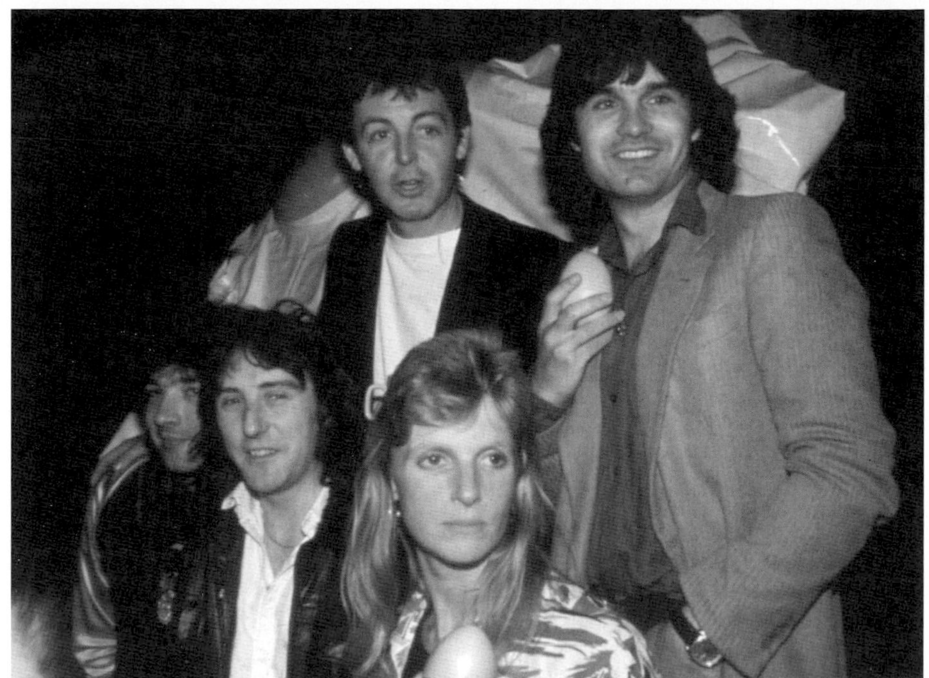

REX FEATURES

Linda with Wings. With Paul and other members of the band.

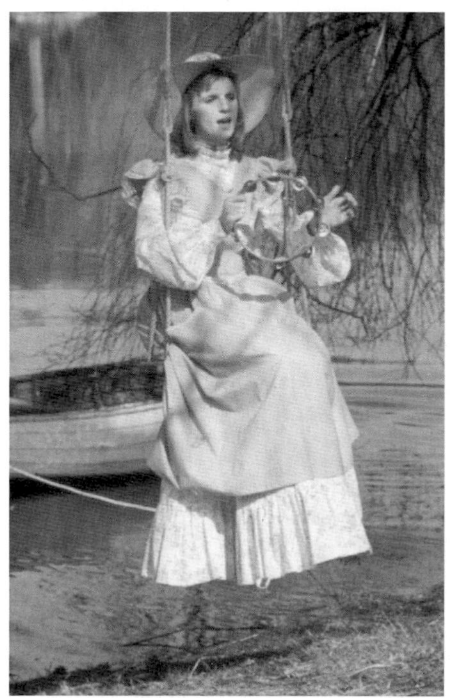

REX FEATURES

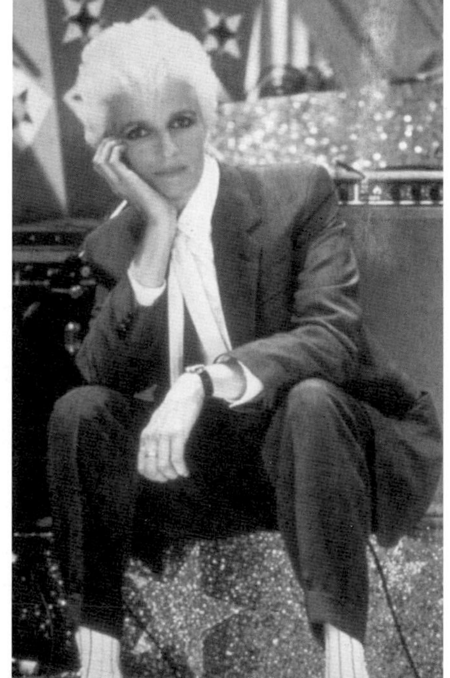

REX FEATURES

A pastoral setting with picture hat and tambourine, and a 1970s glam-rock pose present two contrasting images.

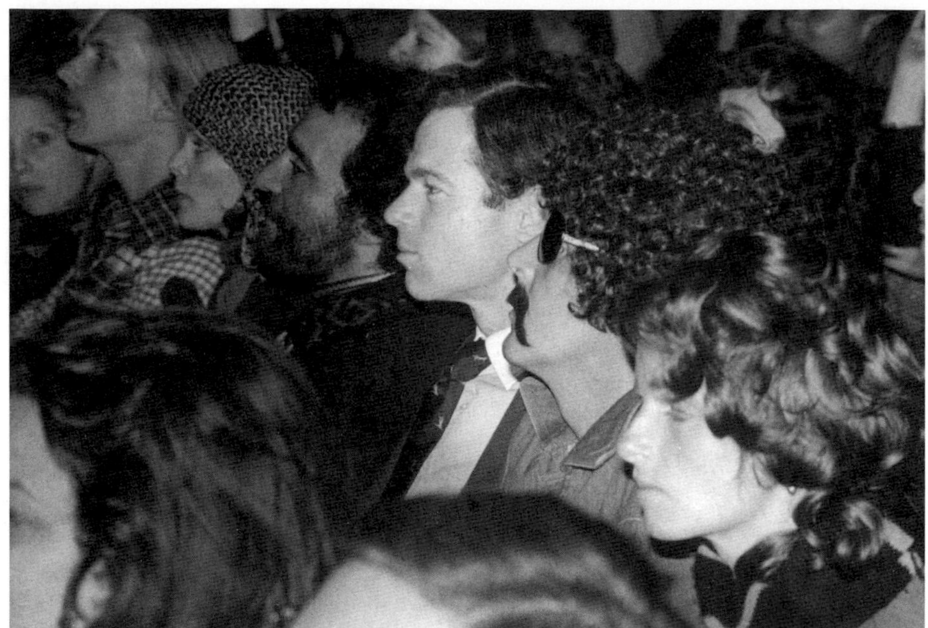

BOB GRUEN

Paul and Linda, with Linda's brother, John, in "hippie" disguise for George Harrison's Madison Square Garden concert in New York in 1974.

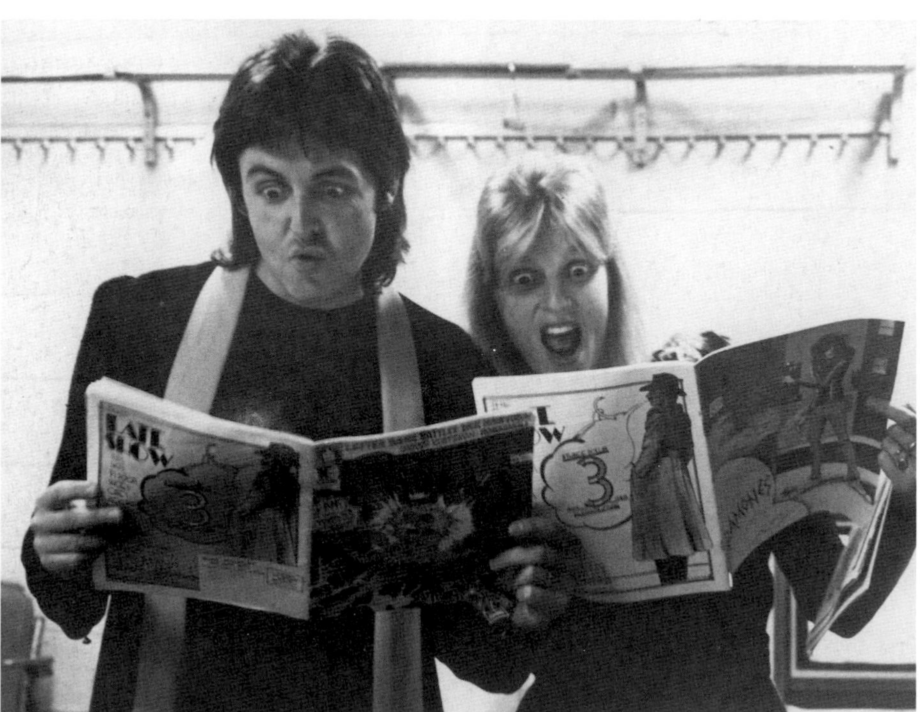

ROBERTA BAYLEY/HUMPHREY OCEAN

Backstage at Madison Square Garden in 1976, feigning shock at early issues of Punk magazine.

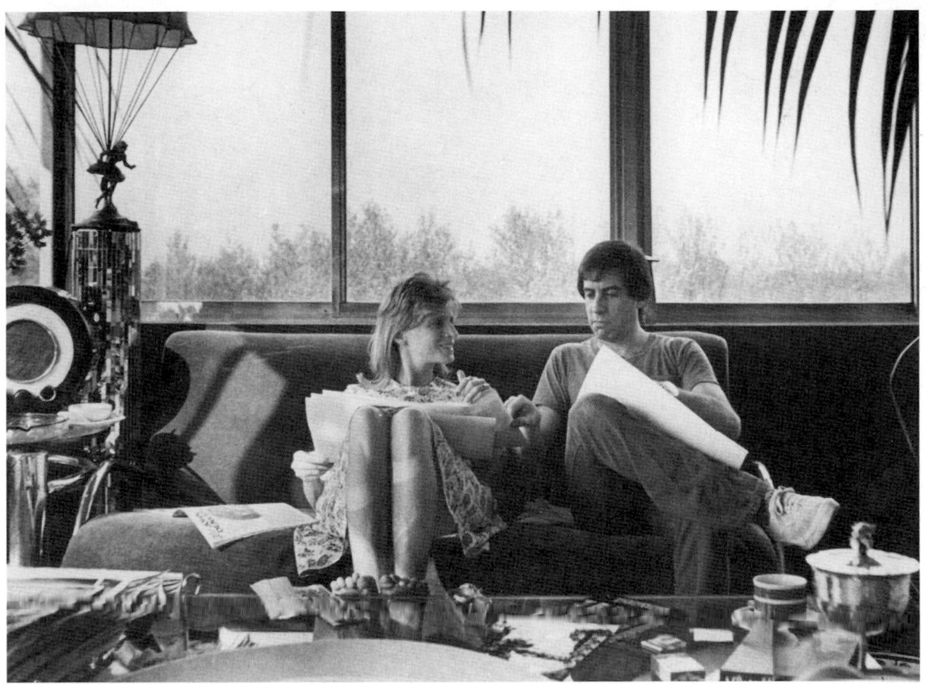

DANNY FIELDS COLLECTION

Linda with the author in London in 1974, choosing photographs for her book *Linda's Pictures*.

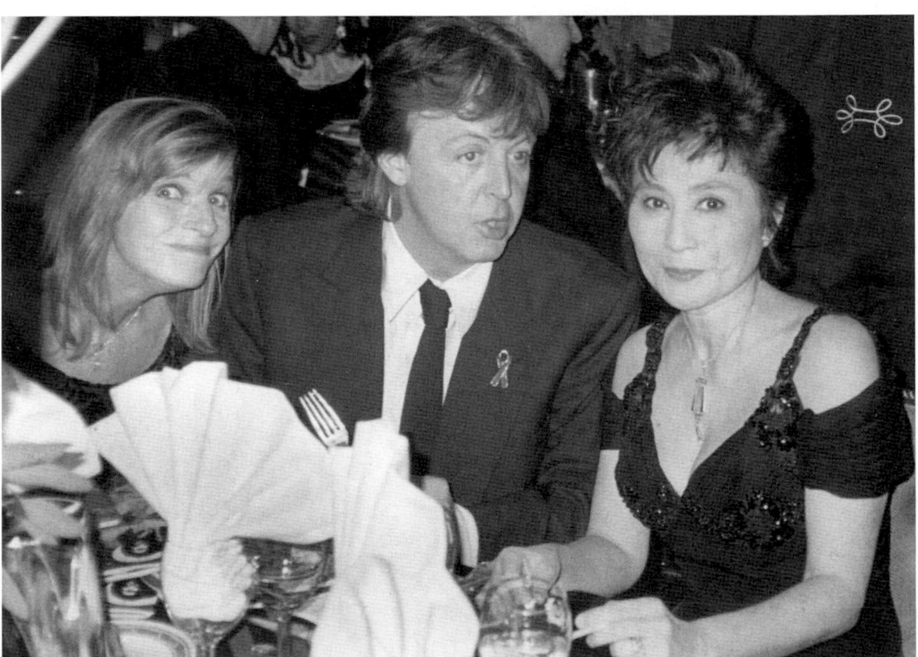

BOB GRUEN

With Paul and Yoko Ono Lennon at the Waldorf Astoria Hotel in New York in 1994 for the Rock and Roll Hall of Fame ceremony at which John Lennon was posthumously inducted.

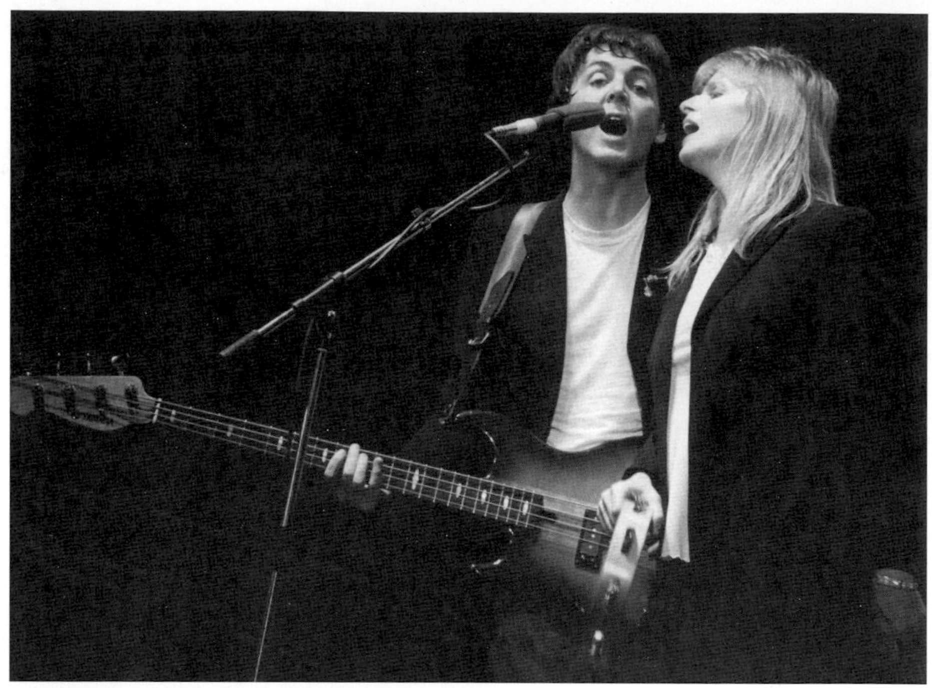

STARFILE/BOB GRUEN

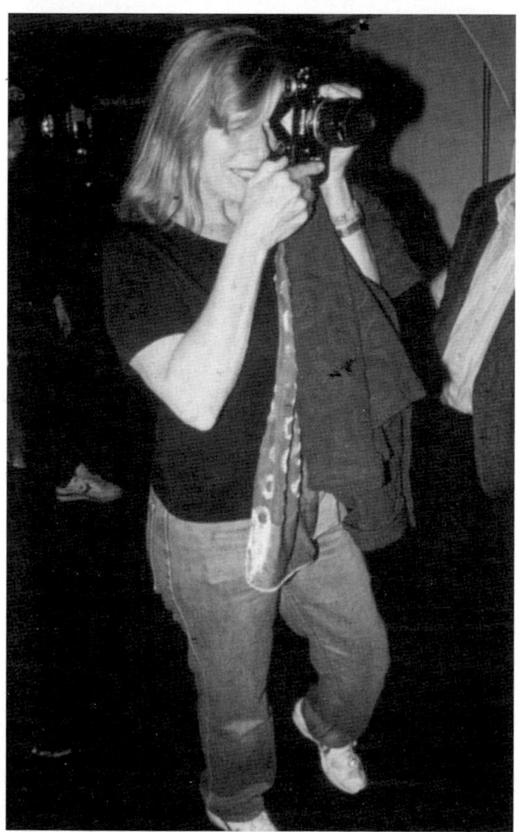

REX FEATURES

Four faces of Linda: Performing with Paul and Wings (above), and backstage with her camera (below).
Top right: Displaying some of her work. Bottom right: Promoting her range of vegetarian food.

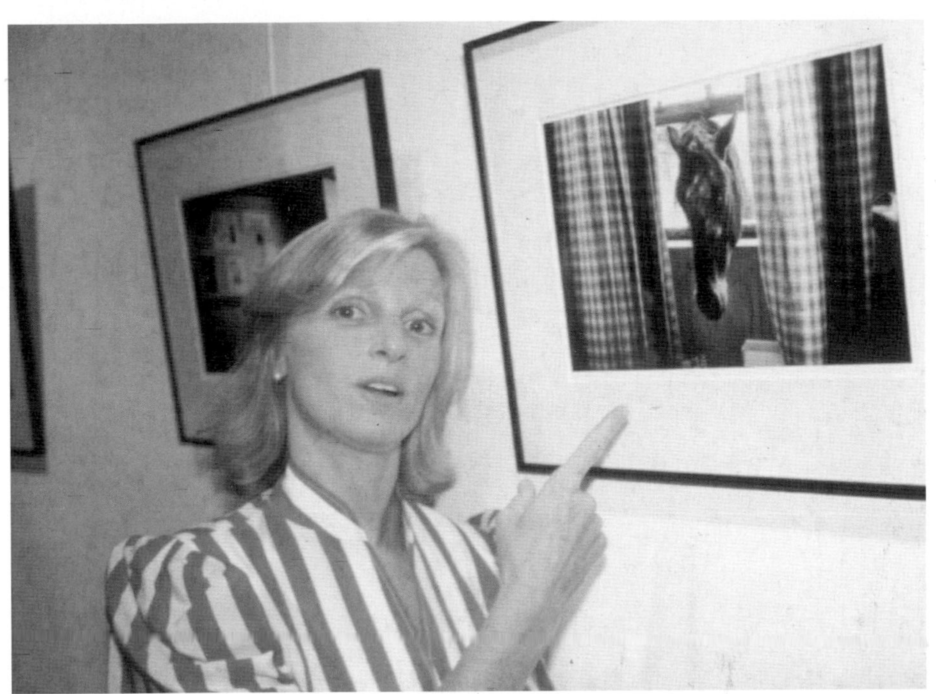

REX FEATURES

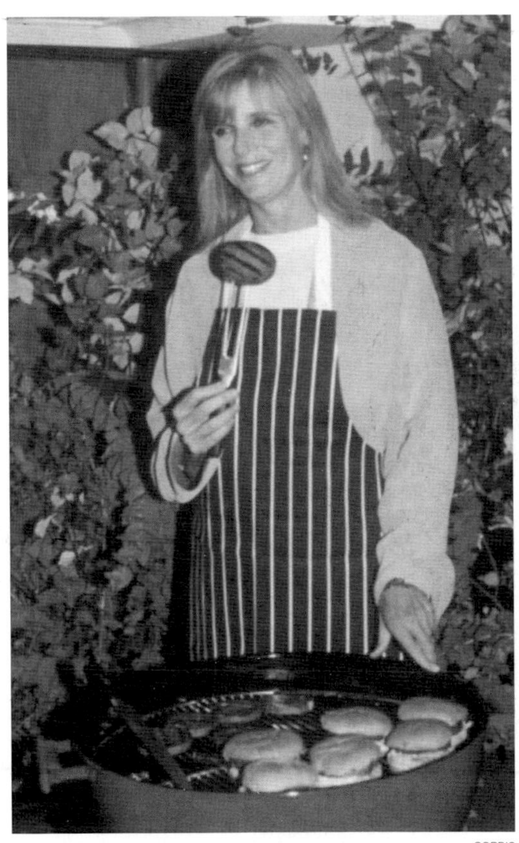

CORBIS

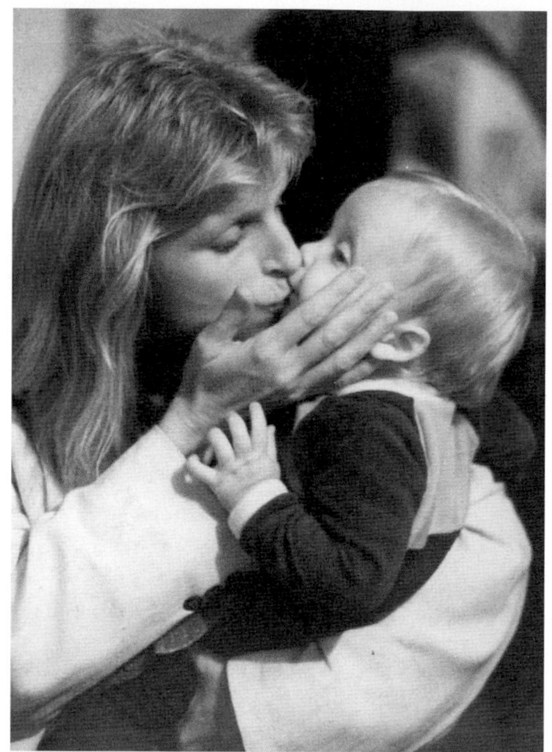

Linda with her son James in 1978.

LAURENCE JUBER

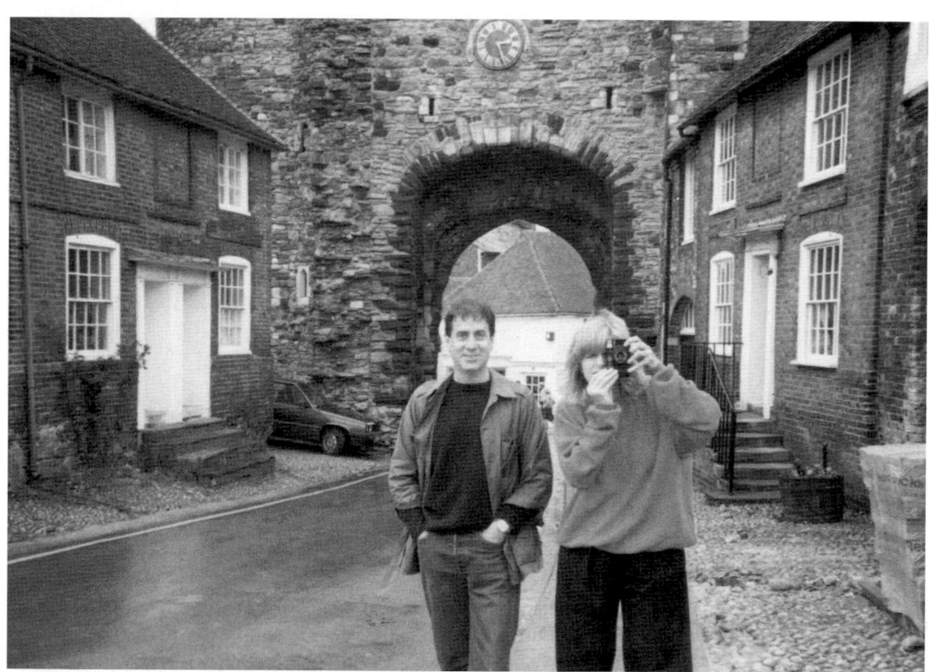

With the author—and the ever-present camera—in Rye, Sussex, 1988.

DANNY FIELDS COLLECTION

Linda in her kitchen in East Hampton, 1992.

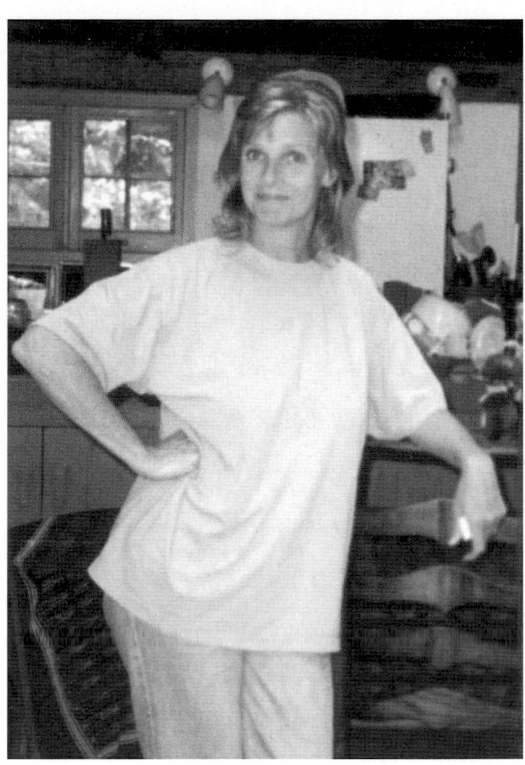

DANNY FIELDS

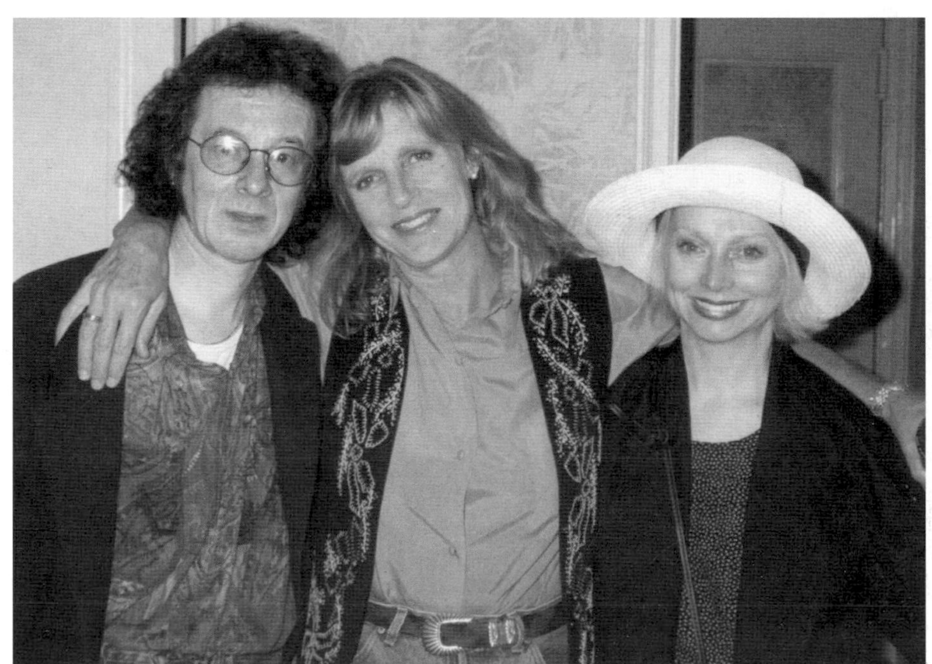

DANNY FIELDS COLLECTION

With Noel Redding and Candace Carell at the Mayflower Hotel, New York City, 1992.

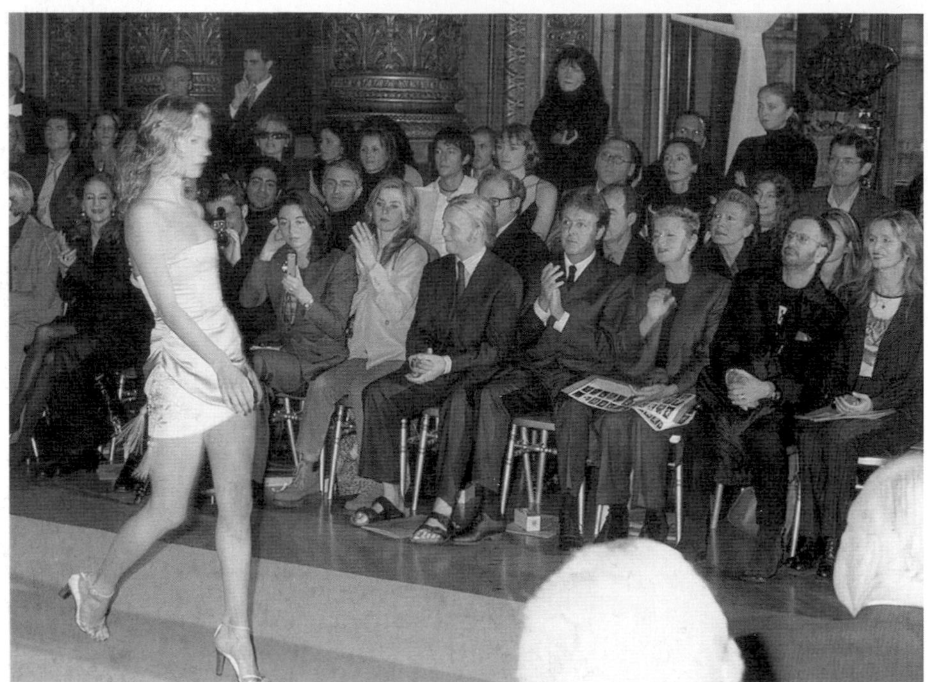

ALPHA/RINDOFF/GARCIA

The McCartney family, along with Ringo Starr and his wife, Barbara Bach, turn out to support designer Stella at the showing of her collection for Chloe in Paris in 1998.

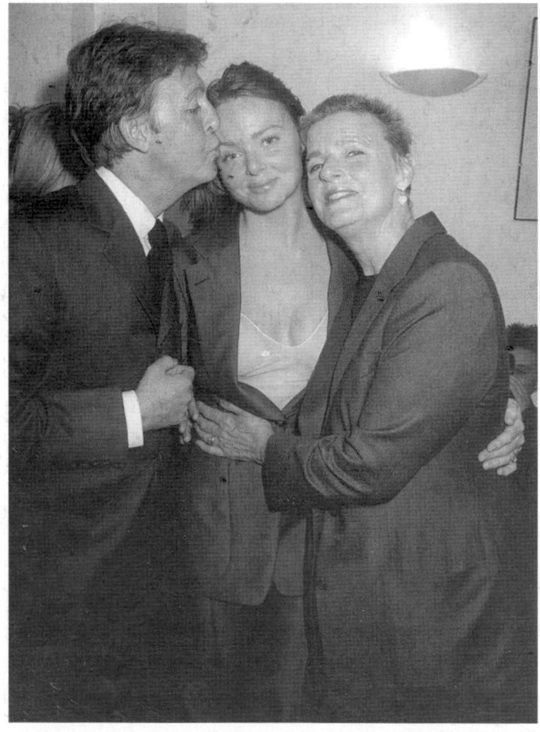

ALPHA/RINDOFF/GARCIA

Congratulating daughter Stella after the show.

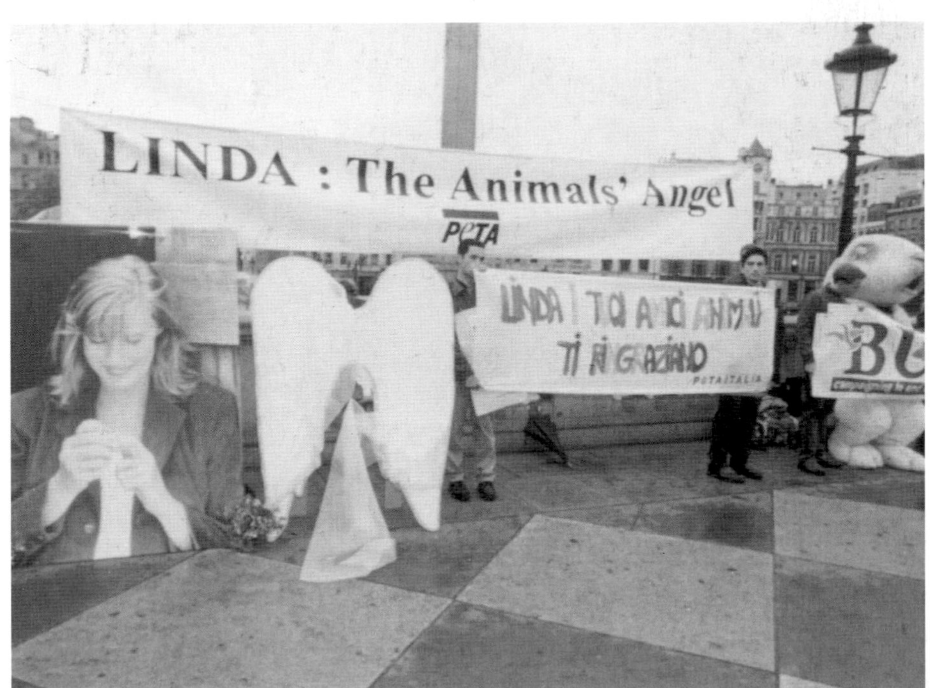

ALPHA/CHAMBURY

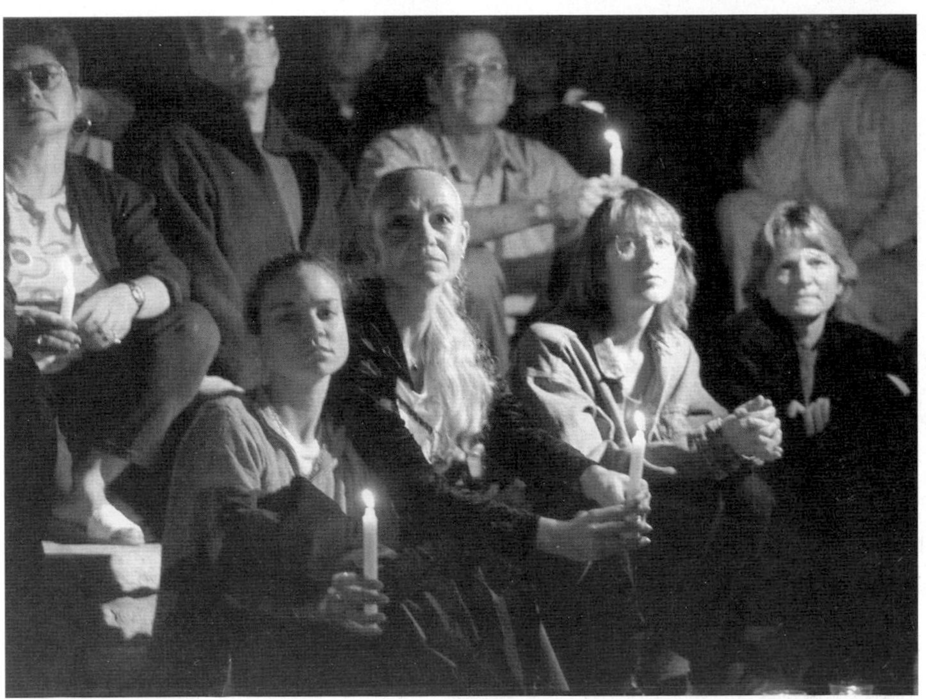

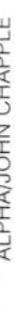

The public reaction to Linda's death illustrated the affection in which she was held on both sides of the Atlantic. Above: The scene outside the memorial service held at St. Martin-in-the-Fields, London. Below: Mourners at a candlelit vigil for Linda in Santa Barbara, California.

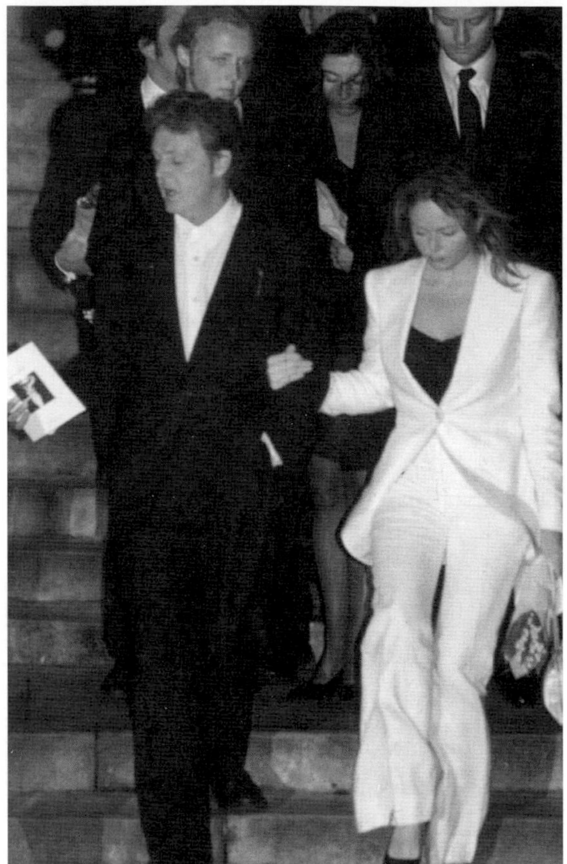

Sir Paul McCartney leaves St. Martin-in-the-Fields with his family after the memorial service for his wife.

ALPHA/CHAMBURY

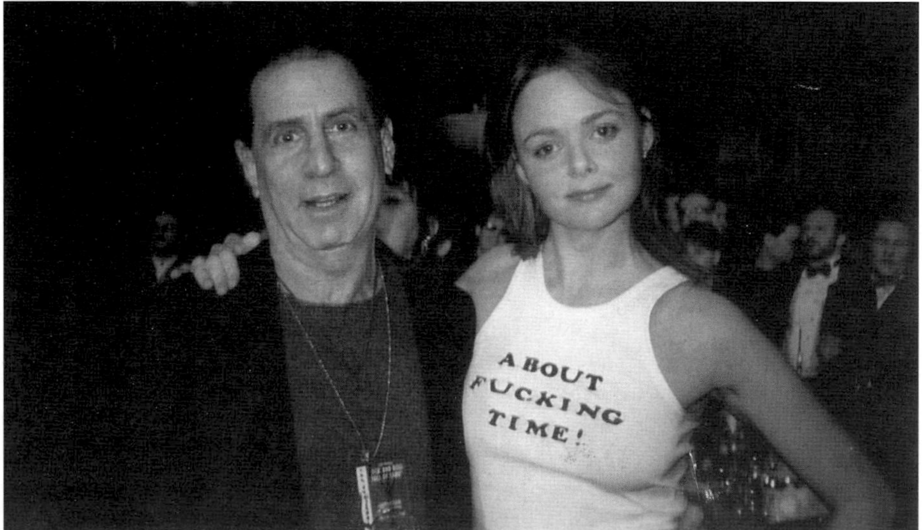

RHONDA MARKOWITZ

Danny Fields and Stella McCartney celebrate Paul's induction into the Rock and Roll Hall of Fame in March 1999.

by drummer Denny Seiwell. As always, Linda and the children were there during the sessions—Heather was eight and Mary was about eighteen months old.

"Linda made tea during the recording of *Ram*," Seiwell recalls. "Mary was tiny and jumping all over; there was a playpen for her in the control room of the recording studio. It was the first time I ever had a cup of English tea. I thought, 'I can get used to this.' Anything Linda did, she really did well."

It was at that time, early in 1971, that Linda called me—it was the first time I'd heard her voice since she had left for London in September 1968.

"Hi, it's Linda. We're in town. Can we come over? Paul would love to meet you."

"Sure."

"Seven West Twentieth Street, right?"

"Right."

"We'll be right over."

Nothing about "I missed you," or "I suppose you're wondering . . . ," or anything to indicate that an unusually long period had gone by for two friends who used to talk every day. Linda was now operating on MST, McCartney Standard Time, and she would for the rest of her life. In their own minds, and in their lives, the McCartneys *were* the Greenwich Meridian. As the Queen is the Fountain of Honor, they were the Fountain of Events—this royal metaphor will be heard many times in this story, and from many sources.

Linda wanted her "new" husband and her old friend to like each other, and there was no problem with that from where I sat; there is no one more charming than Paul, and of course it was exciting to meet him, and great to see Linda again. Except for a certain deference towards her husband in her manner, which was certainly to be expected, she hadn't changed a bit. She took control of the situation, because she had to, and Paul offered the obligatory—and he offered it most graciously—"Linda has told me a lot about you. I'm glad we're getting to meet each other."

One thing about meeting people who are very famous is that you cannot ask them very much about themselves; they have to do virtually all the asking. Otherwise, it's as if you were conducting an interview, and it just doesn't feel right. Besides feeling that it would have been a bit rude to ask a Beatle, "So, what are you doing these days?" I didn't really want to work very hard at this whole renaissance. That was up to them. She'd turned her back, had found greener pastures, was now trying to re-establish something that once was, God bless her. I still loved her, and there was as always a little protective feeling towards Linda; I wanted to see what she'd brought home, so to speak. And I wanted the Beatle to perform, in my living room, to please his wife by pleasing me. I thought I was entitled to that, and besides, we were all too smart and grown-up for anything to go wrong; we were all going to make sure that everything was hunky-dory.

I was working in a dead-end publicity job at Atlantic Records then, and was glad to chatter all about the Rolling Stones, David Crosby, Steven Stills. (Crosby had been a great friend of the Beatles; Stills had been a great friend of Linda's) and my beloved Stooges, whom I was managing on the side. It was very music business, and then it turned into Linda asking me about all our mutual friends; it was instantly clear that I was the only one of the old crowd she had contacted in the course of re-emerging into New York rock-and-roll society.

Steve Paul, the owner of the Scene, was discussed, as was the crowd at Max's Kansas City, the Fillmore, the Chelsea, etc. We shared our devastation at the deaths of Janis and Jimi the previous autumn (Janis's close friend and biographer, Myra Friedman, would have appreciated hearing from Linda at the time Janis OD'd in L.A.; it was known that Paul and Linda had been in New York when it happened, but there was not a word of sympathy offered—the Fountain of Events syndrome starting to take shape), and of course Lillian's name soon came up.

Where I had once described our mutual friend as "not smiling wildly" at Linda's neglect, this time I just said, "She's pissed."

"Uh oh," Linda acknowledged, but I knew she would do nothing about it. She was afraid to confront a pissed-off Lillian Roxon, as was everybody else. I told her she should call, but she never did. (Naturally, I told Lillian all about it as soon as they left. "They must have a new record coming out," she said most disdainfully. "They need all her friends in the press back on their side. I'm not surprised they called *you*." Meaning I was a pussy? I didn't pursue it. Lillian was sliding into deep detestation of her erstwhile best friend.)

Paul was staying out of the sentimental reminiscences, but when I remarked to Linda, "Gosh, I miss your pictures, I wish there could be a book of them," he came vividly to stage front.

"That's *just* what I've been saying!" he said. "Her pictures are great! There should be a book, more than one, definitely!"

"Well it would be beautiful," I replied. Linda asked me if I would work on such a project with her, and I said sure.

The whole mood of the little get together had changed. If they were asking me to line up support for a forthcoming album or musical project of any kind, they were being so subtle that I didn't notice it. What Paul wanted was the rehabilitation of Linda in the public mind, as a photographer worthy of having her name on a book of her work, and he was really, really into the idea. It occurred to me right then that he thought the world should know that he had married a person who was remarkably talented, an artist in her own right. John Lennon had married a woman who was an artist in her own mind, and his; Paul was convinced that he had done just as well in picking a creative mate, probably better. I thought, "Way to go!" It was a very good moment. And it was all about Linda. Paul loved her and wanted her to shine. He was proud of her, proud of the choice he had made, proud of the partnership that his fans and all the press had questioned the validity of from the very beginning. They were wrong; he was right; he had done very well, if they only knew . . . It was my great pleasure to be an instrument in the campaign to prove that Linda McCartney was no groupie, no dizzy débutante, no destroyer of groups—that she was instead an incredibly smart, loving person with an astonishing gift for photography. Her pictures would speak for themselves, and the contempt would start to lift and vanish.

How optimistic we were, and how long the fight was going to take. Because Paul wasn't going to be happy with just a book (or books) of photographs from a beautiful woman who was a perfect wife and mother—he had to put her in his new band and so subject her to a whole new round of ridicule. In the long run, he was right: she rose to the challenge. In the shorter run, Linda would suffer greatly.

Chapter 11

"People would write her really nasty letters; they'd send her turds in the mail."

Laurence Juber

As a Beatle, Paul had always been the member of the group most eager to perform in public. For him, there was nothing as life-enhancing as those waves of love pouring over the footlights; for the other group members, there was nothing as tedious, scary, or boring. Now there was no one on his side of the footlights to complain, and on a roll from his new-found confidence as a solo songwriter and patriarch of a growing family—aspects of his "revival" that owe a very great deal to Linda—it was time to put on a show. The "empty barn" of the old MGM musicals became a series of provincial British universities, where Wings, in early 1972, would arrive unannounced and offer to play that night for an astonished crowd of students.

Musicians, children, and pets travelled in one van; roadies and equipment in another. It was all rather charming, there were no reporters watching and, although physically strenuous, it was rather a jolly little outing. "I'm enjoying these one-night appearances," Linda told a reporter for *Melody Maker* in 1972, one week into the tour. "It's like a touring holiday! And the children love it too. We gave our elder child the choice of school or coming with us, and she chose the latter. Her teacher in London doesn't mind a bit. I mean, this is an education in itself, isn't it?"

(Incidentally, the same article ends with a description of Linda as the "brilliant New York photographer who first met Paul on a Beatles American tour." Where did they get *that*? This is *Melody Maker*, the most prestigious of England's music weeklies; surely it should have known better. Linda may have *seen* Paul from a great distance when the Beatles played at Shea Stadium in New York City in 1966, but she certainly didn't *meet* him until 1967. As the wise man said, "There is no memory, there is no history, there is no truth . . . but we do the best we can.")

If Paul wanted to pretend he was starting all over with a baby band, and that the past ten years hadn't changed him a bit, well why not? Being so famous, he was entitled to do anything he wanted as a performer, even pretending that he was not famous at all. There was no one to tell him that he couldn't "go home again," and in fact no one tells Paul McCartney what he can and can't do when it comes to being an entertainer; Linda could, but certainly no mere mortal on the payroll—and, anyhow, she knew this new band was essential for her husband's continuing rehabilitation as a musician, and that her presence was very much needed in this project.

"Linda was absolutely his support mechanism. There was a lot of ugly stuff going on in the background about the Beatles just then, and he really wanted her around. Paul and Linda would talk about it among themselves, but never in front of the group. That was "the other band," and now we're here. And he wanted her not just around, but in the band, onstage," recalls Denny Seiwell.

"Paul had said when he was putting this university tour together that 'We'll just have Linda play keyboards for a while.' Well, I thought that was a novel idea; I hadn't known she played the piano. As it turned out, she had little knowledge of the keyboard, and Paul would just teach her her parts. And she would just try and stay with us."

Linda's reluctance to be part of Paul's performing band was very real, but so was his insistence that she be up there. It would not have been her first choice as an activity by any means. She was never comfortable in front of a crowd, which certainly showed, and, as she told me many years later, "I'd just as soon have stayed on the farm with the horses and kids, but Paul wanted me there, so . . ." If she felt that she was being forced to do something she didn't really want to do, she was professional enough never to show her feelings on that matter to others in the organization. As far as anyone could see, as far as her behavior would indicate, she was very much involved in the band. If it was going to be that way, she was going to make the most of it, as awfully difficult as it was. Any complaining would have been directly and only to Paul, with no witnesses; there were times when it was obvious they'd just had an argument, but it was, without fail, all kept in the family. And in interviews, she made it quite clear that being a performer was not the thing she wanted most in the world to do, but she did it—next question?

"Everyone respected her musical opinions, because Paul respected them so much; they had the same likes and dislikes in music," says Denny Seiwell. "So if Linda said something, and Paul was smiling, you knew that he was OK with that. She never said anything that was out of line, and she had a lot of good ideas, even though she couldn't pull it off musically or vocally at the beginning. Years later, she'd progressed and she'd become familiar with all of her parts and what she could actually contribute. I think she was pretty comfortable at the end. On the record that was just released [Linda's posthumous "solo" album, *Wide Prairie*], her vocals are pretty damn strong. She didn't care what she sounded like, she was singing from the heart, and that was cool."

The Linda-haters were sure that she had forced herself into the band, as they had been sure that she had forced herself on Paul in the first place—both of which opinions are so disrespectful of Paul that one wonders if these people were really his fans. It was noted earlier that the idea of anyone "snagging" Paul as a husband while he wasn't looking was absurd, and so was the concept that he, the consummate perfectionist, would allow any unwanted or unattractive element in the sound emanating from his band.

Said Laurence Juber,

> She enjoyed that she got to work with Paul. It was tough for her, because she had an awful lot of responsibilities, and when I joined the band [early in 1978] James was just a few months old. The children were always her priority, always. It was very tough. She'd be up early dealing with the kids and Paul got to sleep late, even though they went to bed at the same time. She had her hands full, and maybe he could have gotten up a half hour earlier and helped her out a little more, but he was a really good dad, always talking about something to do with the kids.
>
> I did pick up a certain amount of frustration from Linda at the way she had been treated by the public, the way that people had taken out a lot of anger on her. People would write her really nasty letters; they'd send her turds in the mail.
>
> As a musician, she clearly didn't have the training, but she had good instincts. She'd been around, and she knew what the criteria were for being successful in the music business. I liked her, I trusted her instincts. I mean, she was a great person. And that band, it wasn't just Paul, it was a family unit. I couldn't imagine Wings without her, I don't think the band would have existed as a band without Linda. She was very much the anchor.
>
> Some guys think they're busy being rock-and-roll stars, and the family doesn't exist when they're performing or in the studio. Paul wasn't working like that, he was working from the point of view of being a partner with Linda in this marriage, in raising their kids. The band didn't intrude on the family, and the family didn't intrude on the band. It was a great balance, they figured out a very synergistic way of working. Linda became a bit of a mentor for me in terms of my perception of a strong, intelligent, talented woman being a mother and collaborating with her husband. I learned a lot from her that gave me some sense of what is possible in that kind of relationship.
>
> I never saw the two of them argue. I'd certainly see them angry on occasion, usually when they heard something that Yoko

> had said about them. Or something to do with business that he would get riled about, and she'd follow his lead.

And that she always did. There was always a party line. It was Paul's opinion plus her input, but it became the party line, *the* opinion, the last word. I think I am not the first person to deem Paul autocratic, which is not a moral judgment or an ethical one. He is simply autocratic. He is The Don. There are those on the payroll of his company, MPL; those who work for him at times; those who work with him not directly under his authority; those who collaborate with him occasionally on various projects; those who have worked with him and hope to do it again; those who have and do not hope to again; and those who simply hope to, who are terrified of incurring the displeasure of Paul McCartney. It is not pretty to be on the receiving end of that, which would be true simply because of his immense intelligence, but add to that his fame, his talent and his wealth, and he makes the 900-pound gorilla who can sit wherever he wants look puny by comparison. And nothing that concerns him gets past him without his approval.

His disapproval, manifested as a one-to-one thing, is reserved for those who are on his agenda Right Now, and it leaves strong people shaken. It is a very powerful and upsetting thing when Paul tells you he is displeased with what you have done, or what you have in mind; you will never forget that moment, if you've never experienced it before; the people on his staff have to become accustomed to his wrath. It comes and goes, and it is, after all, a privilege to work for him. They get used to it and remain extremely loyal. They love him, they suffer for him, they know he depends on them, and of course it is valuable for him to know that his "people" are top-notch, can hold up and are going to stick around, which they are, which they do. He is well-served; I would say that of all the very famous people I've known, he is better served by a greater number of very smart and skilled retainers than any other. He has learned the importance of an impeccable organization totally under his control.

And Linda, of course, was so much a part of the ruling mechanism that it was, as Laurence Juber says Wings were, inconceivable without her. Let's not go too far with this comparison, but it works for a certain distance: think of the support the Queen gets from Philip, her husband, father of her children, very much a player in the business he married into—essential, in fact, to her ability to reign. The children, in both families, are at the front of all priorities by far (although, due in part to personality and in part to the inherent difference in the roles played by Mother and Father, Linda's children were fond of her without qualification); the one partner is far more visible, and *must* be seen to be a beloved public figure, while the other survives without mass adoration, requiring at all times, however, the complete loyalty and cooperation of the first. They fight, of course, but when no one is watching. On the other hand, there has never been a question of marital infidelity in the McCartney alliance, and there certainly have been questions in that other one—as I said, one can't take this all that far.

The "royal" thing about Paul and Linda began occurring to me when I spent time with them in London in 1974, working on the book *Linda's Pictures*. Requests and suggestions were not floated by Linda (I had never seen this before from her), but "issued." Their comings and goings were occasions, their opinions were pronouncements—people seemed to walk backwards in their presence, if not literally then very nearly so. Their house was given over to the children, who drew on the walls and furniture (but not on the Magrittes and the de Koonings) as if they, the children, were the most important generation dwelling here—a very royal attitude. Come the summer, Linda told me, parents, kids, and Martha, the giant sheepdog, would all pile into a green Rolls-Royce convertible and drive to the farm in Scotland—you knew that, as informal and proletarian as this journey was, they would not find the farmhouse dilapidated and inhabited by squirrels, that it somehow got taken care of in their absence and that they had to do little more than call ahead in order to find it habitable. I thought that was at least aristocratic, if not necessarily royal.

Once, in the mid-'70s, they phoned me at my strange apartment in what is now fashionable Tribeca, but was then a dingy commercial neighborhood deserted at night, and said they were coming over. Great, always great to see them. We sat on the floor, smoked some "spliffs" (they had been spending time in Jamaica) and marvelled at my view of the Woolworth Building; when it came time to leave, they asked to borrow money for the cab fare so that they could get back uptown.

"Er, of course. Ten dollars? Did you lose a wallet or something?"

"No, we just don't bother carrying money in New York," Linda replied, as I counted out ten singles. "We just tell the cab driver who we are, and then we sign autographs for him and he says we should forget what's on the meter. That's what usually happens. This time, it was someone who didn't know who we were and he didn't know where he was going, and we were afraid we'd have a problem. Sure enough, he wanted money."

"Money? My my! What did you do?"

"Well," she said, quite vexed at the memory, "I had some coins in my purse. I'm not even sure what country they were from, so we told him it was a lot of money in New Zealand or something, and he'd better take it, because that's all we had. But now we're afraid we'll get another one like that, so we'd better have some cash in case it happens on the way home."

"You could lean into the cab and point to yourselves and see if he gets excited, Linda," I suggested, still reeling from this anecdote. "But no problem." I thought that was extremely royal.

I must say I can see Paul and the Eastmans getting red with fury right now, because there was a time when I was truly broke and Linda helped me out, saying, when I tried to thank her, "Let's just not talk about that, it's OK, let's not talk about it." But it is nonetheless, as anyone who socializes above his or her economic station will verify, expensive to have very rich friends, or could be. I don't mean the taxi fare—it's all the "Why don't you come to London and visit?" and "Come and see us next week in East Hampton, don't you have a house there this summer?" On the other hand, it is so petty to complain that people who don't carry cash might not be thinking a great deal about it at all times. I take it all back.

Actually, I'm guilt-stricken for even bringing this up, but they are good stories. Rich friends are a two-edged sword, so to speak. One of the why-don't-you-come-to-London? questions was in response to my moaning that I had heard the National Gallery was having a once-in-a-lifetime show of the paintings of Poussin, who is one of my top ten painters of all time, and I said to Linda, "I just can't, I can't afford the time or the money." A few days later, by FedEx or one of those things, I got from London the catalogue of the show, with a note from her assistant saying that "Linda thought you might want to have this," which was so incredibly sweet and thoughtful that the whole gesture just shines in my memory. It's the kind of thing you would want to do for a friend, but if you don't have an assistant whom you can call and command to do it, then it doesn't get done. So it's wonderful, absolutely wonderful, to have rich friends.

You see, I think it depends on whether something is your idea or theirs. For example, I was in London and on the phone to Linda despairing that the limited run of Dame Edna Everage (the comedian Barry Humphries) in a West End theater was sold out. "Can you help me get a ticket?" I begged. She told me to call her back in one hour. When I did, I was told that a ticket would be at the box office in my name and that I should send a check for the amount of the seat (with no broker's fee, which I'm sure in retrospect there was) to the McCartney office.That was fair.

The utterly gracious Linda.

But she could be a severe, dismissive businesswoman who had power and used it, not always making niceties her priority.

Denny Seiwell recalls first coming to Scotland at Paul's request (the ruined rental car story from a previous chapter). He was joined there by his wife Monique and guitarist Hugh McCracken and his "lady" Holly. After fiddling around for a day at the farm McCracken and Seiwell were asked to come back the next day, but "Leave your wives at home, would you?" suggested Linda, "home" being a typically Scottish "no frills" hotel in Campbeltown. The McCrackens were having no part of this peremptory attitude and soon left for New York. The Seiwells stayed on, taking up residence at a nearby farm. "She just didn't want to worry about having other people around," Seiwell surmises. And she saw no reason why she had to. If anyone had told her it was perhaps a bit rude to summarily dismiss two women who had travelled thousands of miles with their men to be there, and couldn't exactly spend the afternoon at a matinee while the guys played their instruments, Linda would have been shocked at the accusation: rock and roll was men's business, everyone was there to take care of business, and that was that. There was no time for anything extraneous.

People who have worked with the McCartneys are very aware that there's an "us and them" dynamic always in play. I recall a story about a woman who was invited to a garden party at Buckingham Palace and asked someone on the staff what she should wear. "The Queen does not notice what people wear," she was told.

The problems in Wings were never about what people were wearing, but how much credit they were getting, how much dignity they had and what they were being paid. "On the one hand he talked, talked, talked family," says a musician who was with the band for a while. "On the other hand, there was no family here, it was, 'Here's the Pop, and here's the kids.' There was lots of business stuff that wasn't getting addressed and wasn't taken care of, and it was causing a lot of frustration and resentment in the band."

In other words, the musicians weren't getting paid what they felt they deserved (try $175 a week, which was nothing even in the early 1970s or about three or four times that amount in today's money), and the situation exploded on the eve of the group's departure for Lagos, Nigeria, in August 1973, where they were going to record *Band on the Run*. Seiwell and guitarist Henry McCullough, who'd been with them since the university tour, simply quit, in a bitter argument about money. Linda and Paul, with only Denny Laine from the band, went on to Africa and made the record without them.

And were lucky to get away from Lagos alive. Invincible the McCartneys often *felt* themselves to be, but they were certainly foolish to go walking alone at night in an unfamiliar Third World city, carrying cameras and wearing expensive watches. Sure enough, a car that was slowly following them contained not the usual batch of McCartney fans on an innocent stalking mission, but five youths who set upon the terrified couple, brandishing knives. "He's Beatle Paul! Don't kill us, please!" Linda screamed to the attackers, more vicious even than the Apple Scruffs; the thugs settled for not killing them, as we all know, but took everything of value they had, after waving their knives at the jugular veins of our adventurous recording artists. As the legend goes, they were not killed because they were white, and the robbers knew that white people could not identify black people in a police line-up. Muggers whose victims can point to them with certainty are summarily shot in this most populous of all countries in the African continent. Anyhow, Wings, short of members though they were, made a great album, which just goes to show . . . something or other.

Those who have been dismissed from the McCartneys' presence, particularly in the wake of a confrontation about money, recall that "Thanks for nothing, see you never," was Linda's way of saying goodbye to people who indicated they were less than grateful for the opportunity to be in a band with Paul. Whether or not she and Paul agreed or disagreed about the complaints they heard, they responded as one. "Thanks for nothing, see you never." In fact, there were attempts at patching things up over the years, and a major reconciliation backstage in Anaheim, California, between the McCartneys and the Seiwells in 1993. "It was genuine, they were great, the kids hadn't seen Monique in years, and it was really nice," Denny smiles, happy that it ended—for he and Monique never saw Linda again—the way it did. "I really thought that between the four of us, Paul and Linda, Monique and I, there was a great bond, and there had been so much left unsaid and undone that really needed to be addressed, and just never got addressed."

The European tour that began in France in the summer of 1972 was a big-time thing, very much in contrast to the "Surprise! We're here!" tour of universities earlier that year. The shows were promoted in advance, advertised and now subject to reviews in the press, both British and local. Reporters for major periodicals had had a hard—if not impossible—time trying to get to any of the stops when Wings were playing colleges; sometimes the band members themselves had not known where they would be playing in the next few days. But now the knives were being sharpened for the arrival of Paul McCartney's new band; and indeed the eyes and ears of the world were focused on the group, travelling the highways of Europe in a double-decker, flower-power-painted bus that reached speeds of 35 mph. And when the distance between shows was too much to drive, there were private jets and a fleet of limousines waiting. Local castles, run as guest houses by down-and-out European nobles, were preferred to ordinary hotels, and haunted castles were most desirable because they so delighted Heather, now nine years old.

Having to play in British school cafeterias with barely any lighting and a very modest sound-system was one thing for Linda; now she was part of a major concert tour, and she was petrified. "She actually cried on my shoulder the night before we left for France," Seiwell recalls. "It was one of the few times that she and I really shared a moment, we were the two Americans and that was kind of a bond. All of us were nervous, but she was terrified. Obviously, the European press was going to compare whatever they saw and heard to the Beatles. Uh-oh. Linda was actually hoping that she could pull it off, but it was scary for her."

"I didn't want to let Paul down, I didn't want to let the band down," Linda told me over tea one morning in London two years later. "I knew they'd say I couldn't play or sing, and all the who-does-she-think-she-is? stuff, and they'd be right. But I was always hoping that I wasn't going to be the headline, or the part of the review that everyone would remember because it would be so funny. Ha ha, let's think of new ways to say how terrible she is. It was too much to hope that I'd be ignored, like I deserved. Or maybe they'd just put their opinion of me in a separate little box on another page. Yeah, right."

Some unattractive comments were made by Linda in the 1984 *Playboy* interview and one cannot ignore them, wish them away, or pretend that they are professional, because they're not. I find them rather shocking to this day. Paul is called away from the interview, and Joan Goodman asks Linda what the Wings period was really like for Paul. She answers that "Paul felt very frustrated. He wanted it to work with Wings, but we just picked the wrong people. He needed the best to work with, but he had to carry all the weight."

The interviewer then asks if Paul was as dictatorial as some accounts by musicians who worked with him make him out to be. "It's part of the same problem," Linda explains. "Paul is such a good musician, and none of the Wings were good enough to play with him, including me, for sure. They were good, not great."

Well, trying to excuse Linda for her patronizing attitude towards her erstwhile fellow band members, perhaps one can say that it was only four years since Wings ended and the hurts were still raw. That's lame, though; musicians (or any artists or any anythings) do not speak of other musicians who worked for them as "good, not great," not for publication, anyhow. It was not necessary for Linda to make any excuses about the Wings *oeuvre*—it was after all supervised completely and quite thoroughly by Paul, with some advice from his wife. And one wonders if this was the "party line;" Paul could not, would not say that about colleagues (whom he had hired), but perhaps he didn't mind it being said. Speculation—and still, not one of Linda's finest moments.

Though not savagely butchered, literally, in Lagos in the summer of 1973, Linda and Paul could not have been unaware that they had been sliced to pieces most mercilessly earlier that year, when the fearsome journalist Lillian Roxon reviewed their television special, *James Paul McCartney*, in New York's *Daily News*. Her cuts were the unkindest of all—until Linda's other best friend, Blair Sabol, let fly again in 1975. This wretched falling out among girlfriends was a real tragedy of jealousy, abandonment, betrayal, and plain old misunderstanding, played out on a very public level. People who had once loved Linda for all the right reasons now did not hesitate to humiliate her as only they could.

Chapter 12

"I can tell you right now, she didn't marry a millionaire Beatle to end up in a Liverpool saloon singing 'Pack up Your Troubles in Your Old Kit Bag' with middle-aged women called Mildred."

Lillian Roxon, reviewing the McCartneys' TV special

Lillian Roxon had been Linda's closest friend from mid-1966 until Linda left for London in September '68. A member of the radical Sydney bohemian crowd known as the "Push" before she moved to New York (and the person to whom *The Female Eunuch*, by the fabulously famous feminist philosopher, Germaine Greer, was dedicated), Lillian had been described by a friend named Craig McGregor as "mistress of the put-down and the send-up, the come-on and the come-uppance, the double-faced about-turn and, the uncompromising insult." But as the New York correspondent for the *Sydney Morning Herald*, most of what she wrote was, to paraphrase: "Australia's leading entymologist, Dr. ——, and his lovely wife Peggy were in New York recently, where they spent an evening at the theater and then mingled with the likes of Andy Warhol and the Kennedy family at Max's Kansas City, this city's most exciting 'underground' hangout." And, as a columnist for the *New York Daily News*, where she covered the pop music scene, she was unfailingly generous; she was neither a critic nor a gossip-monger, and worked hard at keeping her powerful contacts satisfied with what she wrote. Friends who could read between Lillian's lines could always find some Tabasco sauce in the white rice, but her articles generally concerned whose record was coming out, whose concert was in the near or distant future and what some star had said to her. The uncompromising insults came forth plentifully, but usually over the phone talking to a friend about someone else, or in person; when verbal weaponry wasn't sufficient, she'd just hit someone who'd behaved poorly over the head with her pocketbook.

Soon after Linda and Paul were married, Lillian wrote a glowing story about her in *Woman's Day* which emphasized her wonderful and classy qualities, told from the point of view of an intimate, appreciative friend—which indeed she had been. But after feeling neglected, that is, being neglected by Linda for a few years (and no doubt under pressure from her agents and editors to do an update about her great friend), Lillian grew increasingly bitter and unyielding.

Her support for Linda, apart from her friendship and affection, had been extremely important in settling the question of Linda's "acceptability" with already established professional journalists, particularly women, when Linda first burst radiantly on to the scene in the summer of 1966. Linda had no problem with men, straight or otherwise. Women, on the other hand, were not jumping on her glowing little bandwagon so quickly; it *could* have been said that she was just another pretty face, that she used men, that she slept around, that her main talent was her seductiveness—all those things *could* have been said, whatever their merit, were it not for the very powerful mantle of Lillian's protection. Although a teeny bit prone to flying off the handle, and to some (usually justifiable) vindictiveness, Lillian was a paragon of professionalism; she was a regular contributor to two of the world's largest daily newspapers, was a few years older than most of us, and had been filing columns and articles well before many of us, certainly Linda and me, had arrived with rock's big bang in the mid-'60s. Her judgments were severe, and she did not tolerate frivolity when it came to work—not that she minded people getting laid as often as they could, as long as it didn't interfere with their jobs, and as long as they told Lillian all about it. So when

Lillian said, often literally, to those who were skeptical of Linda Eastman's sudden leap on to the A-list of rock insiders, "You leave this woman alone! She is a fabulous photographer, totally professional and very bright, and she deserves to be successful," potential critics, for the most part, backed off. Linda's enemies became Lillian's enemies, and who needed that? Besides, Lillian was not merely fearsome, but truly adored; she was great fun, knew everything and everyone, and had the world's biggest heart, which went along—sometimes nicely, sometimes not—with the world's longest memory.

In the spring of '73, the shit hit the fan when Lillian wrote a review of the television special *James Paul McCartney* that was the meanest piece she had ever written for public consumption in her New York years. It was headlined "AN UNDISTINGUISHED MCCARTNEY SPECIAL."

> Did you see them in that pub scene . . . Paul as congenial and friendly as all get-out . . . Linda positively catatonic with horror at having to mingle with ordinary people.
>
> I can tell you right now, she didn't marry a millionaire Beatle to end up in a Liverpool saloon singing "Pack up Your Troubles in Your Old Kit Bag" with middle-aged women called Mildred. TV special or not, she didn't crack a smile once in that scene except for a little novocained grimace after, I suspect, Paul had given her a good hard shove in the ribs . . . Take away Linda's ringlets, her picture hats, her tambourine (very *Major Barbara*), and what are we left with? Sweaty, pudgy, slack-mouthed Paul McCartney trying to get across what essentially turned out to be little more than bland easy-listening.
>
> Not a soul I talked to afterwards could remember the names of most of the songs in *James Paul McCartney*, but they certainly had names for Linda's varied hair arrangements—her Stevie Wonder multi-braid, her Los Angeles groupie Moulin Rouge top-knot, her modified Bette Midler forties page-boy, and her quite unforgettable David Bowie split-level crewcut . . .
>
> Paul revealed himself to be little more than an incredibly generous husband and a great piano player—when he could get

> the keyboard away from Linda . . . "You are my sunshine," sang the people who gave the Beatles their original vitality, and Linda sat, her teeth relentlessly clamped in a Scarsdale lockjaw: I could have wept . . . Linda comes across as an incredibly cold and arrogant figure coming to life only when the TV cameras are focused right on her. She is a great beauty and someone should forget about Paul, and make a movie with her. She is obviously dying to become a star, you can tell . . .

Talk about shoot to cripple! "Sweaty, pudgy, slack-mouthed"? "Forget about Paul"? Critics had certainly been less than amazed by much of Paul's work after the Beatles, and the TV special didn't fare very well with the British press either, but Beatle Paul, the Cute Beatle, had never before been described as having lost his looks. Nor had it ever been written that his wife now had the star quality he'd lost—sarcastic as this was.

Linda knew how dangerous Lillian could be if she felt slighted, and I suspect that in four years she'd had time to get ready for the inevitable explosion, although no one is ever quite ready for such a vicious barrage from a former best friend in America's largest circulation newspaper. You may talk about such stuff rolling off your back, but if you don't walk like a duck or talk like a duck or look like a duck, you are not a duck. Still, the worst of it was what was said about Paul. I don't know what he said to his wife about what Lillian had written, but it can't have been very jolly. If Paul "can't handle" criticism, as Linda said in the *Playboy* interview, his reaction to this review was quite likely terrifying to behold.

Lillian Roxon died suddenly four months after this article appeared; she was only in her early forties. I'd been talking to journalist Lisa Robinson, Lillian's closest friend, and she told me that she thought it odd that she hadn't heard from Lillian even once that particular day. "She must be dead, then," I said, seriously. Lisa asked her husband Richard Robinson and their friend Danny Goldberg to check Lillian's apartment, where they found her—she had died of an asthma attack the night before, only hours after she walked home the few blocks from Max's Kansas City, where we'd all been watching a new band perform.

Lisa always said that Lillian's *Rock Encyclopedia* had killed her. Before desktop computers existed, and before rock "scholarship" was even remotely organized, Lillian had undertaken a chore that would have been daunting for a team of workers. The floor of her tiny apartment had been covered with stacks of notes that made her living room impassable by foot ("You're stepping on the Beach Boys!" she'd scream). She was torn between thoroughness and schedules, torn to the point of being tormented, and her fragile health just gave out. Lillian would have been pleased with her very prominent obituaries, and the turnout at her memorial, which included music industry moguls and the élite of entertainment journalism. Life without her was going to be unimaginable; like a mother's love, Lillian's could never be replaced.

If the book killed her, Linda had wounded her deeply and had known what she'd done; but I don't believe that even when Lillian was hating her so vocally and visibly that she had ever stopped loving the woman who had been to her like a younger sister, a daughter, and in fact a best friend.

Linda called me about Lillian just after Wings returned from Lagos, and she was genuinely shattered. She said something about there having been no need to be so mean to Paul, but nothing about Lillian having been so mean to her. And to the end of Linda's life, as was noted before, she would tell me that her greatest regret was not having made up with Lillian. Well, a phone call would have been a move in the right direction, but Linda never made one to her. There could have been letters and flowers and the use as a go-between of less adamant mutual friends, like me, but there were none of the above. Linda told me that she would ask Paul from time to time if he thought an overture was advisable, and although she never said that he was against it, I gathered he did not encourage it either. He is very much a once-bitten-twice-shy kind of person, and he had every reason to be shy of an old and influential friend of his wife's, who knew her before he did, who was a journalist, who was estranged from her and who had written for millions to read that Paul should give up his own career and concentrate on Linda's potential instead.

If Lillian ever had any regrets about what she'd said and written about Linda, she never told anybody about them. But I know she would have melted, eventually, if her old friend had ever really reached out to her.

Betrayals, for large amounts of money, of very famous people like Princess Diana, Prince Charles, Joan Crawford, and Bill Clinton by those who loved, depended on, or served them are sensational enough, depending on what they reveal of course, but not remarkable as events. It is very rare, on the other hand, to be betrayed by someone who was an intimate friend before you married into fame; if the betrayal is done in the course of writing a weekly column, and therefore not especially lucrative, it is very odd. Lillian's review of the *JPM* TV special at least appeared in the form of legitimate critical opinion that fell easily within her purview as a rock writer. She had to write primarily about a show, and therefore about Paul and the music, much as her nails were sharpened for Linda. Lillian was out for revenge, but she had a professional responsibility to make her blood-letting take the form of a critique.

Blair Sabol, writing in New York's "alternative" journal, the *Village Voice*, was free to do as she pleased. Sabol was ostensibly writing about "fashion," but it was for her savage wit that people tuned in; she was always much more fun detesting something than approving of it, and there was very little she approved of. She hadn't approved of the way in which Linda Eastman abandoned her very close friends in New York in 1968, for one thing, and when Linda suddenly popped up in Blair's life seven years later in Los Angeles, Sabol wrote a merciless story that was a landmark in the history of celebrity journalism.

Trailed on the front of the *Voice* issue of April 14, 1975, the story filled a two-page spread and was headlined "LINDA—WHO DOES SHE THINK SHE IS? MRS. PAUL MCCARTNEY?" "At the time it was an incredibly famous piece," says Sabol, now living in Arizona. "And it unsettled me, it really unsettled me. I have been guilt-ridden from that day about that piece. In today's world, there would be no such articles. It wouldn't pass the censors, it wouldn't pass the lawyers, it wouldn't pass a lot of things." What did Blair Sabol do that was so awful? Well, she chopped poor Linda to pieces on every level—as a photographer, as a mother, as a musician, as a friend, and only incidentally as a person expected to display some taste when it came to what she wore.

The story begins with a phone call from Linda. "Now, you must understand," Blair wrote, "the last time I knew Linda was in her groping groupie days . . . [she] was into photographing stars with little or no film in her camera . . . her pictures turned out to be mediocre to poor, but we became fast friends . . ." And then Sabol is off and running.

She chastises Linda for her "disappearing act;" her "affected Liverpudlian accent when Paul is around;" her "nerve to get up and perform onstage with Paul;" and pitilessly for her new-found musical abilities: "Linda then requested that I watch her [in a recording studio] as she played or dabbled at the celesta. She sat down, struck two notes, jumped up and was on to the moog. She hit four moog moans and went on to a guitar. She didn't complete one riff on one instrument . . ." Paul busies himself in the control booth, "not paying too much attention to Linda's childish auditions. Obviously, McCartney takes his music seriously while Linda is just along for the ride . . . [she] decided to become part of his act, if only to talk to him about something . . . Somehow from the tone in her voice that afternoon, I wouldn't have put it past Linda to secretly believe that she is really better than Paul."

The entire second (and hilarious to this day) part of Sabol's story is about the party Linda and Paul gave aboard the *Queen Mary*, docked at Long Beach Harbor, to celebrate the end of the recording sessions for *Venus and Mars*. At the celebration, and skewered by Sabol's pen, were Dean Martin ("who sat at the table next to Linda and Paul and kept booze-bellowing, 'Who the hell is giving this party? Do I know these people?'"), Rod Stewart, Tony Curtis, George Harrison ("with his new artichoke haircut you really notice his lousy teeth"), Bob Dylan, Cher, the Jackson Five, Joni Mitchell, etc. The piece ends as the McCartneys are the last people to leave the ship: "Linda was carrying a yellow and red carnation centerpiece. Which just goes to show . . . You can take the girl out of the bar mitzvah, but you can't take the bar mitzvah out of the girl."

The story was a sensation, the ultimate in Linda-bashing, the ultimate in fame-bashing. It was a watershed; things had gone too far.

Celebrities and their press agents and managers were very careful after that appeared; so were editors and writers. "You write/print anything we don't like, and you'll never get near my client again. You'll never get near any of my clients. And I'll warn everybody else to stay away from you and every paper and magazine you write for." If you think about it, there are very few stories about famous people that are truly mean; by far most of them are "puff pieces," designed to make everybody look good—or else. That is one legacy of Blair Sabol's article about her former close friend. "Now it's all blow-job," says Sabol.

Her thoughts about Linda today are far more measured, and she admits that she was getting even for the dumping of the New York crowd and striking a blow for Lillian, who had died two years earlier, still suffering from Linda's rejection. "The form of journalism that I did in that piece is kharmically hideous," Sabol says now. "There was, more recently, another woman who was a good friend of mine who was a very public figure, and someone close to me keeps saying, 'You knew her! Why don't you speak up?' And I thought, 'Oh, there's that piece, that famous piece that haunts me, it haunts me.' Even though, when it came out, so many people said, 'Oh! That was so true.'"

It wasn't true, not most of it, not by any means. It was, as Blair says today, chock-full of daggers disguised as facts. If you were prepared to hate Linda, because you had once loved her and she had left you in the dust, there is no doubt that Linda herself gave you enough rope with which to hang her. She did get that accent down, but so what? When you relocate, you start talking like "them," whether it's speaking another language or a different version of your own. Big deal. And Linda was learning to play those keyboards, and we know she wasn't all that good, but she was trying, and probably trying to give her old friend living examples of "Look! This is what I've been doing!," even if only to cover the awkwardness of the reunion. As for her clothes, my God, we always knew she was not a Friend of Fashion—and Blair knew it better than anyone.

But did she think herself more talented than her husband? Never—that was gratuitous. Did she decide to "become part of his act"? We know better by now that it was Paul's idea; as Pete Townshend said to me, "What was going on there was bigger than some girl sitting on a stage playing a keyboard, because you know Paul made her do it; he's admitted that to me, he made her do it."

Now, the basic fault-finding premise of the *Voice* story was that an old friend with a history of star-struck dizziness married an extremely famous and talented musician and tried to pretend she was his partner in art as well as life; but that premise is a leap that was not justifiable then, and certainly is not now. A leap to "Who-does-she-think-she-is?" In fact, Linda knew very well who she was, but she had some trouble communicating it, to friends, to audiences, to the press, to the world, in a manner that would not invite scorn and derision. It is, after all, a tragic situation when love and total giving—even sacrifice—invite skepticism and laughter, and you are not equipped to deflect the oncoming arrows in mid-air, because it is just not a thing you do very well. Intellectually, verbally, Linda was no match for Lillian Roxon and Blair Sabol; she could not respond in kind, nor would it have been appropriate for her even to attempt it. Of course, neither of them would have been among Linda's closest friends if she had been deficient in IQ points; her intelligence shone in places other than in the acid-green glow of vitriol.

A moderately contrite Blair Sabol, like so many others, regrets that she took the Linda she knew rather too lightly:

> You know, I certainly would have loved to have connected with her in my old age and to have seen where she went. I watched Linda through the press and wondered, definitely wondered, how she did this one and that one. How difficult it really must have been for her. People don't know that. I see it now, but I didn't then. Forget celebrity, it's incredible what she did. What's more, she and Paul did have this amazing thing about privacy, and they accomplished it. You have to work at it, but you can do it.
>
> That woman had an awful lot to do, she really did. And she had to "create" a world for herself that had little to do with people like Lillian who had been really supportive of her. Linda did something to all of us, and I don't know what it was that made us take the high road like that. Something. I can't

remember to this day what it was, but it was something. I don't know. When she called, the call that triggered that story, I asked her what the hell happened. And she was very, "La-dee-dah, you know, shit happens," and people said to me, "You're just jealous!" and it wasn't that. Maybe it was because we felt like poor relatives. I kept saying, "She'll call." When I heard it was you that she called, I said, "Good! Now she'll break that thing." But she didn't, she couldn't.

Now, I can't imagine Linda coming back to us after she married him. Once you've crossed that river, into that level of fame, it is levelling. It is not what people think it is, and the only thing you can do, and I have respected Linda for this, is go off on your own and make a new world. What is amazing is that the two of them were each other's best friend. How that happened is certainly to be commended.

It is a story of development. It's not as if she started off fabulous and ended up a crone. It's the opposite. We were sort of left shocked by her, it seemed like a bad state of affairs in terms of etiquette. But my sadness is I didn't know her in the end. I came to respect her from a great distance. She was so tough, I thought. She had really grown into something other than the person I'd known.

Linda grew even faster, in some respects, than Blair probably realized—by the time Wings were on their first American tour, in 1976, Linda had come a very long way from the frightened weeping amateur she'd been on the eve of the group's first European concerts. Ben Fong-Torres, one of *Rolling Stone*'s most respected writers, was sent to cover the show in Detroit, and after referring several times to the slagging she'd been taking ("McCartney and his wife and band have weathered six years of criticism and misunderstanding . . . ; Paul says he ignores criticism . . . ; Linda has long been abused, written off . . ."), the writer approaches her ("she is, you can understand, very defensive") at a sound check and asks her about "the criticism that has already built over her celebration of her place in the kitchen [as in the song 'Cook of the House']."

Linda replies: "My answer is always, 'Fuck off.' . . . People don't have to buy it, don't have to listen to it. It's like having parents on your back, this criticizing." Very telling—Linda has put the current situation into a context she can equate with her life before her marriage to Paul. "You have criticism in school," she continues. "When you get out of school, you want to be free. This is a great band, and this is great fun, and that's all we care about."

Denny Laine offers: "We're pretty good critics of ourselves. We don't need all these bums coming along and telling us, "Hey, man . . ."

The writer's back is up. He accuses them of being insular, "with no room for sounding boards and outside opinions." Of course that's his position; he's a rock journalist and he expects to have input. He wants, as we have all done, to have the world think that performers tremble at the words of the critics and reporters, and indeed many do. But the artists believe, for some odd reason, that it is they who are making the music. It is a never-ending battle.

"We always know what's wrong," Linda tells Ben. Spoken like a true musician. Defensive, yes, as he has pointed out earlier in the story. But she's now strong enough to defend herself and her band, in effect telling the critical community exactly how she feels about them, at long last: "Fuck off."

Our heroine is now so much more confident than she had been when Paul first insisted that she become part of his new band. Even if she's not, she's acting that way. She's talking back to *Rolling Stone;* her first photograph used on a *Rolling Stone* cover, by the way, was of Eric Clapton. It is said that Clapton was extremely shaken when he read a bad review of his work by Jon Landau, in guess which publication?

Life in the visible spectrum, as Linda learned in the first half of the 1970s, involved not just a rehashing, so to speak, of private scores for all the world to see, but the playing out of political retributions, directed at Paul and simmering since 1967, and now affecting her most directly.

When the Beatles discovered minor and major psychedelic drugs, they were eager to share with the world their enthusiasm for what seemed to them spiritually and aesthetically enhancing substances that were harmless as well. In newspaper ads and interviews and, many thought, in their music, they "came out" for drugs. For many fans and for many more of their fans' parents, they stopped being adorable at that point; for police and government organizations, who took the menace of marijuana much more seriously than they ever did the dangers of guns, disease, nationalism, starvation, and warfare, the Beatles were now a big problem. Here were the world's most adored arbiters of everything groovy and cool now loudly advocating the Main Menace to the Rule of God's Law and the Governance of Men on Earth—pot. People are still going to jail for addling their own minds with drugs, and this was over thirty years ago. The authorities were not amused. John and Yoko, George, and Patti had already been busted, in their homes or in the homes of friends in England, of all places, and now it was Paul's and Linda's turn, except they got popped in Sweden in the summer of 1972. These advanced cultures still have some archaic laws on the books, after all.

Linda had been enjoying her smoke since she began to hang out with musicians in 1966; she and Paul discovered it to be one of their great shared pleasures when they were first courting each other, and there was no reason to stop just because they were working and raising a family and on the road, all at the same time. It was just something they did, discreetly, never in front of strangers, and absolutely with no guilt. Linda did no other drugs; Paul had dabbled in wilder pastures, but came safely home to grass and a wee bit of Scotch whisky every now and then.

Paul and Linda's first drug arrest was in Sweden late in July (and again back at the farm in Scotland in September, and again at the farm the following March). The bright idea the McCartneys had of receiving their daily allotment of pot via mail from England went awry when someone at their Swedish hotel thought a particular envelope addressed to Denny Seiwell was carrying seven ounces of some peculiarly crunchy stuff that didn't smell like cornflakes. The police waited at the theater where Wings was playing in the city of Göteborg and, when the band were finished, invited them to the local police station, where they spent a few hours in a holding cell and then agreed to pay a fine of a few thousand dollars to have the charges dropped.

The press in England went wild with the story—"MCCARTNEY FINE AFTER POLICE RAID CONCERT"—but the McCartneys sought to turn it to some sort of dubious advantage. They continued to tour in Sweden, Paul calling the incident a "big bother almost about nothing," but Linda felt inclined to tell the *News of the World* that the affair would be "good publicity for the group."

In another interview, in the *Daily Mail*, Paul took the offensive. This story was headlined "WHY I SMOKE POT—BY PAUL" and was accompanied by a photograph of the couple, looking rather haggard, leaving the police headquarters in Göteborg. "You can tell everyone," ran Paul's lead quote, "that we're not changing our lives for anyone . . . We told the police in Sweden the truth. We smoke grass and we like it . . . At the end of the day, most people go home and have a stiff whisky. They feel they need it. Well, we play a gig and we're exhausted and we're elated and Linda and I prefer to put our kids to bed, sit down together, and smoke a joint."

McCartney went on to explain that neither he nor Linda "have gone further than grass" and, rather too ingenuously, compared the general disapproval of their recreational drug of choice to his father's reaction to the "drainpipe trousers" he wore as a kid in Liverpool. "In time things will change," he predicted, ingenuously again, "and all this will seem a fuss about nothing."

But Linda was in a proselytizing mood when she picked up the chat with the *Mail*'s Anthea Disney:

> Every time we appear in public and people see that we are smoking hash or pot it'll make things just a bit easier for an ordinary person next time. I'd love to be one of the reasons for people changing their minds about soft drugs.
>
> Paul always says that a man who drinks beer doesn't necessarily become an alcoholic. Right. I'll say that weed does not lead to heroin, necessarily.
>
> If I found one of my kids on heroin I wouldn't be shocked. I would say to her that I think it's damaging and stupid and likely

> to kill her. And I'd try to persuade her to come off it. But people must lead their own lives. They must make up their own minds. And I know that Paul and I like weed. To us it's just like nothing, and when other people share that point of view, I'll be happy.

The interview ended with Paul expressing regret that they would now most likely be watched very closely on the rest of their European tour, so they would do without it, and without, he implied, experiencing severe withdrawal. "We're just easy people who like to smoke if we can, but now that's out of the question, and I'm sorry."

Not entirely out of the question. There would be several more busts during the '70s, and Paul's farm in Scotland was raided by a local posse who found marijuana plants growing in his greenhouse. There was a capture coming into Heathrow airport, a raid and bust in Barbados, and in 1975 the police stopped Paul's and Linda's car in Los Angeles and found two joints in her bag. She told Blair Sabol, "it happens to everybody and it's time-consuming with the lawyers, but we'll get it taken care of."

The Japanese detention of nine days in 1980 was not quite so casual. "I was so frightened for Paul I can't even describe it," Linda told *Playboy* in 1984. "Your imagination takes off. I didn't know what they would be doing to him. And for what? A bit of nothing. I don't think pot is a sin, but I didn't want us to be a martyr for it." In the same interview, Paul made a "most-dangerous" drug list and placed pot very near the bottom, below Librium, Valium, and Scotch. "That doesn't mean I've turned around and advocated marijuana. I haven't. I'm really only saying this is true for me. I can take pot or leave it. I was nine days without it and there wasn't a hint of withdrawal, nothing."

Backtracking on the advocacy front since 1972? Perhaps, but only to be expected. If the police forces of the world got their jollies from busting Paul and Linda time and time and time again, simply because they could, then something is very nasty. Here, if I may get political, is a new definition of the concept of "victimless crime," which surely the McCartneys believed applied to the consumption of pot. Yes, it was naïve to think, as they did, that being among the most famous people in the world was an inconsequential condition; it is not—if you are a billionaire and you boast of paying no taxes, then some jerk will think he can get away with it too, and if you believe cheating on taxes is a crime (albeit a trivial one), then the billionaire has encouraged the jerk to behave like a criminal. Although for every jerk that gets caught cheating, thousands won't. And there are tens of millions of people who smoke pot, who have never been arrested and never will be; there will also be those who do get busted and can't just phone their lawyers and get on the Concorde, but, for now, that's too bad.

Still, the McCartneys were victims. Not that they are exempt from moral judgment, or aesthetic judgment. But pot-smoking judgment? It was like that guy in *Les Misérables* who keeps chasing poor Jean Valjean for years and years for stealing a loaf of bread.

"We couldn't say publicly how really stupid we thought it was, we found that out," Linda said to me a few years before she died. "When you say that, it makes things worse. They want to show you they're not stupid, and so it starts all over again. We had to say it was just a nuisance, but it was worse than that. We were being targeted all the time. Maybe we were asking for it. Maybe *we* were a bit stupid. But we're not criminals."

When the grand spectrum of the McCartneys' legal problems vis-à-vis cannabis is considered, it seems as if they were being treated not so much as "criminals" (with the big exceptions of the denial to Paul of a U.S. visa for two years, and the Japanese experience), but as almost-criminals, or would-be criminals, which allowed the authorities to flex some muscle and show who's boss without looking completely ridiculous—a doomed effort. In Los Angeles, after the "time-consuming" 1975 vehicle bust, Linda (since the joints were in her bag) was sentenced to attend six sessions of drug counselling, which must have been hilarious. "You should have brought a tape recorder," I told her backstage at Madison Square Garden in 1976. "I leave it to you to think of things like that," she answered, on the edge of being amused, but not quite.

In 1977, while recording *London Town* with Wings on a flotilla of boats docked in Watermelon Bay, a remote lagoon in the U.S. Virgin Islands, the McCartneys threw a noisy little night-time party for their entourage; well into the festivities, the revelers were amazed and amused to see their floating soirée invaded by a boat full of park rangers, who obviously knew whose vessels they were boarding. After explaining that they were there just to ask the crowd to "keep it down," they went on a little snooping expedition and gathered, horrified, near an ashtray which held a few tiny, nearly consumed marijuana cigarettes.

The next day, a letter was delivered to Mr. and Mrs. McCartney, on National Park Service stationery, stating that the agents had noticed "illegal" material on the premises, advising that laws were apparently being broken, and warning that if the rangers were to come back and find more such substances, the people in charge of the boating party would be subject to arrest.

Paul and Linda arranged a little tableau featuring the letter, some rolling paper, and some unsmoked joints, and had the still life photographed by Henry Diltz, who'd been hired to document the recording sessions. "Musicians all smoke grass," remarks Diltz, remembering the carefully laid-out shot. "It goes with the territory. I can't believe those people were surprised to find that out—they probably just wanted a story to tell the folks at home."

Chapter 13

"The McCartneys drinking tea on the afterdeck. The young girls playing cards, and Heather playing her punk rock album . . . We all jump overboard to swim."

Henry Diltz, photographer

The armada docked in Watermelon Bay in the Virgin Islands for the recording sessions of *London Town* was a unique set-up for making an album, perhaps as elaborate, expensive, and sybaritic as any that has ever been organized.

Linda, five months pregnant with James, was the only woman in the company; once again, the musicians had been told to leave their wives and girlfriends at home. A main boat, the *Samala*, contained living quarters for the crew and musicians, and a dining room that seated thirty. Linda, Paul, and their daughters stayed aboard a big trimaran, with a large living room off the main deck and sleeping quarters downstairs. The third boat was a cabin cruiser in which a recording studio had been installed. Transportation between the vessels was provided by motorized rubber dinghies.

"No one wore shoes the whole time," remembers photographer Henry Diltz.

> They'd spend three or four hours in the morning recording, then come over to the big boat for lunch, then Linda and Paul would go back to their boat for a while, then return to the big boat for an afternoon of diving and swimming. They'd go back to shower and change, and then return for dinner, which was always great fun. Good food, lots of wine, lots of laughing.
>
> Everybody was totally friendly, but of course the McCartneys definitely called all the shots—"The McCartneys want to do this . . ." or "Linda needs that . . ." It was their show. They wanted me to document all this, that's why I was there. When I got back to Los Angeles, Linda called and said, "Would you put together a little scrapbook for us, your favorite shots?" And I did, and it was beautiful, pictures of them with the kids, throwing the kids in the water, some recording stuff, like memories of paradise.

Diltz's notes from the *London Town* sessions contain the following entries. May 24: "Dinner is steak and kidney pie with lots of wine." May 25: "Photograph morning session on the *Fair Carol*. Paul singing and playing acoustic on 'Don't Let It Bring You Down.'" May 26: "The McCartneys drinking tea on the afterdeck. The young girls playing cards, and Heather playing her punk rock album, *The Damned*. We all jump overboard to swim." May 27: "Linda shouts over from the *Wanderlust* (their boat) to invite me over. We talk, while Stella draws on our hands with a ball-point pen. I take a few pictures of the family."

Also in 1977, Linda wrote and recorded her first song, "Seaside Woman," performed by the fictional Suzy and Red Stripes. "It's reggae," she said. "I was so in love with reggae music when I heard the Wailers that I wrote a reggae song." Made into an animated short by artist Oscar Brill, the film won the Golden Palm for Best Short at the Cannes Film Festival in 1980. The song is on Linda's posthumous album, *Wide Prairie*, and the animation can be seen and heard on the promotional video that accompanied its release. Ironically, some found the cartoon racist, since its main character, the "seaside woman," is black (of course) and sashays through the short in native Caribbean costume, which the McCartneys always found spectacular during their many visits to the islands. It has been said that she depicts a "stereotype." This is so crazy; Linda was the most color-blind person I have ever known. In her view of life on earth, a beggar, a saint, a king, and a frog were totally equal in ultimate worth; the idea that she judged humans by the color of their skins, or that she had what are called "preconceived notions" about one race or another is like saying that she loved brown puppies more than spotted ones. It is preposterous; Linda never understood what was meant by the accusation, and you would feel foolish trying to explain it to her. She was simply beyond that; it was to be left to people with visions narrower than hers to criticize her for doing something she thought, and rightly so, was as lovely as she could make it be.

Work had begun on *London Town* at Abbey Road back in February 1977. After the sessions in the sun, recording continued in London; the album was finished in January 1978. By most standards, this was spending a luxurious amount of time making an album.

The stated reason for forming Wings, just to be back in a real band and on the road again, was ridiculous from the outset, and increasingly, as the '70s went on, ever more distant from reality. It was, at the beginning, Paul and Linda and the musicians they hired, and although the pretense of a democratic little band of wandering minstrels was floated as an ideal, it was of course one man, surrounded by those who were, except for his wife and children, employed by him.

No group of equal partners, like the Beatles, for example, would ever record aboard a fleet anchored in tropical waters. It is such a costly project that the idea would surely be vetoed by other members of the partnership, management, the record company which as a rule fronts the money for the making of an album, and/or the accountants. But Paul could do whatever he wanted—Wings was selling records and tickets by the millions, the publishing company was booming, so he could simply think, "Wouldn't it be nice if . . . ," and "if" was brought to him to have the wish completed. And brought to Linda and the kids, who were very much part of the "Wouldn't it be nice" syndrome; let everything be fabulous, meticulous, simple, stylish, beautiful, and fun.

How do you not spoil your children, while allowing them to take for granted being whisked out of school at their parents' whim, having at their disposal private airplanes, boats, limousines, bodyguards, mansions, and estates (owned or rented), and a name that's known to nearly everyone in the world? That question is at the heart of Linda's (and Paul's) story, and has been asked by everybody as though it were a great mystery which no one can figure out. Because look at them now—four strong, well-balanced, polite, affectionate, bright, talented, and ambitious children. How did she do it? Nobody can ever know for sure; though I guess she did it by being strict (but not too strict), righteous (but not self-righteous), smart, loving, organized, intuitive, caring, and extremely hard-working. Linda worked hard on a lot of things, but on nothing so hard as her family. That's how she did it—no list of commandments, no book, and no ideal model family on a TV series will teach anyone the secret. It's built-in. Paul knew that when he met Linda and her daughter Heather; he knew she could be the mother of their children. Many people who knew Linda (some rich and famous themselves) and came to know the whole family, walked away wondering: "How did she do it?" All I know is that it didn't just happen to happen. Linda's task as a mother involved not only giving huge amounts of love, but working against many factors that are often blamed for spoiling—if not ruining—the offspring of the privileged middle classes: fame, wealth, isolation from reality, and the absence of close friends of one's own age. Linda's and Paul's children were by necessity each other's best friends because they were so often on the road with their parents, yet somehow it worked.

"The kids never got to rely on school chums being their little friends, having them to tea and all that," says Paul's stepsister Ruth, now aged forty. "That's why the kids are so strong together. Paul and Linda worked at it in a way that had never been done in our family. They worked at it by saying that love is reinforced by always being around your kids, taking them to dinner, taking them on holiday, taking them on tour. They had places in London, Scotland, Sussex, and Long Island, then the ranch in Arizona, and they'd go to the Caribbean in the winter. They would troop en masse everywhere. They were good parents, they just wanted to take the kids wherever they went, and their attitude was, 'Well, it's our marriage, it's our family, they're our kids; time will prove us right and they'll all grow up normal—which they did.'"

It even evolved into something that is almost never seen except in reruns of television series from the 1950s—children and parents were absolutely, genuinely close friends. It was a domestic arrangement that caused the jaws of visitors to drop. Paul might be seen answering the phone and having a little chat with the caller, before saying to Mary, on her way out of the house carrying a tennis racket, that it was her date for that night and could he be half an hour late? "Tell him it's OK," Mary would answer and Paul would relay the message: "It's OK with her. See you later!" Meanwhile, Linda was having a massage in a room down the hall, and famous comedians and songwriters toured the garden with Stella.

Still, one could be sure that Paul knew exactly who it was on the phone, and probably even if the suitor's intentions were honorable, because it was never as casual as it seemed in that household. Linda and Paul were fiercely protective parents without being smothering—it was a delicate road to walk, but the evidence is that it was done well.

Linda Stein, who rented a small house on Paul Morrissey's ocean-front estate in Montauk, near the very tip of Long Island, knew the family well and was glad to see James and his surfing friends pull up in her driveway nearly every day that the McCartney family was in residence in nearby East Hampton. Whereas the westernmost hundred miles of the Long Island coast consist of wide sandy beaches and waves that expend most of their energy on offshore sandbars before breaking, the eastern end at Montauk end is rocky, dominated by huge cliffs, and battered by waves fresh out of the north Atlantic. Hence it is great for surfing, or at least much better than the beaches a few miles to the west. Unfailingly polite, James would ask Stein for her permission to use her beach for surfing, and of course she said it was fine. But unfailingly vigilant herself, and aware of the incident when James went surfing off the coast near Rye, East Sussex, and was missing for several hours before being rescued by the Dover Coastguard, while his distraught parents were near to hysteria on the beach, Linda Stein would periodically check the beach below her cottage to make sure all was well. One late summer afternoon in 1993, when the light was starting to fade, she figured the boys should have been out of the ocean long since, so she started down the steep path to the shore, where James and his buddies were in fact packing up as if to call it a day.

"When he saw me," recalls Stein, "he knew that I had come down to tell him it was way past the time to get out of the water, and he came up to me and said, very seriously and very softly, so that his friends wouldn't overhear him, 'You won't tell my mother about this, will you?' He was genuinely worried about what her reaction would be. I told him I wouldn't snitch, but that I had been concerned as well. 'Oh thanks,' he said. 'Because she'd be furious.'"

The book project that Linda, Paul and I had talked about at my apartment in 1971 didn't get going until the spring of 1974, when I was summoned to London to spend two weeks picking out photographs with Linda. There was always a reason why it had to be "delayed for a while," all of them quite legitimate; in any case, I wasn't holding my breath until all was ready. Stella was born in 1971, as were Wings; the first tours of the new group took up most of 1972; 1973 was spent making the TV special in London and *Band on the Run* in Nigeria; then they had to put Wings back together because only one musician, Denny Laine, was still in the band. I was slotted in for a time period between rehearsals of the new Wings line-up and the group's trip to Nashville in June 1974.

To get my fee, $500, I was called to the office of Linda's father, whom I had known by sight but had never met before. It was as if I were at a job interview; I stood the whole time while Lee Eastman scrutinized me and flung questions at me—"So, what do you think you can contribute to this book?" "How much time do you expect to be actually working in London?"—and similar scary queries. I hadn't known I was expected to pass muster with the old man before getting my check, which he handed to me, somewhat skeptically, at the end of our meeting. In retrospect, it wasn't so much as if he doubted me, but as if he thought this whole idea was sort of nonsensical; in other words, who would want to see pictures taken by his daughter, how could these photographs of rock-and-roll scum deserve being put into a book, why should they have to hire people to pay for this?—and incidentally, that it's a good thing these people don't require first-class air tickets (because I certainly didn't get one).

In London, though, my reception was at least first class. My hosts, thrilled I'm sure that *Band on the Run* had just gone to number one in the American charts, had rented a beautifully furnished apartment for me overlooking Regents Park in a nice art deco building, which was to double as my home and our workplace. Cartons of double-size contact sheets and carousels of slides filled a small spare room, where Linda and I met every day and picked out our favorite shots. As with the work of all good photographers, the eye goes right to the best shot or shots on any contact sheet, and we almost always agreed on which ones we wanted to see blown up. After all, the routine of our early professional relationship had consisted of me meeting her at her lab, Modern Age, looking over the freshly developed rolls of film, choosing our favorites and leaving the marked-up contact sheets with the negatives to be enlarged. It was (it is) always exciting to see what came out of a photo session, and this time around in London it was great looking at the stuff from the early years again and remembering the circumstances of the shoot. Linda forgot nothing: "It looked like it was going to rain, so we . . . ;" "They were so nice, I didn't expect them to be, but we really got along, only they were actually worried about going into Central Park . . . ;" "This was in San Francisco, it was the same day I met . . . ;" "You were there for this one; remember that hotel where they were staying, all the prostitutes in the lobby in pink satin hot pants . . . ;" and always lingering a little longer over pictures of Jimi, Jim, Janis, Brian, and the others who had died in the intervening years.

Linda had been thoughtful enough to provide some creative bachelors with whom I could socialize after hours, and two of my closest friends from New York, Craig and Allison Karpel, were in London then, so it was not all work and no play for me. With Linda, though, it was all work. There were no dinner parties or gala evenings at the theater; the one time I saw the McCartneys after dark was when they came over to the flat where I was staying to look at slides. The book's art director was there, and in three hours we went through twenty-six boxes of slides, each holding 100 pictures. Stella and Mary amused themselves briefly by drawing with pens and markers and demanding a great deal of attention, most of which was supplied by Paul. Linda was raptly looking at the pictures and, as if by prearrangement, left the parenting up to him. Amazingly, his attention to the work at hand was not distracted by his rambunctious two- and four-year-olds, who had the run of the room. He knew every picture, and often commented on the circumstances of their creation himself. It was Paul who organized the finding of the kids' shoes as they prepared to leave. "Get your shoes on, you too mate, get your shoes on, where's your shoes?"

As she was going, Linda gave me my assignment: "You're going to look at stuff tonight. I'd like to finish off the color. So look at as much as you can tonight, and we'll meet tomorrow morning." I remember thinking she was speaking to me as one speaks to an employee; but then again, I was an employee. I was being paid $500 to work on a book of her pictures; she was the boss—there was no need for her to hedge with, "Oh, I wonder if you'd do me a favor and . . ." She was even faintly dictatorial; I liked that, after I got over the shock of it. It was professional and without flourishes. Linda had become very to-the-point since I'd first known her; one might expect that being in partnership with a celebrated autocrat would have made her a bit timid, but it was the other way around. She was learning from Paul how to get what you want from the people who are doing things for you; if the relationship is a friendly one, that part of it can wait until business is taken care of. By 1974, then, as I reckoned it, Linda had become one of the great, tough, working women of her generation.

Linda's Pictures was published in 1976 by Alfred A. Knopf, for a list price of $25. The cover of this very heavy coffee-table book carries the famous picture of a bearded Paul with Mary, as an infant, tucked inside his jacket. It's the last plate in the book as well, and on the cover of Paul's first solo album, *McCartney*. About two thirds of the 150 or so shots are by Linda Eastman—those were the ones we chose together. The rest are hubby and kids and landscapes by Linda McCartney. I was mentioned in Linda's introduction as a friend who had once called her up from Elektra Records and said, "Do you want to photograph Jackson Browne?" Ah well, I guess I didn't do that much work on it after all: about $500 worth, plus airfare and a nice apartment in London for a couple of weeks. No complaints.

Shortly after I left London, Linda and Paul were off to Nashville to record, but Linda was more excited about getting back to England later in the summer, piling the kids and Martha the sheepdog into the Rolls-Royce convertible, and driving up to the farm in Scotland for a month of isolation. But as their touring and recording schedules became more crowded (as did the Rolls-Royce with three growing children), it was not awfully convenient to drive 600 miles to be in the country, so in the summer of 1975 the McCartneys bought a cottage in Sussex, near the ancient town of Rye. The little place, named the Round House for its shape, was lovely and only a couple of hours from London by rail or car, but it was, like the Rolls, a bit cramped. It had two bedrooms, one for Linda and Paul, one for the four kids. "It meant we were a close family, literally," Paul told Chrissie Hynde. "There was no getting away from each other."

In 1978, they bought the farm next to their Sussex property, tore down the house that was there and replaced it with a substantial, although by no means palatial, house that Paul designed himself. Linda was very enthusiastic about a real house in the country at long last, and she described to me some mechanism, invented of course by Paul, that controlled a camera which took one picture a day of the building of the new home. When you flipped through the photographs, you had a time-lapse movie of the whole process.

"It's a very comfortable house that has five bedrooms," Paul told Chrissie. "One bedroom for each of the kids, and one for us, Linda and me. It has limited space, but that's how I wanted it, and that's how Linda wanted it too. Because we always hated stories of people living in these huge stately homes with the children rattling around in the East Wing, and you never see them. We designed something for our lifestyle and for our reasonably simple tastes compared to some other people in our position. It was specially designed to be comfortable, and it is. People come into our house and say, 'Ooh, this house feels lovely,' or, 'This is comfortable.' That, to us, was what was important."

There were stables and a saddle house where the cats lived, an old windmill twenty minutes by car where Paul installed a recording studio and his own office, another old farm building used by Heather as her pottery studio, and lanes, paths, meadows, hills and a cast of animals and birds right out of *Bambi*. It was very beautiful, and on a clear day you could see the coast of France beyond the Channel. Linda and I were walking from the main house to Heather's studio one day, past a stand of giant trees hundreds of years old, and I was plainly in awe at the loveliness of it all. "I was lent all this for a little while," she said, looking up and around, and then at me, "and I have to take good care of it so I can give it back just the way it is."

With increasing success (i.e. big record sales and the thriving publishing business, which was masterminded by Linda's father and brother in New York), the showbusiness team of Linda and Paul McCartney was seen as having truly pulled it off. The rest of the world, even the other members of Wings, were reluctant, in various degrees, to admit that it had worked as Paul had wanted it to, but he knew it had, and she knew he knew. The recovery from the disastrous Beatles dissolution was complete. Linda had told him, wanting and willing it to be true, that the future was all there and theirs, and was all that mattered; Paul had believed her to the extent of metaphorically grabbing her hand and saying, "Let's go then." And off they had gone.

The huge Wings world tour that began with smaller dates in the U.K. late in 1975 and finished at Wembley at the end of 1976, was one of the most extensive and expensive tours in the history of live concerts, playing to well over two million people. It was a mammoth (for its time) production, featuring one of the first laser shows (to "Live and Let Die") audiences had ever seen, and encompassed the "Wings over America" segment which began in May 1976.

I had not seen Paul McCartney live in concert in twenty years. In 1964 I had gone to Carnegie Hall in February for the night of delirious screaming that came with the arrival of Beatlemania in New York, as a rich friend had bought four box seats through his scalper at $150 per ticket—about $900 each today, not so bad for such an historic event. My friend had also taken his entourage to the Forest Hills Tennis Stadium show that summer. As events, the two concerts were most memorable, although one could not hear a single note. In any case, I was more a fan of the Beatles' hair-dos than of their music, so both shows were a visual treat and I got to be there at the Birth Of It All, in New York, at least.

When I went to Madison Square Garden in 1976, I did not expect to be rocked by Paul McCartney. I was wrong about that; it was one of the strongest shows I have ever seen. Also, I was terrified for poor Linda. I could not imagine her whooping it up in front of 20,000 people, and I was right for that, partly. She could not (did not even try to) whoop it up very much, but neither was she hideously out of place. A bit out of place, but not hideously. My friend was a one-to-one kind of person, not a one-to-20,000, and she just never looked to me as if she were born to frolic in a spotlight. But it was not embarrassing. I had her in my binoculars for long enough to ascertain that she wasn't going to make a fool of herself; her eyes were on Paul and her fingers on the keyboard, and her voice blended in ever so nicely.

He travels fastest who travels alone, they say, so I had asked for one backstage pass, and at the end of the show I dumped my companion and headed for the dressing rooms. "Backstage" at the Garden has many levels of accessibility, as does any large venue. The first thing you see when you get there is hundreds of people milling around one big area, all trying to figure out how to get to a more exclusive spot. Hallways leading off the central holding-pen are blocked by security guards, and then the individual dressing rooms are protected by another set of large, powerful-looking men, of whom it will do you no good to ask any favors (or even information).They are under strict orders to respond only to their own bosses. At a concert starring a celebrity as big as, well, as big as anyone big enough to headline an arena, the innermost sanctums are reachable, as a rule, only with the OK of the innermost aides of the star. No laminated pass, even if marked "Performer" or "All Access," the two most desirable of all laminates, will get you into the star's dressing room, especially not Paul and Linda McCartneys.

If you really are expected, and/or welcome into the Presence, the thing is to stand there looking as if there is nothing that you want, and someone will find you. After all, that's one of the things the closest and most trusted staff members are paid to do—find those who "belong" and bring them swiftly inside. The trusted ones will have mastered the process of whisking VIP guests past the security guards without saying, "He's OK," which is very tacky. The guard is expected to stand aside and let the staff member walk right past with anyone they might be escorting; body language tells the guard, "I have this person (or these people) with me, and they are my responsibility." Of course, if you're a groupie kind of guy, you will probably recognize the man at the door and smile warmly; there are very few security companies in the rock-and-roll universe (in America, anyway), and their top people will be in the most important places. It's good to be known by them as someone who might frequently and legitimately appear in the tightest security areas; they can be helpful at times, and they also tend to be among the nicest and least attitudinal of all the people who serve the music industry. Thus I was eventually delivered into the innermost dressing room, a large enclosure with cinder-block walls, benches and a vast showering chamber at one end—obviously, when the occasion demanded, the locker room of hockey jocks or basketball players.

A few members of Linda's New York-based family were leaving, and I was alone with her and Paul. I stayed about half an hour, telling them how great it was (it is nice not to have to lie to performers after a show; then again, it's easy to lie when people really don't want to hear the truth), answering the usual questions like, "How did it sound from where you were sitting?;" "Where *were* you sitting?;" "Did the lighting effects work?;" "What did you think of the new songs?" (always a scary question, because it implies you're familiar with all the performer's material, which I rarely am). Then there are their stories, like how they changed the order of the songs at the last minute, all kinds of musical-technical stuff that I have to pretend to understand and always, of course, always, Paul asking, "Isn't Lin great? Do you believe our Lin? Did you ever think you'd see her doing that? And doing it so well? She's a born performer, our Linda is!" It was by far the most enthusiastic I had ever seen one performer being of another who had shared a stage with him. It looks faintly patronizing in print; in real life, it is nothing but supportive, and totally heartfelt.

What surprised me was that I was alone with them the whole time, and that when I left them, they were alone together. It was not that they gave orders to seal the room after I entered—it was simply that outside of Linda's family, they had no friends. This was New York City, the "tour of the year," Linda's home town, and there was no one back there but me. I may boast from time to time, but this is not one of those times. I was their only friend in New York. (Well, there were John and Yoko, but that is a whole other story. I don't think they were there that night.) I'm sure there were lots of friends in London (I'm guessing who might have been backstage in London), like Paul's contemporaries in other bands; there probably were more friends in Los Angeles, because the McCartneys had lived there the year before while making *Venus and Mars;* but Paul had never spent much time in New York, except, since 1969, with Linda's relatives, and poor Linda's old friends were her friends no longer. It was kind of sad.

(By the time they toured in the '80s and '90s, there was indeed a "New York circle" with backstage entrée—mainly people they knew from summers in East Hampton; rich, self-made businessmen, for the most part, like Ralph Lauren, Lorne Michaels, Jann Wenner, Ron Delsener, and performers like Paul Simon and Chevy Chase—but in '76 no one except me, or so it seemed.)

For a moment, Paul was called away and there were just the two of us. I got to ask Linda how she really liked doing this, and she said it was getting easier. Not that she liked it, but that it was getting easier and that it was what Paul wanted. Then she lowered her voice (I don't know why; there was no one to hear her) and told me Paul's father had died earlier in the year, but they couldn't go to the funeral because it would have "caused problems" and the European leg of the tour was just beginning that day; she wanted to know if, to my knowledge, they were being slammed for it. I told her no, not all that much that I knew of, but they had taken a bit of heat; then Paul came back and, as usual, set the agenda for the remainder of the conversation.

Paul's father, Jim, had died at the age of seventy-three in March, after suffering long and painfully from arthritis, leaving behind, besides Paul and his brother Michael, his second wife, Angie (twenty-seven years younger than Jim), and Angie's daughter from her first marriage, Ruth, then seventeen. Paul subsequently became estranged from Angie and Ruth McCartney, and mother and daughter are now based in the Los Angeles area, where they operate a successful multimedia company. It seems that at one point Paul felt that they were making money from the sale of memorabilia from his father's house in Liverpool; they say they have tried unsuccessfully to re-establish contact, and I am inclined not to judge either side in this very complex business. What matters to me is that Angie and Ruth, who'd known Linda since she married Paul in 1969, both adored her for the right reasons. It bolsters my theory that only people who didn't know Linda didn't like her, and that anybody who did know her saw her fine qualities at once and became an admirer.

"Linda and Paul and Heather came up to visit us just after they got married," says Angie McCartney.

> They stayed for a couple of days, and then I took them to Manchester airport and they flew out to the States. I was a little bit in awe of her, because when you're English working-class, all things American seem to be very exotic, but she was very warm and very friendly. Heather and my little girl got on like gangbusters, playing with their toys and racing around the back yard.
>
> Linda was very down to earth, she was sort of, "Let's go straight into the kitchen, let's make soup, let's make tea;" she made herself very much at home. They were only there for a couple of days, and Jim's health was very bad, so I was preoccupied with him. I must say, Paul and Linda seemed to meld together very quickly, and that was a time in his life when he needed comfort and strength; there was the acrimonious break-up of the Beatles and all that. And Linda was always totally behind him, totally supportive. Even then, just after they were married, it seemed as if she was providing him with something to lean on. I know it was hard for her, we'd heard that people were hanging around outside the house in Cavendish Avenue and throwing things at the car when she drove out, stuff like that.

I started asking Angie about an anecdote in one biography of Paul, which quotes an interview with George Harrison's mother, who claimed that she saw Linda being almost abusive to Heather, and punishing her by withholding food. Angie interrupted me with a decisive, "No! I never heard such bullshit in my life! Abusive to Heather? That doesn't sound one bit like the Linda I knew. Unfortunately, once people have said these nasty things and they go into print, there they remain, don't they? Linda is the one who took abuse. Everything you read in a review of the band, there would be some snide crack about Linda."

What did Angie who had known Paul since 1964, when she married his father, think of all that?

> It was on his insistence that she was in the band. She didn't want to do it, she wasn't confident enough. It was a transitional stage in his life, forming Wings, going off to play universities unannounced, "Can we play in your community hall tonight?" Things like that, just for the band to get their chops. And Paul wanted Linda beside him in the band, he loved her so much and wanted her support; that bond between them was growing, and that was to be a part of it. Linda was so strong—she had the capability to be not just a wife to Paul, but a mother, a lover, a pal, a buddy and even a member of his band.
>
> To us in Liverpool, it was clear that she was breaking the mould of that traditional working-class marriage, where the wife stayed in the kitchen. She became the epitome of the true American woman, with freedom and choices and everything else. But it didn't detract from her being the Mum, the wife, and the lady in the kitchen. She was able to manage those roles and so many more, and wonderfully, I think. Extraordinary woman. A gem.

Was she snobbish? What about the stories of her ordering gourmet food from Fortnum and Mason in London when she stayed with you, and embarrassing you?

Again: "No! Not at all. When she'd come and stay with Jim and Ruth and me, she was very, very flexible, very generous, very good-natured."

I read to Angie from the book I'd mentioned before: "On a few occasions, Jim and Angie went to stay at the McCartneys' farm. They were forced to sleep on dirty mattresses. In addition, says Angie, the whole place was so dirty and unkempt, flies and other insects continually fell off the ceiling into people's dinners."

"I've read that," Angie replied. "I never used the word 'unkempt' in my life. I had told an interviewer that we'd gone up there and they were living a tough-guy kind of life. Paul got us brand-new mattresses and laid them down on the floor of the garage, which he'd just washed—there were only two bedrooms in that house. Ruth slept in Heather's room. And I had said there were flies in the house and Jim wanted to get a fly-swatter and kill them all, but Linda said, "Oh, leave them alone, they have a perfect right to live, like the rest of us." Jim said, "Oh, OK"—and that turns into a story of flies falling into the food! That does piss one off."

When Jim died, on March 18, 1976, Angie called Paul and reached him at a London hotel where he was holding a press conference, on the eve of the European part of the world tour.

> I called Rose, his housekeeper, first, and she told me where they were. I'm sure it was the Royal Garden Hotel. And Paul's PR person came to the phone and I told him that I must speak to Paul, I can't tell anybody else what I have to talk to him about. He came to the phone and I said, "I'm sorry, son, it just happened." He sounded so shocked, he sort of yelled, "Are you sure?" and I said I was, and I'd call him later. He was absolutely and totally in shock. We'd all expected it, but it's always a shock, you know.
>
> We talked later about the funeral and about him coming to Liverpool. They were going to Paris to start the tour and he asked me what I thought. I said, "If you throw everything away and come up here for the funeral, it would just be a circus. It won't bring your Dad back, and he was always so proud of you and your music, you go on with what it is you're born to do."
>
> So Paul and Linda went off to Paris. It was so much more sensible. Can you imagine what mob scenes there would have been if he'd come? There would have been thousands of fans and hundreds of reporters and all kinds of pushing and shoving and

> unpleasantness added on to the reason we were all there. So then the papers didn't get their pictures, but instead they got revenge by criticizing them for not going to Jim's funeral. People will always criticize. You can't win, you know?

So it seemed for Linda. Reviewing the album *Wings at the Speed of Sound* for *Rolling Stone* in May 1976, Stephen Holden finds nice things to say about Paul's musical gifts, and even about Paul and Linda's love for each other in "Silly Love Songs." But when Linda steps out, she gets a non-home-made pie in the face: writing about "Cook of the House," which is proud, ironic, and funny, Holden, after dissing Linda's singing ("colorless, amateurish"), finds that she is politically incorrect as well. "Those with feminist sympathies will also detest this celebration of scatterbrained wife-in-kitchen coziness."

Sometimes you see something and think, "That says it all." Well, in any context, that says it all; that says what an easy, open and waiting target Linda McCartney was in the mid-1970s. So that recalling that quote here would not embarrass the author of it, I called Stephen Holden, now a powerful, brilliant music and movie critic for the *New York Times*, and asked him what he thought today of what he had written then.

"Oh, I was being bitchy," he said. "The review is what I thought of the McCartneys then. It was the prevailing opinion."

Did he mind it being rehashed? "No, it's what I thought then. They were seen as so insular. Unconnected." Then he referred me to a recent interview with the intellectual trouble-maker Camille Paglia, which compared the recently killed (along with husband John F. Kennedy Jr. and sister Lauren) Carolyn Bessette Kennedy to "the very annoying Linda Eastman in the Paul McCartney saga. In both cases, you have an outgoing, warm, pretty boy who takes into his life an often petulant, very private woman who is introverted to the point of neurosis."

And so it goes on. Dear reader, do we still, after all this time, all these pages, believe that, for women, Linda set a poor example? Scatterbrained? Petulant? Introverted to the point of neurosis? (If we are to believe Linda on the subject, and why not, she told the BBC for the bio-documentary that she had indeed been "a bit shy and introverted" until she began taking pictures.) On the other hand, was it wicked to be "in the kitchen" or "very private," or to embrace "coziness"? Was feminism about hating those aspects of another woman? Is it still about that? Was there a deep fear that women would abandon the struggle to be fire-fighters and CEOs and fly back to the pudding bowl? Was Linda going to lead that counter-rebellion?

What the hell was she doing wrong? We still ask that. She gobbled up Paul—it all comes back to that.

And, golly, who is not in awe of Paul McCartney, for mostly the right reasons, but if we thought he was perceived as "outgoing, warm, pretty" all those years ago, do we think that was or is an accurate portrait? I would think the man himself would find it patronizing, or be amused that Camille Paglia thinks of him, to this day, as a Beatles-doll.

"Warm" is a key concept here. Paul was not warm, is not warm—wonderful, perhaps—but warm not. Charming, radiant, smart, gifted, good, a fabulous husband and father, but warm is problematic. Again, the irony of public-private, of what is seen, of what you are meant to think and of what is really going on. Linda was the warm one, Paul the clever one. If you knew them, you knew that. But from a distance, Paul was everything and Linda was, as the shotgun-mouthed Ms. Paglia says, cold and "introverted to the point of neurosis."

"Linda was very, very pro-active in their social life," recalls Pete Townshend, who was a close friend. "When they were driving through this town, she was the one who used to get him to come and visit, even made a couple of surprise visits. She was the one who would call me and then put him on the phone, and we would talk. Then he would be open and entirely accessible, but it was Linda who was always reminding him that he really had friends, that he was likeable as a person, that he could reach and be reached . . . she was constantly there with the idea that there is love between people when the tape stops running and the curtain is down. She was so centered—I think self-possession was her main character attribute, wasn't it? Maybe this marriage was more about Paul than about her, but you know, I don't think so."

Ah, surprise visits! That brings us to one of the most extraordinary surprise visits of all—the night Paul and Linda dropped in on John and Yoko, with whom things were, at the time, on a very rocky footing.

Chapter 14

"John said to me, 'Oh my God! Paul and Linda are downstairs. Can you handle that?' and I said, 'Yeah, so? What's the problem? There's nothing to handle. They're your friends, send them up.'"

May Pang

What of the relationship between Linda and Yoko? many have wondered, as if there were some fascinating matter waiting to be revealed. I rather think there was none—sorry. It was more a question of whatever Yoko/John on the one hand, and Paul on the other, determined their relations to be at any given moment. Not that Linda couldn't or didn't think for herself (which need hardly be said about Yoko), or hold her own opinions, but the women's relationship, however manifested, followed the party line. There was always too much at stake, too intense an emotional field, too much that had gone by and was still being dealt with for it to have been otherwise.

Linda had become the second, and lifetime-it-was-hoped partner of Paul McCartney, whose first partnership, with John Lennon, had been one of the most important in modern history. Nothing involving the two men separately could ever equal, in its significance to the world, what had existed between them; but they had chosen their life-mates, and two other very public partnerships now existed for everyone's delectation. Neither carried the weight of the Beatles, of course, but that immense legacy was not about to vanish simply because the legal, financial, creative and, marital status of the old team had changed most radically. What Paul and John were going to do without each other was, after (roughly) 1970, and by default, as interesting to the public as what they had done together.

Although both men appeared to dismiss their erstwhile partnership as belonging to some past era about which they retained only a distant and dispassionate interest, they fooled no one, and certainly not themselves or their wives. And each admitted, eventually, to having had profound doubts about his ability to ever do anything worthwhile again, as they hovered around the scary age of thirty. A powerful '60s mantra, inspired in large part by the Beatles and the universe that came into being after the big bang that they made, ran: "Don't trust anyone over thirty." How must it have felt to have fathered that sentiment, and to see it come true, but with you now on the wrong side of that arbitrary great divide? It was not easy.

Came the women to the rescue. Yoko seems to have believed, from early in 1968 onwards, that John without the Beatles (and with her firmly at his side) was better than John the Beatle, and she is a very persuasive person, as time has proven; Linda found herself with a Beatle who was one no longer, and whose sense of his own worth, in the aftermath of that very high ride, was going down the tubes. She had to convince him, and did, that, with her help, he could do it alone, and this new team, Linda saw at once, required a very solid front. There were many aspects of Paul's life after the Beatles that Linda was allowed to define, but when it came to John, and by extension Yoko, it was all up to Paul. She knew this both logically and intuitively; if she ever had any doubts, her father and brother were there to reinforce Paul's primacy in that area.

The two women had a few things in common, none of which made them in any way especially compatible: both came from rich families, both were raised in Scarsdale, both were vaguely members of New York City's creative community, both left New York and found true love in London, and both married Beatles. So much for the similarities; they did nothing, to put it mildly, to make Linda and Yoko soulmates. The differences, too many and too obvious to list, weighed much more heavily; in any case, if identical twins had married Paul McCartney and John Lennon in 1969, the way in which their lives would have had to change would have estranged them forever, putting them on opposite and opposing sides of the fence. It was not up to them, but was a function of the choice each woman had made. They stood by their men until the end.

If John said something snide about Paul's solo albums (which he did with unprofessional frequency), then John/Yoko went on the Paul/Linda shit-list. If John's lawyers caved in to Paul's on any of the many disputed items they were always at war about, then John came off the list. If Paul sold more records and tickets than John, he went on the John/Yoko shit-list (or at least he went on to John's, and off; it's hard to believe that the McCartneys were not generally viewed by Yoko with suspicion and distaste, and vice versa).

This is confusing, I know. It's confused me plenty over the years. If it can be summed up, let me try it this way: Paul and John loved each other always—they could be envious, hostile, bitter, and disappointed, but they always loved each other.

Paul never loved Yoko, and Yoko never loved Paul. She tolerated Linda and in fact could be most cordial and gracious. She wrote an appreciation of Linda in *Rolling Stone* after her death that was—not surprisingly—kind and generous and said all the right things. However, I do not know what John thought of Linda as an entity separate from Paul, or if he did indeed think all that much about her in that context. He knew Paul loved and needed her, and that she was an exemplary wife and mother, but I suspect he didn't expend much emotional energy on the subject.

Linda went with the flow according to Paul. I know she participated to some extent in ascertaining what the McCartney Mood of the Moment was vis-à-vis the Ono-Lennons but, once it had been settled on, it was identical to her husband's. In public interviews and private conversations, they spoke as one.

John and Yoko had moved to New York from London (which John would never see again), to an apartment on Bank Street in Greenwich

Village. They began to cultivate the art community, and the art community, which had not been terribly distressed when Yoko left, now welcomed her back as an important artist, a major celebrity, someone to know . . . whatever she wanted. Prominent anti-war activists were also high on their list of collectables.

In 1973, the Ono-Lennons left the Village and headed uptown, to the Dakota apartment house on Central Park West, one of the oldest, finest and most fabulous residential buildings in New York. A fortress of a structure, it was built in 1882 around a central courtyard and houses many rich and famous tenants in its ninety-four apartments. (Yoko now owns two joined-together flats and maintains offices on the first floor; she does not own a dozen Dakota apartments, as rumor and legend say she does.) There are several levels of security a non-resident must penetrate to gain entry. A visitor must check in first at an outer desk, which is under a massive archway leading from West Seventy-second Street into the courtyard, and then again at an inside desk. Ex-husbands, ex-wives, and ex-partners of all sorts have at least as difficult a time getting in as ordinary strangers.

Picture then the unpleasant thoughts that must have passed through the minds of John and Yoko as they sat in their bedroom on the night of December 17, 1975, chatting with their close friend, photographer Bob Gruen, when the doorbell rang. John had recently learned that he would be able to stay in America, permission granted reluctantly by the authorities after a surprise drug bust in England (on the day of Paul and Linda's wedding), a night-time raid on their Bank Street apartment (where a clever attorney got them out of trouble), and the couple's general undesirability in a country whose government had suffered a disastrous defeat in Vietnam, because, it was claimed, peace-nuts just like John and Yoko had (somehow) made it impossible for the military to wage the all-out war they had in mind.

Gruen recalls,

> There was a big flash of paranoia when the doorbell rang. It was like, "Oh my God, who can that be?" In the Dakota, every visitor gets announced from the desk downstairs, so when the bell on

your apartment door rings suddenly, it's a real fright. It wasn't just a little paranoia—they were very scared, very nervous.

They said to me, "Go see who it is, don't open the door until you know what's going on," and I went to the hallway and I heard what sounded like kids singing Christmas carols. So I called back to John and Yoko, "Don't worry, it's some kids from the building singing carols," and when I looked through, it was Paul and Linda. They were singing "We Wish You a Merry Christmas," very cute, kind of adorable, just standing there singing.

I said, "I don't think you're looking for me; come on, I'll take you into the bedroom where John and Yoko are," and they kept singing all the way in. You know, you read about all the animosity between them, about how the Beatles' wives don't get along, but they all seemed like giddy old school chums. Hugging, patting each other on the back, the guys were like high-school buddies who hadn't seen each other in a long time and really liked each other. The girls were very chatty and pleasant. If you didn't read the magazines, you wouldn't know Yoko and Linda were supposed to hate each other, they were getting along just fine. They all went into the next room to look at Sean, who was just two months old. [Yoko had had two miscarriages since she'd been with John; this was the first of their babies to survive.]

Paul told them about the pot bust in L.A. and how they'd been denied a Japanese visa, and how much he and Linda wanted to go to Japan. John and Yoko really loved Japan and went there a lot, so they talked about that. It was all pretty general, nothing about any business between them, and then when they got up to leave there was lots of hugging and kissing, general holiday good cheers. It was so fascinating seeing the two of them together like that with their wives, and everything totally pleasant.

After they were gone, John and Yoko were saying, "Wow! Do you believe that?" And they seemed to be so happy about the visit. Whatever fights were going on between their lawyers, they knew each other too long and too well not to be glad about seeing each other.

In fact, Paul and Linda had seen John a few times in 1974, when he was separated from Yoko and living with May Pang, a vivacious easy-going woman who had met John Lennon when she was working for Yoko as her secretary. (May has written about their stormy affair in *Me and John*, co-authored by Henry Edwards.) The McCartneys had first met May in California, but the two couples became more relaxed with each other later that year. "John and Paul were always one-upping each other, like brothers," remembers May, now married to record producer Tony Visconti.

> John and I had our own apartment on East Fifty-second Street, and we went to see Linda and Paul at the Stanhope Hotel. The first time they ever visited us in New York, the doorman called up and spoke to John, and John said to me, "Oh my God! Paul and Linda are downstairs. Can you handle that?" and I said, "Yeah, so? What's the problem? There's nothing to handle. They're your friends, send them up."
>
> In January of 1975 John said, "I have something to ask you. What would you think if I started writing with Paul again?" My mouth fell open, and I said, "Are you kidding? I think it would be terrific." That was the last time John and I were ever together before we split up. Yoko called him that night and told him she had a method to help him stop smoking, and that he should come over to the Dakota. I told him I didn't like him going over there, and he said, "Stop it!" He was yelling at me. "What's your problem? I'll be home by dinner, we'll go have a late dinner, and then we'll make plans to go to New Orleans and see Paul and Linda."
>
> But when he walked out that door, I knew something bad was going to happen. When he came back, he was a different person about Paul. It wasn't the same. He was saying, "Oh, you know how when Paul and Linda used to come and visit us? Well, I couldn't stand it." Obviously, something happened on the other side of Central Park. Right after that, he was back with Yoko. We split up for good in February, 1975.

> I didn't see Linda and Paul again for a long time. It wasn't until 1989, at Paul's "Buddy Holly Party" in London, and Tony had been invited because he had worked with the two of them. I went over to Linda, and she didn't recognize me. I said hello to her, and she said, "Oh, hi." I said, "It's May, remember John and May?" And she just went "Huh?!" She threw her arms around me and hugged me, she said, "I've always wondered what happened to you! I always liked you so much!" She'd read my book, and she said, "I know it's true what you wrote, I know what you've been going through, I support you, and I'm so glad you've married Tony. We love Tony!" She was so nice. I told her that John had wanted to write again with Paul, and she forced me to be the one to tell Paul that. I said, "Can't you tell him?" She said, "No, I want it to be you," and she brought Paul over and said, "Look, it's May! And she wants to tell you something that John said to her." And so I told him, and he looked very pleased to hear that.
>
> When we were talking about my book, Yoko's name came up, of course, but [Linda] never said anything negative about her. She sort of indicated that Yoko was not one of those people that she welcomed with open arms at all times, but she didn't say it outright.

Something of a mystery hovers over the rekindling of the friendship between the McCartneys and Ono-Lennons in the mid-1970s. It is definite that the last meeting of the two couples took place at the Dakota in May 1976, when Paul and Linda were in New York during the "Wings over America" tour. As John told *Playboy,* Paul and Linda came to visit, and they watched an episode of *Saturday Night Live* on which producer Lorne Michaels announced that the NBC network had told him that he could offer the Beatles the standard fee of $3,200 for an appearance. They thought it would be funny if they hopped in a taxi at that moment and just showed up at the studio while the show was being broadcast, but decided they were too tired. That's a famous anecdote, which Paul also told his biographer, Barry Miles.

But then, Lennon tells *Playboy,* "That was a period when Paul just kept turning up at our door with a guitar. I would let him in but finally I said to him, "Please call before you come over. It's not 1956, and turning up at the door isn't the same any more. You know, just give me a ring." He was upset by that, but I didn't mean it badly. I just meant that I was taking care of a baby all day, and some guy turns up at the door."

One wonders what period John is talking about. After the merry holiday visit, during which Linda described the Los Angeles pot bust that had occurred in March 1975 (indicating they hadn't all seen each other for nine months, at least), the McCartneys returned to England and went into the recording studio to do *Wings at the Speed of Sound.* A European tour began on March 20, 1976 in Copenhagen, and the stateside leg started in May, so there could hardly have been any meeting between December 17, 1975 and May 1976, which, in any case, is acknowledged to be the last time the two ever saw each other. It is possible that Paul came bopping up to John and Yoko's apartment (without Linda and with a guitar) a few times during the 1975 Christmas season, because he was so excited about the surprise visit described by Bob Gruen. John could not have been making it up, but it just seems so very odd . . .

Paul finally got a visa to perform with Wings in Japan, where eleven big concerts were booked for January 1980. For a musician who was so very eager to play in that country at last, as he had told the Lennons back in 1975 (Bob Gruen remembers Paul saying to John and Yoko that it was his dream to go back there, ever since he'd gone as a Beatle), he sure wasn't too cool about taking advantage of the chance when he was finally cleared.

"It took hundreds of lawyers thousands of hours to negotiate with a very slow-moving, unsympathetic Japanese government to let this convicted drug felon into the country," says Gruen, who discussed the Wings 1980 Japanese fiasco in detail with John and Yoko when the headlines announced that Paul had been put in prison in Tokyo for attempting to bring marijuana into Japan. "And when they finally let him in, he walks in with eight bags of pot right on top of the clothes in the suitcase he's carrying. What was he thinking? John said Paul probably just never imagined that anybody would open his bag. He was a Beatle. Nobody every opened their bags or searched their personal belongings. Beatles don't get that kind of treatment."

They don't? After arrests in Sweden, Scotland, and California, the McCartneys must have gathered they were not quite immune from government curiosity about their drug of choice. What is most amazing, as Gruen points out, is that it had taken five years to turn the Japanese authorities around; how brazen it was for someone, even Paul McCartney, to enter a country committing the same "crime" that had kept him out for so long.

Linda, as noted earlier, had been terrified what might happen after Paul was taken into custody. She told me in the summer of that year,

> If I'd known what Paul was really facing, I'd have fallen apart—they told me he might be detained for a few days or weeks, and people caught with less pot were in Japanese prisons for years. Well, they made sure I didn't hear the word "years." At first I thought he'd be out the next day, that it would all be taken care of with a fine or something. Then the days went by, with the kids and me in a Japanese hotel, and we didn't know what was going to happen. What *was* happening! I was thinking they might be torturing him. I didn't know what to tell the kids; James was two years old and he knew something was wrong. Paul and I hadn't spent a night apart in ten years, and now he was in jail. I almost couldn't deal with it. But of course I had to.

The Japanese tour was cancelled; the band members went home with rather bitter feelings towards their boss. Wings "just kind of wound down" during the year after Paul's nine days as a guest of the government, according to guitarist Laurence Juber.

> George Martin was brought in to produce *Tug of War*, but he didn't want to do a Wings record, he wanted to do a McCartney record. There was certainly no more touring planned; I got the

> impression that Paul and Linda didn't want to put that kind of pressure on the family any more.
>
> The feeling was: it's another decade, let's change gears. You know, Wings really had been a band. Paul and Linda were the bosses, but there was always a feeling that this was a collaborative effort. There was an openness to group communication, and I think that was reflected in the way the music came out. Each Wings album tends to have its own identity because of the changing personnel. But at that point, it didn't make sense to do another one. It certainly didn't make sense to George Martin. Nor to any of us, really.

That spring Paul and Linda made the album *McCartney II* at home. It became number one in the U.K. charts, and encouraged Paul to start putting his own name on the package once again. But he and Linda did not do a concert tour until 1989.

"We'd been pretty much on the road for almost ten years," Linda said to me in August 1989 at the Lyceum Theater in New York, where rehearsals (and one concert for special fans and friends) were held for a world tour that was to start in Norway in late September. We sat in a box in the empty theater one afternoon, while Paul did interviews backstage and Linda handled a string of reporters, one at a time, on her own.

"Once I didn't have to play in public," she remarked, "I rather got to enjoy fooling around on the keyboard. I taught myself some things, and Paul would always have some things to teach me as well. I'll do this tour, you know, but I'd rather be on the farm feeding horses and taking pictures." She told the same thing to every writer who asked her, as if she wanted to make it clear, if people still hadn't got the message, that she had never, and was not about to, beat Paul over the head to get herself on stage.

"Paul needs that dose he gets from an audience, and he's getting kind of restless," Linda went on. "We talked about this a whole lot; Paul knew I needed to be convinced that this was the thing to do. The kids are kind of grown up, and that makes a difference. After the John-thing, we wanted to lie low more for their sake than for ours. There were death threats. Some nuts, but we had to take them seriously. We have so much more security around us now, our lives have really changed. We have security that you don't see, you know what I mean? I hate it, I hate all that, I don't like to talk about it.

"Anyhow, he's ready to go out there, and I'll go with him, we all will. I expect it will be fun. You'll see, we're going to do a great show."

The John-thing: December 8, 1980. The McCartneys were at home in Sussex when Paul had a phone call from his office telling him that John Lennon had been murdered on the pavement at the entrance to the apartment building where he lived.

"God, it was horrible that day. I remember everything," Linda said, as we talked on the back terrace of her house in Long Island in 1992. "I'd just taken one of the kids to school, and Paul was home. I drove into the driveway and he walked out the front door; I could tell by looking at him that there was something absolutely wrong. I'd never seen him like that before. Desperate, you know, tears. I can see it so clearly, but I can't remember the words. I just sort of see the image. It's like a picture. Like it's a snapshot. Soul's camera.

"And then he told me what happened, and we were both crying. Later, we sat there with the kids watching it all on the telly. God, it's a weird old world, isn't it?" Linda paused and looked around. "Oh! Look at that female cardinal—see her, under the tree? Sort of a green and a red with an orangy beak?"

"She's not as gorgeous as her boyfriend," I said.

"But when you look at them through glasses, they are beautiful. Even those blackbirds, if you look when the sun's on them, they're metallic blues and browns with yellow eyes. They live here, the chipmunks, and the squirrels and the birds. This is their house, really."

I tried to bring the conversation back to Linda's memories of the day John Lennon was killed. "I was reluctant to call you in London," I remembered. "So I called your brother and asked, 'Are they all right?'—something stupid like that. He said, 'Of course!' I wondered how it could be 'Of course!' but what could he have told me? You must have been freaked out, I didn't know what to say to you."

"But it was lovely of you to call my brother. Freaked out? Slightly. It was awful. Can't you imagine? Paul was in so much pain. Then he started wondering if he was going to be next, or if it would be me, or the kids, and I didn't know what to think. At least Paul and John had been on really friendly terms at that time—they had talked on the phone about John's son, and they were laughing, and Paul felt good about their friendship.

"Boy, people sure fuck up this world, don't they?"

Linda and Paul had gone to New York to see Yoko soon after John's death. "We all cried so hard, you know, we had to laugh," Paul told the *Sunday Express*. "Yoko wanted to get us something to eat, and she mentioned caviar. We all said, "Let's do it!" Her houseman brought it in, mumbling, and he backed out and there was the caviar tin with just a little bit in the bottom. Her servants had eaten it all! So I said, "Ask for some wine." Sure enough, when it arrives there's like a quarter left in the bottle. They've had all the wine too! We were all just hysterical, and the relief was indescribable."

It was not to be all giggles between the widow and the McCartneys from that moment on. In the spring of 1981, Yoko told an interviewer that Paul had hurt John more than any other person. Paul did not take too kindly to that statement. In 1985, when the Beatles' song copyrights went on the market, Paul claims he was relying on Yoko to retrieve the catalogue for both of them, but that she let the deal slip through her hands: Michael Jackson ended up with the Beatles' songs, for $47.5 million—Paul was furious.

In 1988, the year the Beatles were to be inducted into the Rock and Roll Hall of Fame, Paul was aligned on one side against Yoko, Ringo and George on the other, in a dispute about recording royalties. He signalled that he didn't want to appear with the three of them on a stage accepting this great honor—then he said he might come after all. It was very big news that Paul might not show up, and I phoned Linda every day in the week preceding the event to find out how the land lay. "I don't know," she said one time. "Paul doesn't feel like pretending everything is just fine, when they're all getting up a legal case against him." The next time, it was, "We might come, we haven't really decided." It was left at "might" until the day of the ceremonies, when Paul's office faxed a statement to the Hall of Fame board saying he regretfully could not go through the hypocrisy of smiling for the cameras with three people who were, at that moment, his enemies. His absence was extremely noticeable, as one might imagine. (Neither did Diana Ross join the other Supremes, reportedly because of some fit of temper, so two of the biggest stars being inducted that night weren't there.) I was kind of stunned; I had really thought Paul and Linda would come to New York after all.

The next morning, I had a "casual" phone call from Linda at my office at the radio syndication company, MJI. "Hi," she drawled. "So what's happening?"

I answered, "You were sorely missed last night. I wish you had been there—by the way, I taped the whole show; would you like to hear it?"

"Hmm, maybe. Paul? I have Danny on the phone, he taped the Hall of Fame thing last night. Do we want to hear it? Oh, Paul says yes."

Not entirely unprepared for this call, I had a cassette deck close by, with the tape cued to Mick Jagger's terrific speech inducting the Beatles. "OK," I said, "here's Mick. I'm going to hold the mouthpiece of the phone next to the tape machine." I played Mick Jagger's thing, which was followed by enormous applause. "Could you hear that OK?" I asked.

"Yes, he's great," Paul said.

"OK, now everyone is standing up and George, Ringo, Yoko, Julian and Sean are coming on stage. I'm putting the phone back near the deck."

"Uh-oh," Linda said.

Ringo and George bantered a bit—George drawing a big laugh from the audience with, "I don't have much to say because I'm the quiet Beatle. It is unfortunate that Paul's not here because he was the one with the speech in his pocket." The phone receiver I was holding over the cassette deck seem to grow a bit chillier in my hand. Then Yoko stepped up to the microphone.

"I wish John was here. He would have been here, you know. He would have come. He was that kind of person . . . etc. etc."

Now the phone receiver seemed to turn distinctly icy. "Umm, could you hear all that, guys?" I asked, trans-Atlantically.

Paul answered with some rather unkind words about Yoko, and left Linda and me to pick up the pieces.

"I guess we missed a big night," she said, clearly with no regrets. She'd been thrust for a moment into the Beatle-hell that had engulfed her new life as the consort of Prince Charming nearly twenty years ago, and the memories were not pleasant.

"That much bigger since you weren't there, my dear. You and Diana Ross." I had to bite my lip to stop myself adding something about "prima donnas."

"Diana Ross didn't come? How can they have the Supremes without Diana Ross? Well, maybe we better not get into that. Goodbye my love." Click.

The whole Rock and Roll Hall of Fame thing would have become a non-issue with the passing of time, but for the induction of John Lennon for his solo recording career in 1994. His first records, post-Beatles, were the three albums he made in 1969, all with Yoko, thus making him an eligible nominee; artists become eligible for the Hall of Fame twenty-five years after the release of an album with their name on it. Lennon would be the first person to have been inducted twice into the Hall of Fame, once as a Beatle, once as himself; as a member of the nominating committee, I was wary of that precedent as a real can-of-worms opener. I also truly felt that his inclusion was in large part a sentimental one; he was, after all, a martyr and the first entertainer in history to be assassinated. I do not mean to question his stature—he was certainly one of the most brilliant and important men in the second half of the twentieth century, a wonderful songwriter, a true celebrity. I just happened to wonder if these past years defined a real "rock-and-roll" career, and I saw some handwriting on the wall that contained the names of a married couple very dear to me, who would certainly feel that this honor should come their way as well, and as soon as possible.

Of course, there was no one who could make John's induction speech but Paul himself, and he was persuaded to do it with vague reassurances of his own imminent induction. And so, on that January night in 1994, there was a re-lighting of the flame, as Paul, Linda, and Yoko sat together and chatted away amiably, with Paul at one point putting his arm over the back of Yoko's chair and laughing genially at whatever it was she was saying. His speech inducting John was as full of love as it indeed ought to have been, and when Yoko came out to accept the statuette, and they embraced, there was not a dry eye in the grand ballroom of the Waldorf Astoria. After the ceremonies, she had a small get together at her apartment in honor of the McCartneys.

I wondered when "it" was going to start, and sure enough, "it" began but a few weeks after that night, with a phone call from Linda. "So," she asked, "is Paul going to get into the Hall of Fame now that John is in?"

"Paul is already in," I said (and would say to her many, many times again).

"Yes, but John is in as a soloist. What about Paul's solo career?"

"Linda, permit me to be blunt. John is in because he's dead. Do you want Paul to qualify by being dead?"

"No, I just want to see him inducted, as he deserves."

Linda was working her half of the partnership. I was on the nominating committee, where I was assumed to have some "pull," which I didn't, only opinions.

Some variation of this little interchange between Linda and me on the subject of the Hall of Fame occurred with dismaying frequency. I had no answers, except to reiterate my belief that John Lennon was already in because he had been murdered. When Neil Young became the second person to own two statuettes, one for his solo career and one as a member of Buffalo Springfield, Linda turned up the heat. Neil was very close to the McCartneys (he spoke at Linda's memorial service in New York in June 1998); being a friend made the Hall of Fame Business worse, not better.

One time I found a little phrase to use in my argument that has come to haunt me. It's one of the most terrible things, in retrospect, that I have ever said to anybody. "When Paul gets into the Hall of Fame, Linda, you will be the Widow McCartney."

Paul got in six months after Linda died; she never knew that this dream was coming true, and Paul, on the night of the ceremonies, was feeling—as I interpreted it, knowing Paul a little and having worked the induction ceremonies backstage for several years—somewhat bitter towards the whole institution of the Hall of Fame for depriving Linda of this moment. As if it were in anyone's control. Daughter Stella McCartney, aged twenty-seven, the rising star of the international world of fashion as chief designer at the House of Chloe in Paris, was Paul's "date" that night, and he called her up to the stage to share the moment with him. She wore a white tank-top shirt that said "It's About Fucking Time," which I'm sure would have been Linda's exact words. Stella's "statement" had to be blacked out for TV transmission.

Chapter 15

"I'd see her at the studio, and I'd notice one sock would be down and the other pulled up, and she had this handbag that must have been twelve years old; she was always kind of a shambles, you know? And I thought that was so cool: here was a woman who could have anything, and she probably never had a manicure in her life."

Chrissie Hynde

On a summer's day in 1984, my housemates Susan Blond and Roger Erickson and I piled into Roger's neat Alfa Romeo and drove from our beach bungalow in the Sagaponack neighborhood of East Hampton to Linda's brother's house a few miles to the east. Susan, Michael Jackson's publicist, had just flown back from the first dates of his world tour and Paul was most interested in knowing everything she could tell him about Michael, at that moment arguably the biggest star in the world. He was also fascinated with the Alfa, and how I'd managed to get myself into the tiny cavity that served as a back seat. James frolicked on the lawn, and a pleasant time was had by all.

As always, since around 1982, Linda had greeted me with, "Have you gone veggie yet?" and as always I told her that I was a little more veggie than the last time we had seen each other and that I was getting there, gradually. That made her happy.

During our visit, Linda suddenly asked me if I liked bacon. Was this a trick question? "Mmm," I replied, trying to duck having to give a direct answer, "I've enjoyed it in the past . . . it's been a while, I think. I'm trying to remember when I had it last."

"You can admit that you like it," she said. "I have a reason for asking. They're making vegetarian bacon now, and Paul and I are really interested in someday putting out something like that and making it available to everyone. So I wish you'd try this." She went into the kitchen and came out with a stack of cartons of veggie bacon. They were made from something called TVP, or textured vegetable protein. Sounded yummy!

"Try this," she insisted, "and you'll never eat real bacon again." We put the bounty in the little space that remained in the trunk of the car and were starting to drive off when Linda, who'd been waving goodbye to us with Paul, called out, "Just a minute!" and dashed back into the house. She came out with her arms full of more vegetable things disguised as meat. "We're getting on a plane in a little while and there's plenty here for my brother and his family. Besides, I didn't give you enough; here, take these," she said.

"Oh, they've got so much, Lin," Paul pointed out, as I mumbled something like, "Gee, the trunk is kind of full, what with the car cover, and Roger's cleaning fluids, and . . ."

"Well, here," she persisted, "you hold on to them," dumping the boxes into the back seat so that only my head rose above the ocean of packaged food. We waved goodbye anew, or at least Roger and Susan did, because my arms were nowhere to be found. When we got home, we stuffed the freezer with as many shiny little boxes as it would hold, where they stayed for days, unopened.

"I know Linda is going to call to ask how we liked this stuff," I said from time to time to my friends in our bungalow. "We have to try it." We'd pass around one of the packages, examine it with great interest and put it back in the freezer. Finally I decided, "Let's do it!" Roger and I unpacked the "bacon" and stared at it, blinded by its orangeness and perfect symmetry. Into the pan the strips went; as they fried, they turned a deeper, different shade of orange and stayed perfectly flat, never curling or crinkling or even making much of a sizzling sound. Except for the color, and a vague crispness, they didn't look too different from the raw product; they tasted OK, if a bit weird, but not at all like bacon.

"What did you think of that frozen food?" Linda asked when next we spoke.

"Very impressive!" I responded.

"Now you keep eating that, even if you don't go completely veggie for a while," she advised, "because every time you do, that's one less animal that had to be killed so that people could eat meat. Let me know when you run out, and I'll have more sent to you."

That was the idea behind it all—eating this "bacon" was saving the life of a pig. It would have been better if the food were fabulous but, meanwhile, it was a pound of flesh not slaughtered.

We had been given a prototype of what would become, six years later, Linda's own line of frozen vegetarian food. The quality of TVP-based foodstuffs, by the time Linda put her name on the packages, did improve a great deal, the range of products grew vastly and Linda's revolutionary culinary idea, vegetarian food disguised as meat, became an enormous success in Britain. Like McDonald's, they're now counting sales in the billions.

Tim Traharne, the food entrepreneur who helped Linda start her business and now runs it for the family, says about the first batch of frozen dishes given a public launch, "I can only flinch at their crudeness, compared to today's products." And he's talking about the stuff they came up with in 1990—you can only imagine what that first "bacon" I ate was like, before six years of research, development and taste tests. Then again, maybe you cannot.

It's understandable that Linda could gladly accept a gradual move towards vegetarianism on anyone's part, for she and Paul did not go the whole hog (so to speak) into a meatless and fishless life all at once. There is an oft-told story about the family having a leg of lamb for dinner in Scotland one day, when a lamb either came into view frolicking in the grass outside the house, or wandered into the dining area—there are various versions. In any event, at that moment Linda and Paul supposedly forswore meat forever. This incident is said to have happened in the late 1970s. When Linda's foods were about to be launched in the U.S. in 1994, the accompanying promotional literature claimed that the McCartneys had been strict vegetarians for twenty years; in one interview, Paul says that started when Heather was six and Mary a tiny baby, which would have been around 1969, but members of Wings recall a Thanksgiving dinner with real turkey, and meat and fish were certainly being served aboard the flotilla in Half Moon Bay in the spring of 1977.

Then there's the big caviar controversy. If, as we've seen, the McCartneys were eager to partake of Yoko's caviar when they visited her in early 1981, they cannot have been orthodox veggies at that time. In fact, Paul told an interviewer they had continued eating caviar even after they'd given up eating fish, because "we thought it's only eggs, OK. Until we inquired into it and someone said the mother sturgeon gets slit head to toe. We said, "We thought they milked her." That stopped caviar." Milked?

This is not to quibble, and not to question the extent of Linda's and Paul's total commitment to the right, as they defined it, of all things with a heart not to be eaten by humans. One night Mike Fisher, my companion at the time, and I arrived at a party for the McCartneys given by Linda's brother, John, and his wife, Jody, at their home. I had some CDs to give Linda, and my favorite shoulder satchel was then a soft, dark blue plastic, insulated and marked with the brand name "Petrossian," a famous importer of . . . caviar. Linda was in the entrance hall as I arrived in an elevator full of guests, and she lost no time in embarking on a major harangue: "Petrossian! Caviar? Do you *know* how they get caviar? They cut the mother open, from one end to the other. They cut her open! They take out her millions of eggs, and that's what caviar is. Oh, that's horrible, Danny, how can you carry something from that horrible place?"

Over Linda's shoulder, her daughter Stella looked at Mike and winked.

"I'll get rid of this, I promise," I told Linda, and went into the room where people were putting their coats and hid it under the bed. I still have the bag—it's great for keeping iceberg lettuce sandwiches cold, and the Petrossian logo has long since worn off.

One brings up the subject with caution and, it is hoped, some sense of humor, but for Linda this was no laughing matter, nor is it now for Paul, who is the very dedicated keeper of the flame. As a couple, they were the world's most prominent animal rights activists and advocates of vegetarianism; as an individual, Linda McCartney was purely, totally, famously and successfully a protector of all species not human. Directly and indirectly, she probably saved the lives of more animals than any person in history, at least in the history of the West.

Her name in Britain is now synonymous with frozen meatless food; there is even a dog food marketed there that is "Lin-tested," with a little icon of her face on the package; a cat food is on the way. There are celebrities who are passionate about animal rights, and their passions are commendable, but somehow I do not think that a picture of Bea Arthur or the B-52s on a bag of dog food or a package of frozen "sausages" would be very meaningful. Linda really was the "animals' saint," as activists have called her. "When she died, the animals of the world really took a hit," comments photographer Dave McGough. "There is no one to take her place."

I think Linda was born to be the animals' saint; as a child, she brought home injured animals and was more comfortable, and more fulfilled, with her horses and even with the birds and tadpoles that she would sit watching for hours in a woodland area near her house, than with many of her own species. Motherhood, career, marriage, and family diverted her energies, and she was a brilliant success in those areas, but I think her kinship with all non-human creatures was simply dormant for about twenty years; it manifested itself as her children needed less nurturing and started going full-force in the early 1980s. For the last ten years of her life, it was total and, amazingly to all who watched her, growing all the time.

Laurence Juber, who was a staunch vegetarian at the time he joined Wings in 1978, recalls that the McCartneys were "transitioning into being full-time about it when I first met them." While working with them at George Martin's Air Studios in London, he would buy loaves of bread, bags of bean sprouts, and other non-animal delicacies for Paul and Linda, which they accepted with enthusiastic interest. "One day Linda wasn't at the studio and I gave a bag of stuff to Paul, and the next time I saw Linda I asked how they had liked it. She said, 'Uh oh, you shouldn't have just left that with Paul. It's not in his nature to remember that there's a bag of groceries in the back of the car.' Sure enough, she went to look inside the car and there was a container of very gooey bean sprouts in the back seat. It wasn't strictly vegetarian back then. That's the way most people start—they certainly came the distance, didn't they?"

"Gradualist is a good way to describe the way they got into it," remarks Chrissie Hynde, a very close friend of Linda's and Paul's and an outspoken animal rights activist.

> I think Linda did it the right way, and went public with it very effectively. You know, I would do phone-in radio shows and women would call in and say, "I'm a vegetarian and I'd like to convert my family, but my husband is a real meat-and-potatoes man." And I'd say, "Well, then leave him." That was always my take on it, probably a little bit hardline.
>
> Linda's approach was, "If your husband is a meat-and-potatoes man, don't tell him. Slip him a veggie-burger and if he says it's delicious, say, 'Good! Well it's healthy too.' And she got all those women who read her cookbooks and bought her food to do just that. What she was up to was not primarily about the beauty of vegetables, or the science of nutrition, but about saving animals' lives. If she could do that, her goal was accomplished.
>
> She was always telling me how many dinners she had sold, how many units of non-animal protein, and what the equivalent of that was in terms of animals' lives. I don't think she ever saw it in any other terms, not in terms of a business or her personal success in marketing food, or that she herself had done well, but that every time a cookbook was sold, animal lives were saved. And she'd call in for the latest sales figures, and I think she'd just get on a horse and go for a ride feeling great that someone became a veggie that day.

It was Hynde who encouraged Linda to come out from behind the cookbooks and the frozen foods and to establish herself as a vocal and active spokesperson on behalf of the animal kingdom. "She was the least pretentious person I've ever known," says Chrissie, who first met Linda in 1983.

> I got a baby present, some clothes, when I had my first child, and it said, "Love—Paul and Linda and the kids," and I'd never met them. I was just amazed. Well, about a month later I was rehearsing and Paul was in the next studio; it wasn't easy for me, but I walked over to him and said, "Gosh, thanks for the baby clothes." He looked a little embarrassed, and he said, "Oh. My wife." Then I met Linda a few weeks after that, and I liked her instantly. I'd see her at the studio, and I'd notice one sock would be down and the other pulled up, and she had this handbag that must have been twelve years old; she was always kind of a shambles, you know? And I thought that was so cool: here was a woman who could have anything, and she probably never had a manicure in her life, and she obviously just didn't give a fuck.
>
> Then, I hadn't talked to her for a few years, but she sent cards and I knew, from being a new mother, that it can take up all of a person's time taking care of one kid, and she had four. She was being a superlative mother and, for me, that was an inspiration. I had been very anti the whole American nuclear family thing, I was such a product of the Vietnam War, but when I saw how nurturing she was with her children, it was obvious that that was the right thing to do. When her children were getting old enough that they didn't need that much nurturing, we began to talk on the phone more often, and most of that was about animal stuff.
>
> I'd been thinking about starting something really big, like the vegetarian answer to McDonald's, and one day she called me and I went straight into it. I knew that the one way to get her attention was to imply that she was a snob, because that was the last thing she would ever be, or wish to be.
>
> I said, "Listen, McCartney, why don't you get off your high horse and do something? We're starting a revolution, and you should be part of it." I knew she'd be horrified if anyone thought she was above the cause. And she stammered a bit, and she

answered, "Look, no one wants to hear what I have to say, they just want to see me standing next to Paul when he gets awards." I told her, "Wrong! People are so impressed with fame that they don't care why you're famous. You've got a voice and you can use it, and people do want to hear what you've got to say. And whether they like it or not, you've got the voice, and you can do whatever you want with it." She just happened to get me on a day when I was on a tear.

She was reticent, and I understood why. She'd been preoccupied with her family until then, and the press and the public certainly hadn't made her feel as if she had any great contribution to make on her own. She'd always been portrayed as jolly and up and optimistic, all peace signs and good-natured stuff, but I said, "Come on, get your fist in the air, no more mister nice guy, this is serious stuff." Soon after that, she and Paul were at some premiere, and there was a picture of them and Linda had her fist in the air! And the caption was about her. It said something like, "Linda McCartney, seen here with her husband, punches the air." I thought, "Whoa! I'd better shut up, I don't want to inspire her to do that again." But I knew the energy was there, and she probably just needed a kick in the ass to say, "Yeah, you can do it." Because we both had this intense appreciation and love of nature, and we felt how noble animals are. To me, the whole animal kingdom is God's link to man, and it will give you all the answers. But Linda and I never had discussions about religion and we never talked about God. It was always Man *vs.* Nature.

By the end of the 1980s Linda's first cookbook, *Linda McCartney's Home Cooking*, was published. Although she was performing with Paul on his first world tour since Wings had broken up, she clearly had her own agenda, and being one of her husband's back-up musicians was not her main concern. The kids were still with them on the road, but James was twelve, audiences were no longer scary, the critics had long since said everything condescending about Linda that they could, her photographs were being acclaimed at museums and galleries around the world, and now she had a passion and identity of her very own.

Not that she was at all indifferent to Paul's success on the road, or to her part in it. "The crowds have been incredible, and if it carries on like this it'll be great," Linda told me in a phone call from Madrid in November 1989. "Although you do forget where you are. When you leave a country, you feel like you're still there. I think we went to Italy after Germany, I can't remember. During the day, you know where you are, but then you come to the halls at night, they're all the same. Even though I love seeing the excitement in people's faces, and their happiness at being in the same room with Paul. And I'm still amazed at the way they carry people out of the audience after they've fainted. I counted sixty in Paris."

"You counted them?"

"Well, I know the set pretty well, and I can do more than one thing at a time, in spite of what you may think."

Since I was doing a story on the tour for the syndicated radio show I was writing and producing for MJI at the time, I put to Linda the usual cliché question: "What are you looking forward to as far as the United States' leg of the tour is concerned?" She was off and running.

"Well, Paul is definitely just playing to all his fans, and I love the idea of him just doing that, and of course I like coming back to America, but you know me, I want to get my point of vegetarianism across, Danny."

"How are you doing that?" I asked dutifully.

"Well, my cookbook which—do you have one?"

"No, you said you'd send me one. But I wrote about it anyhow."

"Bestseller."

"Congratulations!"

"I will send you one, I'll bring you one personally. I want to talk about things like that myself, because that's really all I'm interested in: no slaughter of animals and no experiments on animals. That's what I'm about. I don't want to drive people crazy with it, but you know me, I'm just outspoken that way. If I believe in something, I'm gonna say it. And what it's about is, if you love animals and don't want to eat them, this is a very non-cranky way to do it."

"I see that the tour will be in California at Thanksgiving, and then you'll be in New York?"

"Yes, and that will be a turkey-less Thanksgiving, because turkeys shouldn't be murdered!"

"Now, Linda, you promise that this will be non-cranky? I mean, the press, Paul's fans, they've stopped hitting on you; now you're telling them they're murderers?"

"Well, that's what it is, isn't it? And I'm showing them a nice way to stop." Linda went on to tell me that they'd been to the Prado that day and it was fantastic: "Bosch, Goya, El Greco, Breughels, Velazquez. Oh my God! We go on in fifteen minutes! See you next year in November."

Of course, it wasn't perceived by everybody as non-cranky. All the backstage catering on the tour was vegetarian, naturally, but the crew were told that as long as they were part of the McCartney organization, they were not to eat meat anywhere. No sneaking off for real sausages, or the job was in jeopardy. There was some resentment on the part of the "real men" who hauled equipment and drove trucks, and there was no doubt some illegal consumption of sausage. If anyone got fired for that, which I doubt, it was certainly not publicized; the bosses would indeed have seemed cranky, and people who work tours cannot risk being seen as trouble-makers, but the point was made. "This is a vegetarian tour, like it or leave it."

It was, as I said to Linda, and as her friends certainly noted, brave of her to challenge the world on the subject of food just as she was becoming "acceptable." The girls who hated her for marrying Paul must have got over that in the intervening twenty years, and the guys who hated her for presuming to be in Paul's band had realized, it was to be hoped, that there was nothing to get all that upset about. Experienced musicians had known that, although she appeared to be amateurishly playing keyboards with only one finger, as Paul told Chrissie Hynde in a wonderful interview he did with her for *USA Weekend* in November 1998, "You can't play those instruments [Moog synthesizers] with more than one finger. Well, you can play with as many fingers as you like, but only one will register. She was synthesizing a whole orchestra, and that's really difficult to do. She learned it all, and she did it all, and she took it kind of seriously." And as Pete Townshend says, Linda's voice was integral to the sound of Paul's music after the Beatles, whether or not most people knew that.

In any case, the mockery had died down by the time Linda decided to hit the world over the head, albeit nicely (at first), with the "Go veggie!" motif. It was, after all, courageous of her to provoke the public all over again, but she had long since realized that she was not going to do well in popularity contests. Popularity was her husband's province, and it was not only unattainable for her, but not very desirable either. So what? It was nothing compared to what she believed in, which was essentially a complete reordering of the relationship between humans and animals. I made the mistake once of asking her about the requirement that the road crew "go veggie" for the duration of the 1989–90 world tour, and told her I'd heard some of the guys were complaining that the McCartneys were being "a pain in the butt" on the subject. "A pain?" she replied, fixing me with a look that was both anguished and shrivelling. "Let me tell you about pain! Do you know what kind of pain . . . etc.?" The annoyances borne by humans were as nothing compared to the suffering of animals—nothing; not in those exact words, but certainly as a doctrine, this was the mantra of the last decade of Linda's life.

If Chrissie Hynde convinced Linda that she could say something and do something to promote the cause of animal rights, it was Dan Mathews who showed her what there was to do, and exactly how very effective she could be. Smart, handsome, funny, creative, and totally dedicated, Mathews works at People for the Ethical Treatment of Animals (PETA), one of the more radical ("We're theatrical, but not violent," he cautions) animal rights organizations, and I first met him in March 1989. He was organizing the first Rock Against Fur concert in New York, and after talking to him for a while on the morning of the concert, and being totally charmed, I asked him if he knew Linda and Paul, or if they knew of him or the work PETA was doing. He said he didn't know, but that he would love to be in contact with them. I called Linda that same day and told her there was someone fabulous I had just met who was doing animal rights stuff and that I thought they would adore each other. I gave her his phone number. She lost no time in contacting him. As Mathews recalls,

> It was right after the Rock Against Fur concert and we were having our department heads meeting, when the secretary burst into the room and said, "Dan, there's a call from England, and she says it's Linda McCartney calling for you." Sure enough, it was Linda. She said, "Hi, Danny told me about you, and I hear you're doing great things and it's not just fur, and by the way, are you veggie?" She was asking me if I was veggie—I answered, "Well, if you only knew. Of course." We talked for about ten minutes, and I told her some of the things we were doing, undercover exposés in slaughter houses and fur farms, and she was very enthusiastic. Very casual, almost as if we'd been friends before she even called, and then at the end of the conversation she said, "If you ever get over to England, please come and see us; here, take our number down, it's just for friends, but please call." Here was Linda McCartney calling me, sight unseen, giving me her home phone number.
>
> I was going to England a month or two later, and I called, and they invited me to their house and said they'd have a car pick me up at my hotel in London and take me to Sussex. Well, everybody knew I was having a heart attack because I was going to visit them, I was going to see these mega-celebrities. But I never felt intimidated, mainly because of Linda's tone in that first phone call, that mellow voice. So simple, so direct; she'd heard about something she thought was cool, and she wanted to help, and called. She was as interested in us as we were in them.
>
> It was a two-hour drive, very beautiful, and we went past the gatehouse up this long drive, and there's Paul and Linda, standing side by side, their arms around each other and waving with the other hand, all smiles on the front porch. I guess I thought the house would be bigger and more sprawling, but it was just a comfortable size, and we went right into the kitchen, where it seemed everything happened, and she asked if I wanted

> a cup of tea or coffee, then she fixed it. No maids, no servants, none whatsoever. Paul was so sweet and smiling, their eyes were so enthusiastic and they actually seemed to be excited that I had come to visit them.
>
> They explained their motivations to me, it was important for them to do that. Linda's was purely from the ethical issue of animal cruelty, whereas Paul was more concerned with the environmental impact of the meat industry and there were things about that which really upset him. He was being very supportive of the Friends of the Earth organization at the time, he was planning to give them a special prominence on the upcoming tour. Eventually, their attitudes came to be nearly identical, but at the beginning, she was interested in one aspect of the humane movement and he was into another part of it, and they reinforced each other over the years.
>
> Paul's never been afraid of the more radical stuff we've done. There was a concert promoter once whose wife worked for the Ringling Brothers Circus, and they saw that PETA had a booth at the show and the guy said to Paul, "Do you know about these people? They dumped a ton of animal manure on the Ringling Brothers' corporate headquarters in some kind of protest," and Paul replied, "Whatever works. Sometimes you have to do that kind of thing." That told me a lot about Paul. He's never been afraid of the more radical stuff.

The McCartneys joined PETA in campaigns against General Motors, L'Oréal cosmetics, Gillette razors and meat in general. In the Midwest, the pork lobby learned of the association and 300 pig farmers in Iowa returned their tickets to Paul's concert. It was front-page news in the region, with protesters at the concert carrying signs saying, "I Wanna Hold Your Hoof" and "Paul, Don't Have A Cow, Man!" Paul and Linda loved it.

Mathews remembers,

> When they were on tour, I would hook up with them. In Florence Linda and I had a press conference, and she urged Italian

women to honor St. Francis of Assisi and stop wearing furs. I held up a fur coat, and she spray-painted it. It was all over the papers. In Paris, L'Oréal had just stopped their animal tests, and Linda had been a big part of that campaign, so Linda and I and Cliff, my lover at the time, did this photo opportunity with Cliff dressed as a rabbit, and we opened a giant bottle of champagne and challenged other companies to join L'Oréal.

Paul was often busy doing his thing to publicize the concert, and I always sort of felt that Linda and I were like Lucy and Ethel, going off to do these things while Ricky led the band. She would say that he had to do whatever it was, but "Let's do this." You know, it was practical. She did it with him, she did it without him.

One of Mathews's favorite memories of Linda is of walking round her house with her one day and emptying the live mice from the mousetraps she'd installed.

When I got there she said, "Oh good, you're just in time, we've had some mice in the house and I want to go check out the traps." She had these little cages where the mouse can get in, and then the cage closes but the mouse is not injured. She'd check them every day, take the cages with the little mice and get in the car, then she'd let them out at the edge of the forest. It was part of the routine—get the papers, make coffee, check the live mousetraps. No grandstanding, just a normal part of her life.

You know, never once did I see her snap. Never once did I see her roll her eyes at somebody. And she was never one of those fake air-kissing people. She was a breath of fresh air in any world, but especially in the celebrity world. Linda already had some baggage, what with marrying Paul and playing in the band, and then she did what she thought was right and fought for what she believed in. Nobody has done what she did, it's made her an icon in the humane movement. People, especially women, are told, "Oh shut up about animals, there are more important things

> to worry about than animals," and Linda changed that. She spoke up about it when nobody that prominent was saying anything, and she helped initiate a change which will be a permanent one. She popularized something that was almost unimaginable before. She became effective and respected, and I thought that was pretty great, and it had to have been encouraging for her, after all she'd been through. And she stayed involved until the end of her life—two weeks before she died, she faxed us asking for vegetarian cat food recipes. There was such a thing, it had just been developed.

The last time I saw Linda at her house in Long Island, we were having a dinner of corn and salad and she was quoting statistics on how much water and land cattle consume, down to the gallon and the acre. My East Hampton hostess that particular weekend was Naomi Rosenbloom, who had actually dated Linda's father many years earlier. She was utterly charmed by the family—so charmed that she overruled me when I responded to Linda's dinner invitation by saying that Naomi and I actually had plans that evening, knowing that Naomi is not a veggie kind of gal. Well, we could always raid Naomi's fridge afterwards, and did. "I didn't love the food," Naomi has said to me more than once in recalling that day, "but that was the nicest family I've ever met in my life. Those children! The most beautiful, polite, most naturally affectionate children I have ever seen in any family—and in a rich family! Because you know they're usually the worst. How did they do it? You tell me she really was a famous cook? Well, OK—a famous mother I can see, but . . ."

Anyhow, I interrupted Linda's agronomics lecture, interesting though it was, and asked, "Linda, what do you feed your dogs?"

"Aha!" she exclaimed. "Vegetarian dog food! There is such a thing. They love it—you take soya and mix it with [whatever] and you start feeding it to them when they're puppies, and they'll eat it forever, and they'll never care about meat again."

"OK, then what do you feed your cats?" I'd seen an army of felines in the (non-leather) saddle house on their farm, and they didn't seem all that veggie from a distance.

"Nh," was what Linda's answer sounded like. She looked away, sort of covered her mouth with her hand, and said what sounded like, "Nh."

"What?"

"Nh," she repeated.

"Oh Lin," Paul said, "tell Danny that we give the cats fish."

"I hate it! I hate it that we have to do that!" she burst out. She was genuinely upset at the thought.

"Do you stand on the shore of the ocean and think about all the fish out there?" I asked, incredulous that she seemed to be so angry at herself for participating in the carnivorous food chain, however indirectly.

"Yes, I do," said Linda. "But you know, they're working on a veggie cat food right now. The next time we meet, I hope I can tell you that our cats have gone veggie."

Linda never had a chance to tell me that, but by golly, it is happening.

A great fan of Linda's home-cooking was none other than the poet Allen Ginsberg, who had first met Paul through Barry Miles (Paul's and Allen's biographer) in 1967. In 1994, when Miles was working on Paul's book, Allen came to the U.K. and was eager to renew the acquaintance, so a Sunday dinner at the family homestead was arranged. Miles and Ginsberg both noted how physical and affectionate Paul and Linda were with their children, who were all there; "lots of hugs and touching," Miles recalls, "more like a big Italian family than a usual middle-class English one—but then, of course, they were neither of them English middle-class."

The crowd sat around the kitchen table, clearly the social center of the house, and dined on vegetable lasagne and a veggie loaf, which the guests found delicious. "Allen rather greedily helped himself to seconds before anyone else, and then polished off the last portion, proclaiming it to be the tastiest food he'd eaten in a long time. He genuinely seemed to love it," Miles remembers, but then, if you've eaten Allen's cooking, you'll know why he enjoyed it so much. Linda and Allen talked about vegetarian diets and health problems—alas, they would both succumb to cancer within a few years.

"Linda behaved as if Allen was an old friend," Miles wrote to me on e-mail. "It's something he sometimes brings out in people, but by no means always. She touched his arm while speaking, and Linda indulged her nostalgia for New York, because they were the only two New Yorkers in a roomful of Brits. Allen liked her very much, which is rare, because he was notorious for not even being able to remember women's names—he just blanked women from his life, but Linda remained there, possibly because she was famous, but also because they had a rapport.

"When we left, Mary drove us back to town, and I was very struck by the hugs and kisses between Linda and her girls, and also the way they unselfconsciously spoke about how much they loved each other. Linda often came across as strident in public, but in private she was much softer, vulnerable, open and loving."

Allen, Paul and Linda saw each other again at the McCartney home in East Hampton; they wrote haikus together (Allen's revenge for them serving him veggie loaf?), which sadly are lost, but, as Barry Miles recalls, they were formal seventeen-syllable haikus, and pretty good.

Simply as good hosts, the McCartneys had not cracked open Linda's Frozen Meals, tasty as they were, but served the freshest ingredients available, usually produce grown on their own farm. Typically, when they had decided to explore the world of mushrooms, they flew over a French mushroom expert and went around the grounds with him, photographing all the local toadstools and annotating the pictures for future reference; these were divided into two piles—edible and poisonous—and kept on file.

Food manufacturer Tim Treharne was named by Linda in 1997 as one of the "main men" in her life, besides her husband and son, in the magazine *Woman's Journal*. "[He] heads up my food company and made a reality of my dream to create a range of veggie meals. We work well together because he's a good, kind man."

Treharne was in the meat business and, through his vet, who was also the McCartneys' vet (although they lived sixty miles apart), learned of Linda's and Paul's eagerness to market vegetarian food. "We met," he remembers. "The whole situation was bizarre, in that we were obviously worlds apart. They were devout vegetarians and world famous, and I had been in the meat industry for thirty years and was unknown outside of it. So we were not people that anybody would logically have put together."

An understatement but, as novices in the business of marketing a line of food, the McCartneys were made to understand two simple facts. First, their name on the package would result in one sale per customer, but what was *in* the package would determine whether or not the customer came back for more. (Treharne used the example of Frank Sinatra's sauces and Paul Newman's salad dressings; Sinatra's products were off the shelves within a month, but Newman's products delivered the goods, and the rest is history.)

Second, and a very bitter pill to swallow, was that Linda was going to have to deal with the meat industry as it existed, if she were going to be in the food business putting out what was not merely a niche product. It was not appropriate to be in one branch of the industry while being seen to tear down another part of it. And even more important, according to Treharne, "the technology and manufacturing expertise needed to produce Linda's products was in the very industry she was against, the meat industry. As she said, she had to learn to 'sleep with the devil.'" Research in such critical areas as transportation, refrigeration, marketing and so on is financed, in fact, by the producers of meat—you cannot put out a line of frozen foods to be sold in supermarkets without relying on that (hated) area of the industry. So be it.

Cleverly, Treharne and the McCartneys aimed their products not at pure and devout vegetarians, who make up only a very small percentage of the food-consuming public, but at what they called "Mrs. Slightly Green," a category which accounts for an astonishing 56 percent of the food market in Britain. Mrs. Slightly Green has to feed a family on a budget; probably has a daughter who doesn't like meat; and has a husband whose health she's concerned about who doesn't exercise, is overweight and is very much a "meat man" who won't change his habits. So Mrs. Slightly Green has to feed her husband, says Treharne, "non-meat products without making him feel 'wimpish.' She has to give him food he recognizes and relates to." As Paul has said many times, most people expect to see some sort of meat in the middle of their dinner plate; the meat comes first, the other items on the plate are complementary. Hence TVP disguised as meat, and a good disguise it had better be.

On April 30, 1991, Linda McCartney's Meatless Entrées were launched, in a colorful package with a photograph of Linda on the front. The six initial products, the names of which might mean more to British consumers than to English-speaking people from other countries, were: Ploughman's Pie, Ploughman's Pastie, Beefless Burgers, Golden Nuggets, Lasagne, and Italian Style Toppers.

Linda's bestselling cookbook had preceded her foods by about two years, so a television and press publicity and marketing campaign was a natural for the public to digest, so to speak. In a typical spot, Linda introduces herself and talks about her meat-eating early years and her conversion to vegetarianism. Some vivid examples are put in to appeal to animal lovers and all the Mrs. Slightly Greens of the world. ". . . We were behind a truck of chickens, tightly packed, beautiful chickens, and [then the truck] turned into a chicken processing plant . . . People [say that] fish don't have feelings. Yeah, pull them out of the water, they're so happy, they say, "Hey thanks! I didn't like it in my own kingdom. You want a few of my friends?" I mean, everything has feelings, who are we to murder them? It's just something that's in me, I think. I love life, and nature and animals are life."

In one of her sweetest vignettes, Linda stands in a meadow talking about cows and walks over to them, saying, "Hello, hello ladies, young ladies, hello! Cuties! Moo!" Then, standing adoringly next to a cutie, she talks about how she once rode a cow, how the young ones are taken away from their mothers and how they give you nice dairy products, in much the same way that chickens give you eggs. Without seeming to notice that Linda's been standing there, the cute cow just turns and walks away. "Goodbye," Linda says with a loving smile, as if she knew the cow was not going to be cuddly with her and she didn't at all care. If a dog behaved like that, or even a cat, one would expect to see the affectionate human get a tiny bit insulted, shrug for the camera, indicate, "Oh, it doesn't matter, I know she loves me." But Linda does none of that. "Goodbye." It's a cow, it's being a cow, Linda does not expect it to act like a person, or demonstrate training, or be appreciative, or do anything cute. It walks away. It's a cow. For Linda, it can be nothing more, and nothing better; it's quite perfect as it is.

By the time Linda McCartney's Home Style Cooking line was ready for an American launch, in 1994, there were eighteen of her products in the English supermarkets. Meals were selling by the millions, and the industry (and the McCartneys themselves) were very impressed. Clearly, Ploughman's Pasties were not going to be a hit in America, where the word "pasties" is understood to mean those little adhesive circles that strippers put over their nipples. Nor is the ploughman associated with nutrition . . . as a rule. So for the U.S., and with the help of a manufacturer named Fairmont Foods in a small town in the center of Minnesota hog-country, nine new vegetarian entrées were readied: Spaghetti Milano, Lasagne Roma, Pasta Provençale, Pasta Primavera, Rigatoni Marinara, Chili Non-Carne, Burrito Grande, Fettucine Alfredo and Bavarian Goulash. Market research had clearly indicated that dieting Americans, or those going veggie—even if temporarily—seemed to be in a mostly pasta frame of mind.

A huge publicity tour, complete with politicians and Paul, did little to help, and because of some confusion with the manufacturing company and its new owners, the line failed to get off the ground. One food reviewer only found four of the nine entrées in his local supermarket, a bad omen.

There were other setbacks too. In October 1992, steak was found in a batch of about 3,000 of Linda's Deep Country Pies. Linda was quoted as saying she was "horrified," and added that "there could simply have been a mistake in the packing, or it could be something more sinister." A spokesperson for the U.K.'s Vegetarian Society got the final quote in the *Daily Telegraph* coverage of the disaster, talking about "immense distress" and "revulsion."

Nor were the food writers enchanted. The meals were found to contain a good many calories, one third of which were fats—a proportion that is severely frowned upon by the gurus of healthy eating. Linda seemed not to care, admitting that something had to be done to make these things taste good, and better fats than meat. The nutrition gurus were unmoved. "Animal welfare is a proper concern, but the health of humans is equally so," wrote Glyn Christian, who was appalled by the fake-meat concept, in the *Sunday Telegraph*. "If you are to give up meat successfully, it is surely best to reduce it slowly rather than playing pretend."

Cruelly, one writer in the *Arizona Republic* compared Linda's foods to Paul's music after the Beatles: "The Pasta Primavera reminded me of McCartney's album, Pipes of Peace—there was nothing there, really. Certainly nothing memorable. Creamy, but mostly bland. The Rigatoni Marinara fared better, like maybe Venus and Mars. A little spicier. Zesty. Catchy, sort of, like the clarinet solo in 'Listen To What the Man Said.'" Clever, very clever. "Linda McCartney oozes with the sincerity of the seriously rich," begins an article in the *Observer* from 1995, headlined "LOVE, LOVE ME DO, NO COW IN MY STEW." (Sue Whitall in the *Detroit News* turned the music connection into a positive, with "LINDA MCCARTNEY SAYS HER VEGGIE ENTREES WILL SEND BLAND ON THE RUN.")

But everyone seemed ready for a reaction that focused first on Paul, then on Linda. No one believed that "Linda Eastman's Home Style . . . etc." would ever have gone anywhere in the first place. And on the tour designed to promote the U.S. launch of her products, Linda gave press conferences all over the country, which were interrupted halfway through by the voice of Paul, on the questioners' mike, asking something like, "How does your husband like your food?" Then he'd join Linda onstage, the photographers would go insane and the questions thenceforth would be about a Beatles reunion. "Any more food questions?" from the organizers would be met with more Beatles questions. Once again Linda was sidelined, even when it was her project in the spotlight, but it was ultimately to her advantage, of course, that the possibility of Paul's presence guaranteed a large press turnout for her beloved frozen meals.

But although it didn't work in America (the first time out; there are still plans to do a U.S. launch), in the U.K. Linda's food line was, and is, a sensation. In 1995 a factory dedicated solely to the manufacture of Linda's products opened in Fakenham, in Norfolk. It employs nearly 500 workers and no meat is allowed on the premises; it is the only completely vegetarian food plant in all of Europe. A professional bicycling team, the Linda McCartney Pro Cycle Team, is now on the roads and proud of consuming 8,500 vegetarian calories per day per cyclist, mostly in the form of Linda's own foods, of which there are now forty-two varieties. And early in 1999 the billionth box of her food was sold in the U.K.

At the time of her death, and in her own right, Linda was one of the richest women in England. What's more, Linda's third cookbook, *Linda McCartney on Tour*, is another bestseller; she is now the most successful author of vegetarian cookbooks in the history of publishing.

Linda's picture was taken off the front of the food cartons, at her request, when news of her cancer was made public. There is now a picture of her, with her hair short and dark as it grew back after her chemotherapy, on the back, a quote from Linda and assurance from the McCartney family that "this product meets with Linda's ideals for a great-tasting quality product."

"Everything Linda stood for is in the name on that package," says Tim Treharne, managing director of Linda McCartney Foods, now owned by her family, who still approve every new development in content and packaging. "This was a tremendous achievement for her. She had become more comfortable with it over the years, and I saw her go from being 'Paul's wife' to being Linda herself. She was her own person, and with her ideas, and all of us working together, we succeeded beyond anyone's dreams."

Dreams that began, I suppose, when she discovered that there can be bacon, or almost bacon, with no blood shed. Everything grew from that.

"We're coming to America to launch my frozen food line," Linda called to tell me, early in 1994. "We're going to start with supermarket chains in the Midwest—soon it'll be everywhere."

"Wow," I said. "That is so great. It means I'll get a chance to taste it."

"You haven't tasted it? Well, maybe because you can't get it there yet. But you are using my cookbook that I gave you, and Mike is using it too?"

"Oh, religiously," I fibbed, as I grabbed a copy from the kitchen cookbook collection, where it had sort of languished. "We going to try Aubergine Fritters tonight! Hey, honey, what's an aubergine?"

"It's eggplant, but it's not a good time to buy it now. Did you actually ever use my cookbook? Those recipes are really good."

"You've honestly cooked sauerkraut? Come on."

"They've all been tested and tasted, that I can promise you. Listen, I'm going to send you some of my frozen food."

"You know, I have such a small mailbox. The mailman folds everything, CDs, everything. Maybe it's not a good idea."

"Well, soon you'll have them in your neighborhood . . . what?"

"D'Agostino," I answered; the name of my local supermarket.

"I'm going to make sure they're in every D'Agostino. I'll call you when we're in New York. Do you like Mexican food? There are two Mexican meals."

"I can't wait, but mainly I can't wait to see you. You'll give my love to Paul and the family?"

"Paul's right here, I'm sure he wants to say hello. Oh . . . he's waving hello, it looks like he has to run somewhere. Well, I love you. If you go veggie, you'll live longer and I can love you for a longer time."

"Goodbye my darling."

Chapter 16

"Her decision was that she was never going to be apart from him, and I think that was the smartest and most amazing choice."

Judy Collins

Linda once said that if she hadn't married Paul, she would have been a professional photographer and would have been quite satisfied with that as her life's work—as long as she could have a horse and did not have to live in the city. As it turned out for her, Linda did indeed get her horse(s) and her house(s) in the country, but she also married an eligible and famous man and stayed with him for the rest of her life; raised four children; wrote three bestselling vegetarian cookbooks; became the world's most celebrated animal-rights activist; created a line of food products that was enormously visible and lucrative; performed onstage in front of a cumulative audience of about ten million people; and . . . well, the book tells you all the things she was and did.

With all that, her obituary in the *New York Times* of April 20, 1998, was headlined, "LINDA MCCARTNEY, PHOTOGRAPHER OF ROCK STARS, DIES AT 56." It was at the top of the page, and five columns wide out of six. Still representing the mind-set of the public when it came to Linda, the headline was, I thought, struggling to be correct, but patronizing and inaccurate. (In all fairness to the august *Times*, there was a subheading that read, "An animal-rights activist, vegetarian entrepreneur, and wife of a Beatle.") If Linda were to be remembered as a photographer, then her achievement certainly went beyond doing pictures of "rock stars;" but it is still remarkable that she was identified as a photographer at all, because that is not exactly what came to mind when one thought of Linda, the celebrity. Or, she *was* a well-known photographer, went the prevailing opinion, until she became Mrs. Paul, and became truly famous being his wife. Always, there was the implication that her best work was done in her "freewheeling" days in the late '60s (as in "Photographer of Rock Stars") and that her portraits intimately captured the spirit of that era; after her marriage, well, she got some good pictures of the Beatles, some really good ones of Paul, and then went on to other things, which were not quite as fabulous as those shots of Janis, Brian, Jimi, Jackson, Pete, and so on.

It is not astonishing that her early portraits have overshadowed her subsequent achievement—her shots were beautiful portraits of fabulous people and she was certainly in the right places with her camera, where few got to go and fewer still took pictures, let alone memorable ones. Her early talent jumped off the contact sheets like a genie released from a bottle. What's more, those pictures are looking better all the time, and the public's appetite for them seems to be growing as well.

I drove with Linda Stein to Greenwich, Connecticut, in March 1999, to the opening of a show at the Bruce Museum called "Linda McCartney's Sixties: Portrait of an Era," an exhibition due to tour American museums until August 2001. Of course, the local press was rampant with speculation about the possibility of Paul being there, but wisely (as ever) he didn't go; instead he sent a modest bouquet of flowers which was prominently displayed at the entrance to the exhibition. (He and Linda rarely went to the openings of the many shows of her work in the U.K.; they knew all eyes would be on them, so what was on the walls would get much less attention than the people standing in the middle of the room.) It was a beautifully mounted show, the place was packed, vegetarian hors d'oeuvres were served along with top-shelf spirits, and the gift shop was well stocked with Linda's books, her posthumous album and even Beatles memorabilia (there's no getting away from it, is there?) consigned to the museum by local collectors.

Greenwich, about thirty miles from New York, is one of that city's richest suburbs by far; the event we attended was a preview for sponsors and supporters of the museum, which occupies a large and magnificent building on a hill overlooking Long Island Sound and is a beloved institution in the town. Which is to say, the crowd that night was made up of the élite of the élite; chairmen of the boards of the world's great financial institutions and their wives were there in abundance. Collectors and connoisseurs themselves, impeccably dressed and extremely sophisticated, hardly a bunch of rockers, the preview-goers were ooh-ing and ah-ing like six-year-olds at Gorilla Jungle theme park.

The local reviews were joyously positive, quoting many of the guests at the reception. Jane Chase of Greenwich said, "I'm really amazed at how talented she was and it makes me sad that she isn't around to give us those gifts any more." There was the inevitable and terribly clever ten-year-old who commented, "In most of these pictures, I don't know who they are. But I like the fact that she does a lot of pictures in black and white." "Stunningly compelling" was the first line of "LOCAL EXPERTS REVIEW EXHIBIT FAVORABLY" in *Greenwich Time*, but it was a quote from a curator at the museum. Photographer Jeff Wignall told the writer, "It was Linda Eastman who took most of the pictures before she met Paul McCartney. In reality, she was a superb photographer." The catalogue of the exhibition claimed that Linda had "earned her place among the great photographers of the Twentieth century." Wow.

Current and subsequent assessments of Linda's work toyed with the word "great;" although some were reluctant to grant that accolade, others did. It's telling, though, that among the more reluctant was Reuel Gordon, editor of the *British Journal of Photography*, who wrote in the *Independent*, just after Linda's death, about her "haphazard approach to photography . . . [her lack of] affinity with the mechanics of the medium and scant knowledge of films, shutter speeds, and so on," resulting in a lack of "consistency that separates the good photographers from the truly great ones." One begs to differ; Linda knew a great deal about film, processing, chemistry, light and composition, and studied and worked on these areas with acknowledged experts. Mr. Gordon may not find her achievement great—that is his opinion—but she had learned her craft quite meticulously. (And I cannot comprehend what "consistency" the critic is referring to; Linda, like all photographers, exhibited and published the images she wanted to, and, like all photographers, kept the rest in a box, although she emphatically did not take dozens of shots to get one good one. The pictures she showed demonstrated a fine grasp of light, processing, and composition, or they never would have been hung in galleries and museums. I sniff here the implication that she was perhaps spoiled and indulged because of who she was—it's the same old story. The article ends: "Not one of the greats, perhaps, but certainly one capable of producing striking and memorable images." How grudgingly generous.

More interesting to me than the patronizing quibbling of Mr. Gordon is the opinion of Lee Fleming in the *Washington Post*, who wrote about Linda's portraits in 1993: "in a contest between work like that of Annie Leibovitz, which manipulates and plays on public perception of her subjects, and McCartney's low-key revelations, the latter's pictures win hands down . . . [her] images reveal something of the source, not just the surface, of her subjects' creativity."

Bonnie Benrubi, whose New York gallery handles Linda's pictures (and work by Walker Evans, Dorothea Lange, and Alfred Steiglitz as well), was working closely with Linda on a show titled "Wide Open" that went on view just months after her death. Benrubi does not hesitate to call Linda's work "brilliant." She praises "the composition, the vision, the kind of clarity and freshness, the perfection in printing, the overall accomplishment of it." Benrubi had known the '60s pictures, but then became familiar with the sun prints (experiments, almost abstract, with light and chemical processing), the still lifes, the horses, landscapes, and the pictures of decidedly non-famous people. Her last conversation with Linda, about the forthcoming show, took place three days before Linda died: "We talked about the exhibit; I had no idea how sick she was."

She continues: "I miss her a lot. I think she was a great person, warm and trusting, not bothered by silly, small things. She never seemed to be distracted when she focused on something and, more impressive, she was able to grow, she really grew and she never stopped growing. Linda would have been so proud of that show."

And in a review in the *New York Times*, Margaret Loke wrote that Linda "never seemed to feel fame's constraining effects on her life or her photography . . . Ms. McCartney brought an engaged, intuitive and minimalist eye to her black-and-white landscapes and still lifes of the 1980's and '90s . . . Her photography could be disarmingly earthy, but her eye was definitely precise." Ms. Loke found Linda's work "paradoxically, intensely private . . . the pictures of sea and sky, of trees, and of clouds share a profound aloneness," and called the landscapes "quietly elegiac."

Those quietly elegiac (and very beautiful) pictures will never be as famous or as widely beloved as Linda's celebrity portraits, and she never deluded herself that they would be. She pursued photography because she loved everything about it, and she knew as well as anyone that there were not going to be many more Hendrixes or Joplins in her life making music that she loved, inspiring her to "get them down" at their creative heights. What's more, never needing to prove (except to herself) her viability as an artist, Linda just went on creating, and her output was immense. She had five books of photographs published, exhibitions at New York's International Center of Photography, the Museum of the City of San Francisco, the San Diego Museum of Photographic Art, and of course her galleries—Fahey-Klein in Los Angeles and Benrubi in New York. Her "Sixties" show has been or will be at museums in ten American cities. In England there were one-woman shows of her images at the Royal Photographic Society in Bath, the National Museum of Photography in Bradford and the Victoria and Albert Museum in London. Her photographs of John Lennon and Paul McCartney are on permanent display in the National Portrait Gallery in Trafalgar Square. Her work has been exhibited on the European continent, in South America, and Australia. In 1987 she was voted "1987 U.S. Photographer of the Year" by *Women in Photography*. With Brian Clarke she created stained-glass windows that were widely and extravagantly admired; for her private delight and close friends, she produced calendars and datebooks and a series of scarves using images from her pictures.

"She would always send me things she was working on," said Judy Collins. "Beautifully cut velvet scarves, and then the ones with her photographs of leaves and flowers that she had translated into fabrics. These glorious things. She was an artist, you know, all along. This connection she had with her art was very strong. In a sense, she gets the prize for her continuity in her work; it was the real thing at the start, and then always the real thing."

At very rare moments, Linda took a break from cloudscapes on the moors and went back to where her career as a photographer began—shooting stars. The last she ever photographed was Chrissie Hynde. Chrissie was planning the cover of her 1998 album, *Viva el Amor*, and called Linda's daughter Mary, now a successful photographer as well as custodian of her mother's pictorial legacy.

> I wanted a militant-looking thing, fist in the air, as if we'd won the revolution, and when I talked about it with Mary, she said, "Well, why don't you call my Mum? I'm sure she'd like to do that." I knew Linda hadn't been well, and I didn't want to bother her, but the next day my manager called and asked, "Did you organize a photo shoot with Linda McCartney?" I said I hadn't. She responded, "Well, guess what, there's one organized." I called Linda and said, "Hello, my personal photographer!" and she told me, "I love this, I love your idea because it's strong, and I love strong. I've turned down so much work this year because they were things that just didn't interest me, but this does."
>
> So I went down to Rye, to the windmill where Paul had his recording studio and Linda had her photography studio. I was in my crappy old jeans and Linda had the camera set up, and I said, "Is there a mirror or something?" "Oh yeah, I think so," she replied, and she walked me into this little lavatory that had a tiny mirror and a couple of lightbulbs next to it. Not what you're used to when shooting an album cover with a famous photographer.
>
> While we were setting up, Paul was in the other studio recording tracks for Linda's solo album, which he seemed really eager to get on with, and she showed me her lyrics. Then in

between doing the shots of me, she'd run out and get on the phone, putting the finishing touches to her last cookbook; she's going, "No, no, no! Not parsley"—things like that. She was always working on lots of projects at once, but this time I had a sense of her needing to finish whatever she was doing just then. After the session, she told me she was going to the States for a holiday and would be back in a couple of weeks. I never saw her or talked to her again.

This was one month before she died. A few days after the shoot she sent me the contact sheets, and I marked the one I wanted and sent it back to her. And then the news came over the radio.

A week later, her photo agent called my office and said, "There's a picture that Linda wanted hand-delivered to Chrissie," and the next day this package was brought over. It was the picture—she had instructed her agent how to print it up, which was exactly how I wanted it, and to deliver it to me, and there it was. The only message that came with it was, "Do whatever you want with this," and it was her last portrait. I think her way of saying goodbye to me was doing this picture for my album cover.

If Linda was reluctant to rely on words, she was not troubled by her verbal non-brilliance, because her vision was so extraordinarily developed. I, on the other hand, like to talk things to death, which led to occasional little communications battles between us. One day in 1968 we were walking past the Frick Gallery on Fifth Avenue, going to meet a musician for a photo shoot in Central Park. Linda was scrutinizing the sky and the foliage across the street, when she suddenly grabbed my arm and steered me towards the gallery's entrance. "There's a Constable I must look at," she said. "The landscape with Salisbury Cathedral. I want to see something about the light on the trees."

"Why?" I asked. "Why now? You've seen it a million times. We're late; what do you need to see?"

"I can't describe it," she answered. "We have to see it, not talk about it. We're wasting time; come on, it's free."

Chapter 17

"The doctors would always say, 'She wants to beat it, she's doing well.'"

Candace Carell

In December 1995, Linda called to tell me that a malignant tumor had been found in her breast. "I wasn't feeling well, so I went to the local doctor. He told me I had some kind of cold, and to take some pills and wait two weeks. Two weeks later, I still didn't feel better. So we went to London and they tested it, and it's cancer."

I was stunned. "What's going to happen?"

"They'll take out the lump, and we'll see."

"Could you feel it?"

"Yes."

"Had you had a mammogram or whatever?"

"No."

"They just cut it out, and it's over. They told you that, right?"

"Yeah, that's what we hope."

Well, Linda lived another sixteen months and died of metastasized breast cancer on April 17, 1998 at the age of fifty-six. We saw each other several times in those months, sometimes on the fly, sometimes laid back, but she never ever mentioned her cancer to me again. The McCartneys made the diagnosis public, announced a positive prognosis in 1997, and never talked to the press about the cancer until after Linda's death.

In fact, the prognosis was grim after the doctors looked at Linda's lymph nodes when they removed the tumor. Many were affected. The cancer had spread before it was discovered, but nothing is or was hopeless, and Linda and Paul kept hoping. They had the best doctors in London, New York, and Los Angeles, and relied mainly on traditional medicine with an overlay of holistic therapies. If there was a slim chance that something might work, short of nonsense like swimming with a dolphin (which the anguished couple had been asked to consider), they took it. As Paul told Chrissie Hynde, as long as they didn't hear the dreaded word "aggressive," they wanted to believe they might come out OK, that there was a chance—and indeed, there is always a chance.

I approach this subject with great caution. This is for many reasons, and the first of them is that, I'm sorry, but I cannot find out everything that happened, every treatment, every surgical procedure. The records are confidential and locked away, as everyone would hope theirs would be; the doctors who treated Linda of course won't talk about it, nor would one ever expect them to; and, what's more, people who claim they are telling me about the true course of Linda's final sickness often contradict each other.

Sometimes Paul has said that he knew more than Linda about the gravity of her situation; close girlfriends of hers whom I've interviewed say that there was nothing Linda didn't know, that she in fact knew more than Paul. Some have said that she knew how fragile Paul was in the face of her illness; his mother had died of breast cancer when he was fourteen. These are two very, very strong people, but cancer rearranges things, it seems. Again, what is the truth? Are we going to play who-knew-what-and-when-did-they-know-it? Or, will we salute a very brave little group of people who suffered elegantly and privately, and hoped powerfully?

I have more close friends with breast cancer right now than I ever would have imagined. My mother had lots of friends and sisters and there were women all around when I was a child, and I never heard of one of them having breast cancer. Other cancer, but not that. Or perhaps it was simply not "mentionable." Is it an epidemic? I ask doctors, cancer specialists; some say no, others say it's too soon to know. Is it horribly hopeless? One doctor told me it's among the most treatable of cancers, that there's an excellent survival rate, especially if it's detected early on. Another doctor told me it's always very alarming. No surprise here—as anyone knows who has sought opinions from specialists about an existing or potential condition.

It struck me that there was a parallel between the way Linda dealt with her cancer and the way she dealt with the overwhelmingly hostile reaction to her marriage to Paul. She looked very carefully at her situation, considered the indignities and the possibilities, and although there were moments when it seemed she might go under, she came out of her corner fully expecting to win in the end. What's more, Linda McCartney, who was certainly not shy when speaking to the public, who had risked and experienced scorn and skepticism for her activities and beliefs and who would never back down in her advocacy of highly unpopular subjects—Linda chose to keep the details to herself and her husband. She and Paul had obviously decided not to tell people about her medical progress unless it was necessary for them to know.

When this crisis first came upon them, they divided their world, and the people in it, into those who had to know what was happening at all times and those for whom it would serve no purpose to know. This was not a matter of "closeness," although clearly those who were indeed closest, the family and those who worked for and with them in crucial positions, had to know. It had nothing to do with affection; in fact, when possible, they preferred to have very close friends believe that recovery was at hand.

Says Chrissie Hynde, recalling the photo session she did with Linda one month before her death, "When she said goodbye, and that she'd be back in a few weeks, she didn't embrace me like she always did. I knew there was something going on in her mind, and when I thought about it, it didn't surprise me that that was how she behaved when she knew it was going to be the last time she was going to see me. She didn't want to be sentimental about it, she didn't want me to be sad, she certainly didn't want pity. She wanted, I guess, our last memories of each other to be a dynamite photo session."

Tim Treharne recalls a phone call early in 1998, when Linda told him she was losing the fight. There were a lot of things about the future of her food business that they had to talk about, and soon, so that continuity would be assured in the absence of the person whose name and image would be forever on the product.

Me, I got the party line. "She's fabulous, she's doing great." From her daughters, for example: in 1996 there was a huge reception at New York's International Center of Photography for Linda's "Roadworks" show. It was crowded, and of course people were looking for McCartneys. Mary was in charge, very much so; when I asked where her mother was, she told me they'd just had dinner and Mum and Dad were outside in a car, not wanting to deal with what would happen if they walked in.

"How's she feeling?"

"Great!"

Linda Stein introduced me to Evelyn Lauder (of the make-up empire), who had donated the breast cancer center named for her at Sloan Kettering Hospital, cancer treatment center of the world and the home base of Linda's treatment. Evelyn, a photographer herself, was eager to meet Mary, and so I brought her over. Mary instantly thanked Ms. Lauder for the beautiful and comfortable clinic where she often accompanied her mother for chemotherapy sessions. "Everyone loves your mother there," Mary was told. "She radiates hope." (More than that, Linda was actually thought of by the other patients as someone who had beaten the disease and was showing them it could be done. She never said that, but she seemed that way.) Mary's tone and manner were gracious and warm, like Linda's when she met someone she liked; Mary and Evelyn were soon talking about different kinds of 35mm black and white films. Two women, I thought, so beautiful, so rich, so blessed, and it's goddamn cancer that's brought them together.

I am very fond of Jody Eastman, Linda's brother's wife, who seems aristocratically formidable but is really a lot of laughs. I literally cornered her at a party and said, "Look, Jody, nothing on earth is that fabulous; what's really going on?"

"She's doing great," Jody answered, looking me right in the eye. "Great."

It was from Paul that I learned how things really were. Paul Morrissey, Linda Stein and I had driven from the compound Morrissey and Andy Warhol had shared in Montauk to the McCartney house in East Hampton. Linda McCartney, who had shaved her head rather than having to see her hair fall out because of the drugs she was taking, was wearing a bandanna. She took Morrissey and Stein on a tour of edible flowers in the gardens behind the house (I dropped out after chomping on something quite unpleasant), while Paul was tending to the barbecue. Zucchini and peppers, I think, but I was shocked to see Paul starting the charcoals with lighter fluid.

"You? A "friend of the earth"? You're burning gasoline!"

"This is the way to start a fire, Danny."

"It's a lousy way, that's poison!"

And we were actually having a barbecue argument, just like any two guys in any garden, each of whom thinks only he knows how to start a good fire. We were mock-yelling at each other, and it seemed a good time to broach another subject. "So, Paul, how's Linda doing? She looks great."

"Well," he answered, "the first round of chemotherapy sort of didn't turn out all that well, so we're going to go through it again, and this time it's going to work."

That's when I knew the situation was very far from fabulous.

Prior to her diagnosis, Linda and Paul had been primarily reliant on orthodox medicine, yet hopeful that alternatives existed, or might be found. At a 1989 party at the restaurant Lucky Strike, in New York's SoHo neighborhood, they were regaling my baffled roommate Michael Fisher with theories, apparently learned rather recently, about the mystical aspects of the "water balance" in the human body, how all health concerns were a function of this water thing, which modern science had completely—and to its shame—ignored. But, as Paul told Chrissie Hynde in the interview she did with him about six months after Linda died,

"Everyone's got a miracle cure. And some of them say what you really don't want to do is go the traditional medical route. I hate to tell you, I still don't know the answer. For instance, when Stella was born we had to go the traditional medical route, as there were complications at the birth. If we hadn't, both Linda and the baby would have died. So we'd learned that there were times when you need traditional modern medical science and we opted for that route."

Threading through the entire course of Linda's illness and her treatment was the issue of animal testing on the drugs that were being administered, and the added complication, as if there weren't already an overwhelming amount, of the implications of her diagnosis for her advocacy of vegetarianism and the loyal consumers of her food products.

When she first introduced her frozen foods, Linda listed, among the benefits of "going veggie," a reduced risk of cancer. Other advertisers making a similar claim tend to put it much more equivocally, as in "some studies have shown that eating a certain amount of this cereal may reduce the possibility of getting some forms of cancer," but Linda had never been equivocal; and what always mattered most to her was getting people to eat less meat, thereby saving the lives of animals. To be sure, vegetables are healthier than red meat, but no food can come with a guarantee of being anything other than what it simply is—certainly it seems extravagant to claim that anything will prevent cancer.

Candace Carell had become friendly with the McCartneys when she designed the disguises they wore to sit in the audience at George Harrison's 1974 Madison Square Garden concert. They met again in 1992, when Linda and Paul were in New York shooting footage for the documentary *Behind the Lens;* Candace at the time was the girlfriend of Noel Redding, bassist for the Jimi Hendrix Experience, and Noel was working with Linda re-creating the photo session she'd done with the group in Central Park in 1968. The two couples became friendly enough for Candace to tell Linda that she'd been diagnosed with breast cancer and was having chemotherapy. When she heard that Linda was stricken, she wrote her a long letter from Ireland; Linda in return sent Candace and Noel a scarf and a blanket made from the wool of their own sheep. (I had once asked Linda if they made wool from their own sheep; "No, it's cruel," she said. "They nick the sheep terribly when they're shearing them. We're trying to find a way of getting the wool without cutting their skin." I guess they found a way.) Candace told me,

> We talked on the phone a lot. I was always complaining, and she never was. You know you're not in great shape when you're getting chemotherapy, but her spirit was so profound and so strong, and we'd agree that hot baths made you feel better, things like that, but she never talked about being in pain. I'd ask if she was eating, and she'd say, "Are you kidding? I eat all the time!" She was putting on weight and she didn't like that at all, but I told her that was an effect of the therapy and it would pass.
>
> In New York we were both being treated by the same doctors, and I would ask how she was doing, and of course they're not allowed to talk about other patients, but the doctors would always say, "She wants to beat it, she's doing well." There was a period when it seemed hopeful, but then in September 1997 she said to me, "I get so depressed," and I knew from the tone of her voice that there had been bad news. I'd been carrying on and complaining as usual, and she said that, and I just got scared. I put Noel on the phone, and he said, "How are you, lovey?" and she said she was all right, she was looking forward to getting a call from Paul, who was doing a charity concert in London, so Noel told her to just smoke a joint and that we were thinking of her and loved her. She didn't tell me what she'd heard, but fighting cancer, you get very intuitive, you get the message, whether or not it's put into words.

Candace confronted her doctors with her intuitions about the progress of Linda's condition, and, again not in words, they confirmed her belief that Linda had been told the cancer was terminal—barring the miracle which both Linda and Paul never stopped believing would happen. What amazed the doctors, inasmuch as they would discuss the matter with Candace, was Linda's reaction to bad tidings. "She was asking them what to tell people," Carell says. "And she meant what to tell people who had stopped eating meat because she had convinced them to! Would they think they'd been deceived?" Worst of all, Linda worried, would they become so cynical about the benefits of a vegetarian diet that they'd start eating meat again?

Linda could deal, somehow, with her own death sentence. But to think that it might turn into a death sentence for animals unknown and probably unborn was a thing, one of the few ever in her life, that she could not deal with.

I would never suggest that Linda was not afraid of dying, but I do think she was far less obsessed with it than are many physically sound people. Like everything else in her very organized and attentive existence, dying was added to her agenda, and not, if this can be understood, for morbid or self-pitying reasons, but because it affected so powerfully everything else in the program. What would Paul and the children and the animals do without her, or rather, what *will* they do?—and let's be prepared. Plans for the food business, for the photography show, for Mary's imminent wedding—plans even for the first Christmas she would not be there for her family and what gifts they would be getting from her. It looked as if dying was a likely and not very distant end to this hateful disease; her legacy was to be that the work, and the love, went on.

The last time I saw Linda was on November 19, 1997 at Carnegie Hall in New York, at the premiere of Paul's *Standing Stone*. My date that night was my dear friend and colleague Bonnie Bordins, one of the world's great Paul-fans and, when I'd first met her, a Linda-hater since childhood. Bonnie literally wore mourning clothes to school for weeks after Linda and Paul were married, and referred to her as "Beast Woman," which was not a reference to her animal rights advocacy. When Linda walked into the party, we hugged each other and I introduced her to Bonnie. "This is my friend who wore black when you married Paul; she really hated you," I announced, in my customary way of breaking the ice.

"That's OK, I'm almost over it now," Bonnie said, faintly mortified, as I'd planned.

With a great smile, Linda shook Bonnie's hand, pointed to her dress and remarked, "You're still wearing black! All these years, Bonnie?"

I whispered to Linda that I never got to be alone with her, that we always met at some "occasion" or talked on the phone for a few minutes every few weeks, at best. "Let's do it now," she said. We sat down at a little table in the corner, were surrounded by security guards, chatted about the concert we'd just heard, were joined by Bonnie and then by Paul, and in less than ten minutes Linda and Paul were summoned away by someone on their staff and were out the door. The last memory I have is of her and Paul walking through the corridors of Carnegie Hall, surrounded by a phalanx of bodyguards, and of Linda turning around and waving goodbye. We never did get to talk much that night; I asked her once how she was feeling, and of course she said, "Fine." What else could she say? There were about 200 people staring at our little tête-á-tête, and even if we'd really been alone, I think she'd have said the same thing. We left each other a bunch of phone messages over the next few months, and talked a few times, always with the understanding that we'd talk again soon. It was all the usual:

"Hi, how are you?"

"Great, how are you?"

"I think of you."

"I think of you too."

"Will I see you soon?"

"Oh, I hope so, we'll figure it out."

"Goodbye, I love you."

"I love you too."

This routine was so standard, just an affirmation of an old friendship, that it doesn't matter who said what, except there was always an exhortation to "go veggie" somewhere in there.

On a Sunday in April, I came back to New York City from my little house at the beach, the first time I'd been there since October, when it had been closed for the winter. There was no phone and the TV sets were wrapped in their blankets, and I had spent the weekend sweeping away the parting presents of all the little forest creatures who'd invaded in my absence and eaten some books and the labels off the canned food.

When I got back to my apartment in New York the phone was ringing, and a gentleman identified himself as someone from the *New York Daily News*. I began to tell him I didn't want a subscription, when he interrupted me and said, "No, no, that's not why I called. I wonder if you have any anecdotes about Linda McCartney?"

"Linda McCartney? Why?"

I had that awful hollow feeling even before he answered, "Oh my God! I guess you didn't know and I have to tell you this. She's dead."

I apologized for being unable to speak to him at that moment, and called Laura Gross in Los Angeles; she was the producer of almost everything Linda ever did for television, and in fact we'd met because Linda suggested that we'd like each other. I wondered if she thought I should call Paul, and she said by all means, so I did. When he took the phone, the first thing he said was, "Wasn't she beautiful, Danny? Wasn't she beautiful?"

Paul told me about Linda's last days and ended up consoling me, when I had called to console him. At the end of the conversation, he said, "By the way, we've told the press it happened in Santa Barbara instead of Tucson. Don't want a bunch of reporters swarming around down there, you know; just a little fib, so will you back us up on that?"

I did the obligatory round of television, radio, and print interviews over the next few days, the press having been steered my way by Paul's New York public relations company. For the first time since Linda had become famous, the media were inclined to say kindly things about her; it was neither unexpected nor inappropriate that the coverage was about "the love of Paul's life," but if I had something to add to that, I was absolutely going to do so. I was dismayed to see people who barely knew the McCartneys being interviewed by the cable networks about their dear friends Linda and Paul, but all I could control was what I had to say, not the list of chosen vultures.

Very unfortunately, the decision to place the scene of Linda's death in Santa Barbara had some rather unforeseen consequences when the coroner in that city said he had no record of Linda's passing there—where a memorial service was held, and innovative scoundrels were charging money to show people "the house where Linda died." The name

"Santa Barbara" was a code word, and not a very serious one, used by the McCartney staff as a substitute for Tucson, Arizona, where the family had a ranch—the region was among Linda's favorites on earth and was where she lived when she briefly attended the University of Arizona. "Oh, when will they be coming back from Santa Barbara?" was the kind of thing people in the organization would be able to say comfortably to each other, not having to mind the snoopy computer repair person waiting to tell his family where he'd spent the day. But very famous people caught in little lies are automatically going to be suspected of concealing bigger ones, and at the end of the week the tabloids were theorizing that Paul's office had misidentified the place of Linda's death because it had been an assisted suicide. Why else would they not say where it happened, unless they were trying to cover something up, and what else would they be trying to cover up but that? (Naturally, once the press found out that Tucson was where Linda had died, there was virtual helicopter gridlock over the McCartney ranch and photographs of their desert home in every paper: just the thing the family had wanted so badly to avoid.) In any case, I was back on the air at the end of the week dealing with this revolting speculation.

I had one simple response to the whole matter: Linda had wanted more than anything to live long enough to be at Mary's wedding to Alistair Donald, and in fact the date of the wedding was moved back when it was known that Linda had only months to live. I cannot imagine that a mother planning for the first time the marriage of one of her children would choose to die beforehand. It makes no sense on any level; furthermore, Linda was not in great pain at the end and was on the phone that very week, for example to Bonnie Benrubi in New York discussing her upcoming photo exhibition. And that was the case I made: "I have no problem if someone makes that choice, but I have a very great problem believing that Linda did; it fits in with nothing we know." Take it or leave it—and the whole issue faded away after two days in the headlines, not because of what I said, but because it so obviously lacked any merit whatsoever.

It was a great honor to be asked to speak at Linda's memorial in New York, and I found it touching that the McCartney office followed up that invitation by inquiring if what I planned to say was going to be "original," as opposed, I assumed, to reading a poem—in which case they wanted to make sure that no two people were going to use the same literary source. This was pure Paul, the perfection of all arrangements, and indeed it showed in the magnificence (there is no other word for it) of the event itself. I was even asked to call him to discuss what I would say—he suggested I speak "from the heart" (and to keep it at three minutes or less). I assured him that my heart was the only place I could come from, and not to worry; I had, alas, spoken at many services, in front of many distinguished mourners, in memory of many beloved friends. Still, this was the "biggest" one of all and I was terrified. Fashion-fright even sent me to Brooks Brothers, where I hadn't shopped since college days, for a shirt and tie, an alien costume these many years.

Laura Gross, staying at an uptown hotel, sent her car for Mike Fisher and me, and we had drinks before heading to the Riverside church, one of the most beautiful in America, in a quiet neighborhood "way uptown," overlooking the Hudson River. I was agonizing about memorizing my speech or reading it; an actor friend told me to memorize it, but others warned me that an actor would say that and that I should have the assurance of a written text. I also had, in my little black overnight bag, a two-pint Evian bottle filled with ice-cold vodka.

The very select crowd of several hundred (Paul had cut the guest list several times) was awed by the interior of Riverside Church itself (most, like myself, had never been there), the flower arrangements (there were something like 400,000 blossoms) and the gravity of the ceremony, but by the third speaker there started to be a smattering of applause at the end of each eulogy. Not for me, and although Paul gave me a thumb's up when I caught his eye as I was coming down from the podium, I was convinced I had made no sense at all. "It's because everyone was crying," someone told me afterwards, and I thought, "Good, job well done after all, they should be crying."

I certainly was—back in my seat I broke down, to hell with dignity, and didn't recover myself until Stella McCartney, walking past me as the family left the church ahead of the crowd, punched me in the shoulder and said, "Stop it! Stop it! She wouldn't want to see you like that."

I was one of the first to arrive, in a car provided by the organizers of the event, at a restaurant called Zen Palate in the theater district, where a very small party was held for family and participants in the ceremony only. The proprietor of the restaurant greeted the arriving guests standing next to a niche where sat a statue of the Buddha, to which I made a hesitant ritual bow. "You like the Buddha?" she said with a beautiful smile, and I replied, "Yes, I love the Buddha, and I'd also love a drink."

"Ah," she returned, "no alcohol, no liquor license, you bring your own."

Mary McCartney, who'd come in at the same time, said, "Uh oh, Dad is not going to like that," and summoned Paul's personal assistant, John Hamill, to remedy the situation as soon as possible.

"There's a temporary solution in my bag," I told Mary, and poured three stiff ones for her, Alistair and myself. What a good idea that had been.

It was truly a party, with a high level of good cheer and laughter (especially after John returned with cases of wine and Scotch). I remember most of all looking down the table at Linda's sister Laura, now married to a fabulous Italian landscape architect and living near Florence, and being staggered at her resemblance to Linda. I had the same rush months later at a Linda memorial concert to benefit animal rights charities, produced by Chrissie Hynde at London's Royal Albert Hall; Heather had brought me into the family box to say hello to Paul and to meet Arthur, Mary's son, the first grandchild, then just a few weeks old. Heather bent over to kiss Paul, and when she turned around and looked at me, I saw Linda—and told her so. "That's the nicest thing anyone could say," she responded.

In the summer of 1998, I set aside a corner of my garden at the beach for white flowers only, as a little shrine to Linda's memory. I'd buy or plant anything as long as it was white—something I'd never done before, having been afraid of white flowers, that they'd never really be truly white; but they were, and it was great. I told Paul about it and he wanted to know what I was growing, so I sent him pictures and labeled them; things like, "JFK rose, smells beautiful too." The rose bush came back, by the way, after a winter planted in the sand behind the house, more beautiful than ever.

Chapter 18

"Linda had no answers, only her will and her spirit; she helped me, it was encouraging just to know what she was bringing to this fight."

Linda Stein

Linda McCartney's death sent shivers through women all over the world, whether or not they knew or cared about anything she had done or believed in—she was famous, she was rich, she was a strict vegetarian, she had access to the best advice and best treatment and yet she died of breast cancer. What was to become of women diagnosed with the disease who were not so rich and could not command such resources? What was the point of having everything and living such a healthy life if you could be fatally stricken with a condition that is thought to be relatively "easy to beat"? Where was hope to be found, or optimism, or good sense? Well, if we knew the answers to those questions, we'd have a cure for cancer, and we don't.

One good friend of mine went for an examination as soon as she heard that Linda had died; "I was overdue for a mammogram, and that made up my mind," she told me. A malignancy was found, and treated, and her prognosis is now excellent. I would think that her reaction was incredibly sensible, and it demonstrates as much as can be learned from Linda's example, which is a great deal. Anything one does is better than nothing—beyond that, I certainly am not qualified to address the subjects of risk, therapies, survival and so on. Women have asked me, simply because I knew Linda, what she did, what the time intervals were, if she did anything wrong, could she have done it differently, what drugs she had; and all I can say to them, or to anyone, is that it's something for a woman (or, in rare cases, a man) to talk about with her doctor. Linda and Paul fought a good fight, and if there are regrets and soul-searching, it was an inspirational battle. They never gave up, and what more can be said? I would like this story to be hopeful, because the McCartney family was always hoping, and it made those last years that much the better for all of them, and for us; I would like to be helpful, but I cannot be specific: every woman is different, and every health problem is different.

"Did you ever know her to be shy?" asked Linda Stein, a friend who is battling the disease herself. "Did she not say what was on her mind? Did she not have advice to give, and answers to give? But only when she believed she had something to contribute, only when she thought it would be helpful to others, if they were people or animals. She never said anything in public about her cancer. She would write me notes saying, 'My love is with you,' and when we met we talked about green tea and skin moisturizers, but never about the disease we both had. And we were going to the same doctors at the same clinic. Linda had no answers, only her will and her spirit; she helped me, it was encouraging just to know what she was bringing to this fight. Now I'm here, and she's gone. There are no answers; Linda's life was her answer, but only to her own questions."

The only medical subject I will even go near is the subject of animal testing on drugs, which became a contentious and most unwelcome issue for Linda and Paul as they were struggling to conquer her illness. There were people who had a simply great time criticizing the treatments Linda was getting, because it was likely that the drugs administered were tested on animals. (As Paul said to Chrissie Hynde, they opted for orthodox medicine.) And those who accused the McCartneys of hypocrisy were actually lobbyists working against the humane movement, trying to embarrass Linda, the world's most visible animal rights crusader.

For what I hoped would be a sensible and sensitive answer to the question of animal testing, I asked Dan Mathews of PETA for guidance; he is by any definition a radical activist. "I think most people recognized that assault as a cheap shot," he replied. "Auto tires contain slaughterhouse by-products. Does that mean none of us should drive? If you take aspirin, you're using something that was tested on animals. Should we not take aspirin? That's not what the animal rights movement is about. It's about having a sense of practicality, and at the same time taking a look at mistakes that have been made; it's about finding alternatives to animal testing. When we find them, and we will, and if they work as well as anything we have, and we expect they will, then we'll be ready to make the basic changes. But we have to live in this world in the meantime."

In the meantime . . . she's gone from this place. There's no taking just yet of the measure of her loveliness. From all the people I spoke to, who were all people who knew Linda at one time in her life, there was never a sarcastic word, not a sneer, or even the faintest question-mark over her remarkable goodness, her selflessness, her lack of conceit or attitude, her energy, her frankness, the clear and strong picture she had of herself and her obligations. Amazingly, neither are there any question-marks about her children, which is a tribute—and one that she would probably have appreciated more than any other—to their upbringing that was defined with great care and watched over with great love. And about her marriage, I think we have heard more said than we can probably comprehend, so unlikely was it at the start and so incomparable for all those years until her life was over.

Animals will be spared because of her work, and the fight against cancer will be enhanced because of the way she fought it and the assets she brought to the struggle. Although she didn't survive, others certainly will, and there will be more of them. Her husband will continue to be part of one of the most amazing and joyous teams ever to come before the public, for there is much to be done and he is now carrying two torches—but who better than he in all the world to see it through? And all her friends, and everybody who was aware, or will become aware, of what she did, will keep remembering and learning, and that is perhaps the greatest legacy of all.

The last time we spoke, there were Linda's standard questions, and my standard answers.

"Have you gone veggie yet?"

"Well, not yet."

"You always say that. I'm not giving up on you, you know."

"I know. I love you."

"And I love you. Talk to you soon."

Epilogue

The point has been made, I think, that people who knew Linda had very strong and positive memories of her. (Even Blair Sabol, who savaged her in print twenty-five years ago, recanted—to some extent). Many who only knew of Linda also had astonishingly warm opinions of her, as evidenced by the thousands of "tributes" posted on the Internet after her death.

Those friends and acquaintances of hers to whom I talked for this book gave me more wonderful quotes than I could ever use, or fit into the context of the story at all neatly and yet I would not want to see them left out, so here are some sentiments that didn't make it into the preceding chapters, but certainly stand on their own.

Chrissie Hynde: She always made you feel like everything was OK, and I thought, well, it made me feel like I wasn't so afraid to die because, when I cross over, she'll be there. I can just imagine dying and Linda saying, "Oh, it's all right, come in. Don't worry about anything—you know you don't have to wipe your feet."

Yoko Ono (in *Rolling Stone*, June 11, 1998): Linda and I did not meet up and have coffee and muffins in a corner café or anything like that. But we communicated. We communicated in deeds more than in words. When she was strong I felt strong.

Carolyn Jobson (Linda's masseuse at Roundhill, Jamaica): There are people who nurture everybody else more than themselves, they're always very giving. Linda was the most nurturing person. I was thinking about that, that she was like a sponge, really, and the whole family was in that special space. She wasn't somebody who worried about clothes and fixing herself up, she was really down to earth and I think that was it; she spent all her time looking after animals, looking after other people, that kind of thing. She was, to me, the ultimate earth mother. People who didn't know her might have been surprised that she wasn't like a fancy lady.

She never lost that way of dealing with people—whatever walk of life you were from, I think she just treated people the same. It didn't matter, nobody was any more special than anybody else because of where they came from or whatever. I would just thank her for what she has done for the animals and say that we're going to continue the cause. I'm raising my children vegetarian.

I have a friend who's an alternative doctor but who also practices intuitive medicine, and she's very "sensitive," as they call it. I was taking her around Roundhill and I showed her the house where they stayed. The next day she said to me, "I've been picking up Linda's presence very strongly, but it's a good feeling. I think she's OK. She feels very happy where she is."

Eddie Pumer (producer of Paul's and Linda's radio shows): She just carried on telling the truth, loving her family, her husband, loving the music, being a musician, a photographer, being totally honest, being Linda; her strength as a woman won that battle, without a shadow of a doubt. She never went out there saying, "You're all wrong, don't do this to me." She never did. She just gave it time, and in time everybody understood the truth and she was the most truthful person; she never bullshitted in all of the years I knew her. She won because she was Linda McCartney and she did not sell, publicize, try to push; not at all. She won because of truth and the love of a family, the love of the music, and that's what makes her a remarkable woman; as far as I'm concerned she will remain a very prominent and loved figure. It's very rare—she was a wholly good and loving person and that's what won the day. She just carried on as Linda.

Eddie Kramer (record producer): She did something for me in a strange sort of way which I really appreciate now. I wasn't sure about it when it was happening, when I went to see them at the house and they were all vegetarian and she was trying to encourage me to go vegetarian. And in the vegetarian cookbook she gave me, she wrote, "Go veggie, Eddie!" You know she does that to everybody, I guess, but it was so nice that she did that after I had heart surgery. I decided, "I'm gonna change, that's it, no more meat for me." I always appreciated that phrase, it always stuck with me: "Go veggie, Eddie." I've been vegetarian for four and a half years now.

She was very special, very, very special. I just loved her warmth and it's an interesting thing: how does a person be warm and tough at the same time? She was that. She was tough. You know she had to be, but what a wonderful, sensible person. The way she treated her kids, her love of art and photography and music, animals and the whole package; it was great. I think she just evolved into this. Do you remember how she was in '68 compared with how she was in '98? Look at that fantastic upward curve! It was brilliant; look what she evolved into, she just kept growing, each step of the way.

Dave Marsh (author): I think the key to a relationship that strong is kids, because at some point, whatever your differences are, if you have this big thing in the center of your life, that's a bond. You know one thing that typically happens with couples is that the kids grow up, start to go off to college or whatever, and that's when the trouble happens in the marriage. That is a very stressful moment; it was for my wife Barbara and me. Paul and Linda seemed to have escaped even that. The other thing was that Paul and Linda both strike me as being people who had their adventures, and then they met each other.

Dan Mathews (animal rights activist): When I heard she had died, I went outside to the harbor at Norfolk and looked at the water and listened to the wind and I remember waving goodbye to the wind. I felt her in the wind, I sort of said my goodbyes then and there.

Ron Delsener (concert promoter): She was of another era. She was of the land. I could never see Linda McCartney wearing a fur coat, I could never see Linda or Paul McCartney using a cell phone, I could never see Linda McCartney taking garbage and burning it in the backyard or throwing it off a boat or out of the window of a car. They were trying to tell people, "Become veggie, do this, do that," and I wish that she had lived long enough because she would have had her own television show and got that message across to everyone.

Linda Stein (prominent New Yorker): Sadly, in her death she's separated from Paul: she's not Linda McCartney, Paul McCartney's wife; but Linda McCartney, the late, great Linda McCartney. And I think people were so jealous of her, especially women. Other people criticized her because they really didn't get it, they thought that all she wanted was to wave a tambourine and be onstage, but it was the last thing that she seemed to want. She was discussing the music of Wings, she was enthusiastic about organic vegetables, art, flowers, green tea, saving animals, and certainly being a mother. I think that she was devoted to pleasing Paul and she fed his needs. She's nurturing and that nurturing was sometimes responding to "Give me a little Scotch, honey," or "Hold my hand;" it was whatever he wanted. But not in a snap-your-fingers, here, "Jump, honey" way. I could never call it subservient, because there was nothing subservient about her. If she gave him a glass of water, she was regal in giving it. She anticipated his needs and she met them, but not as if she was beneath him in any way or beneath anybody. That was part of the gracefulness and beauty of her personality, because she just was who she was.

Judy Collins: Nobody was warmer than Linda. That hug! Boy, when she hugged you, did you know you were being hugged!

Laurence Juber (guitarist with Wings): Linda really represented for me an epitome of a certain kind of womanhood and I think that the things I learned from her are probably the same things that Paul fell in love with: her strength of character, her artistic sensibility, her natural beauty, and all the things that those of us who had any direct experience with Linda can really appreciate—her sense of humor, and then there was that kind of skeptical aspect to her personality. She had something that I'm never going to forget.

Denny Seiwell (drummer with Wings): The kids, the love; I mean, it was just a very genuine thing there. They were best friends and Linda had some incredibly intuitive ways about her that Paul really respected. I think the way Paul saw her was the way she looked at him, as the genius of the Beatles and the writer and the performer. I think that he looked at her and at her talents and that he believed she had as much going for her as he did. And that kind of mutual respect—I believe that was the thing.

Tim Treharne (managing director of Linda's food company): I'm not a big follower of newspapers but she always seemed to be Linda McCartney, wife of Paul. In the end, though, in the last few years, she became Linda McCartney, herself. And I think that was a tremendous achievement for her. She was her own person.

Denny Evans (in an Internet posting): Having lost my mother at a very young age, I was constantly searching for role models. The searching stopped when I got to know more about Linda. Besides being so extremely talented, she seemed to have the biggest heart. What lucky people her friends must have been to have known her personally. I wish I could have told her what an inspiration she has been to me. I have gone vegetarian because of her and I hope that others will follow her example. Even though she is not on earth any longer, I know she is somewhere watching over us, trying to guide us in the right direction. So, Lovely Linda, I hope you can hear me when I tell you that you were the most beautiful person inside and out. Your time with us was filled with happiness, but was much too short. You left us all so much love, you were one incredibly amazing person. I will remember you always.

Index